The Law of
Subordinated
Debt

AUSTRALIA AND NEW ZEALAND
The Law Book Company Ltd.
Sydney : Melbourne : Perth

CANADA
The Carswell Company Ltd.
Agincourt, Ontario

INDIA
N.M. Tripathi Private Ltd.
Bombay
and
Eastern Law House Private Ltd.
M.P.P. House
Bangalore

ISRAEL
Steimatzky's Agency Ltd.
Jerusalem : Tel Aviv : Haifa

43.00

The Law of
Subordinated
Debt

by

Philip R. Wood, B.A. (Cape Town), B.A. (Oxon)

Solicitor of the Supreme Court

*Visiting Professor, Queen Mary and Westfield College,
University of London*

Visiting Fellow, Kings College London

LONDON
SWEET & MAXWELL
1990

Published in 1990 by
Sweet & Maxwell Limited
South Quay Plaza, 183 Marsh Wall, London E14 9FT
Computerset by MFK Typesetting Ltd., Hitchin, Herts.
Printed in Great Britain by
Butler & Tanner Ltd., Frome, Somerset

British Library Cataloguing in Publication Data
Wood, P. R. (Philip R.)
    The law of subordinated debt.
    1. England. Companies. Insolvency. Law
    I. Title
    344.20678
    ISBN 0-421-42670-5

Po2998

DEDICATION

To my wife Marie-elisabeth, my twin sons
John Barnaby and Richard, my daughter
Sophie and my son Timothy

PREFACE

Subordinated debt has been widely used for many years in a variety of contexts. Sometimes shareholders have preferred to capitalise a company by subordinated debt instead of equity. Banks in workouts have required that insiders or suppliers should subordinate their claims to those of the banks. Subordinated debt forms a fixed capital component of many banks, investment businesses and others who are subject to a capital adequacy regime. And more recently subordinated debt has been raised in highly leveraged takeovers and management buyouts in order to increase the finance available.

Nevertheless, notwithstanding the fact that subordinated debt is now a mature transaction in practice, many crucial areas of the law are relatively undeveloped. Subordination is undoubtedly quirky and idiosyncratic from the legal point of view: it does not fit easily into conventional legal concepts and some twisting and wrenching is required to get it to work.

This book is an attempt to provide a reasoned legal basis for subordinations, to provide some answers to the questions, so far as one can, and to indicate the practice. Where the law is doubtful, I have endeavoured to aim at common-sense solutions which meet legitimate expectations but nevertheless adding notes of caution where this seems desirable. Unfortunately, even so specialist a topic as subordination seems to require a gargantuan knowledge of all areas of law, other than gavelkind and burglary, and hence I fear that I will have been guilty of many infelicities.

Nowadays many commercial and financial transactions have an international element. Accordingly Chapter 12 contains a summary of the law in a number of other jurisdictions prepared by leading practitioners in the countries concerned. Some reference to the law in the United States, Australia and elsewhere appears in the rest of the text: these essays into foreign law were written by myself, though not without trepidation.

Finally I have included some forms and precedents and also a checklist: I hope that these will be found useful.

I have endeavoured to state English law as at May 1, 1990.

Philip R. Wood
9 Cheapside
London EC2V 6AD

ACKNOWLEDGEMENTS

I am grateful to the international correspondents who gave up much of their time to prepare contributions for Chapter 12 as to the law of subordinated debt in their jurisdictions. As with all leading lawyers, they are busy people but nevertheless they devoted considerable time, expertise and skill to the development of their contributions (at very short notice) and I would record my appreciation by listing them as follows:

Belgium	Wilfred Goris of De Bandt, van Hecke & Lagae, Brussels;
Canada	Simon B. Scott Q.C. of Borden & Elliot, Toronto;
France	Jacques Terray and Sophie Boyer Chammard of Gide Loyrette Nouel, Paris;
Denmark	Jens Zilstorff of Plesner & Lunoe, Copenhagen;
Finland	Lauri Peltola of Procope & Hornborg, Helsinki and London;
Germany	Dr. Wolf-Dietrich Krause-Ablass of Bruckhaus Kreifels Winkhaus & Lieberknecht, Dusseldorf;
Greece	Theodoros B. Karatzas of Law offices, Karatzas & Perakis, Athens;
Italy	Dr. Disiano Preite of Chiomenti e Associati, Milan;
Japan	Takaki Takuoka of Blakemore & Mitsuki, Tokyo;
Luxembourg	Janine Biver of Loesch & Wolter, Luxembourg;
The Netherlands	Mark Blom of Nauta Dutilh, Amsterdam and M.P.M. van de Ven of Moret, Ernst & Young (tax);
Sweden	Olof Waern of G. Sandströms Advokatbyrå, Stockholm.

I gratefully acknowledge the help which I derived from a number of private papers prepared by law firms in the United States, England and Australia and from numerous seminar papers.

My partners and colleagues at Allen & Overy gave me much assistance in discussing points with me and clarifying my thinking.

The manuscript and its frequent amendments were typed magnificently and rapidly by Sue Bristow.

My publishers put the book through the presses with efficiency and speed and bore the author's whims with their usual philosophic patience.

As an inadequate record of my continuing appreciation of my family's forbearance when it comes to book-writing, I have dedicated this book to them.

TABLE OF CONTENTS

8: Secured senior and junior debt

9: Protective clauses: the guarantee analogy

TABLE OF CASES

INSOLVENCY RULES

LEGISLATION OF OTHER JURISDICTIONS

Australia

Belgium

Canada

Denmark

Finland

France

DIRECTIVES OF THE EUROPEAN COMMUNITY

CHAPTER 1

MEANING AND PURPOSES OF SUBORDINATION

Definition 1.1

Subordination is a transaction whereby one creditor (the subordinated or junior creditor) agrees not to be paid by a borrower or other debtor until another creditor of the common debtor (the senior creditor) has been paid.

Like security, subordination is relevant only if the debtor is insolvent because until then both junior and senior creditors can be paid in full. Hence the fundamental object of a subordination is that it should be successful on insolvency.

A subordination on insolvency may be achieved by:

— a turnover agreement by the junior creditor to hold dividends and distributions receivable by him on trust for the senior creditor for application towards the senior debt, or (less commonly) an agreement by him to pay to the senior creditor an amount equal to recoveries on the junior debt; or

— an agreement between the debtor and the junior creditor, with or without the senor creditor, that the junior debt is entitled to be paid only after the senior debt has been paid in full.

These two techniques of a turnover subordination and a contractual subordination are studied later: paragraphs 2.3 *et seq*.

Hierarchies of claims 1.2

Apart from subordination contracts between creditors, there are many number of methods whereby one claim may rank junior to another:

— share capital may be divided into preferred, ordinary and deferred shares ranking down the ladder of priority on the liquidation of the company concerned;

— shares rank for payment after debt;

— unsecured debt ranks after secured debt;

— both claims may be secured on the same assets of the debtor but the junior debt has second-ranking priority;

— a claim may be subordinated on bankruptcy of the debtor by virtue of a mandatory rule of insolvency law: paragraph 11.8.

This book is primarily concerned with the subordination of unsecured debts, not the subordination achieved by share capital. Something is also

1

said about intercreditor arrangements between secured creditors since many subordinations also in practice involve secured debts.

1.3   Purposes of subordination

Some usual objectives of subordinations are:

(a) **Insiders.** A senior creditor, such as a bank, wishes to subordinate insiders of the debtor, such as a parent company or major shareholder (especially in project finance). The insider's debt is treated as proprietors' capital which must remain locked in until the outside creditors are paid. The senior creditor relies on the cushion of the subordinated capital and the junior debt is postponed to ensure that the senior loans are used for the business and not to repay the insider's debt.

(b) **Capital adequacy.** The debtor wishes to increase its capital base for regulatory purposes. Thus subordinated debt may rank as primary locked-in capital or as near primary capital for the purposes of central bank supervision of the capital adequacy of banks: paragraph 11.1. Supervision of the capital adequacy of business is common in the banking, insurance, and securities sectors. This type of debt is often intended to rank as more or less permanent capital and is sometimes perpetual debt.

(c) **Change of control financings: mezzanine debt.** Where the loans are to finance a takeover or a management buy-out on highly leveraged terms, lenders may be prepared to lend on a subordinated basis. This increases the money available. The senior creditors benefit from the cushion of the junior debt and therefore may lend more. The junior creditors benefit from a high interest rate to compensate them for the larger risk and may be further sweetened by warrants for shares in the debtor or the ability to convert their debt into shares. The junior creditors may be institutional investors or a shareholder who agrees to take a portion of his purchase price as subordinated debt and who is thereby able to squeeze out extra price. The terms of this type of subordination are by far the most complex, partly because the junior creditors expect to have some control over their investment, partly because the junior debt is intended merely to support a transaction and may therefore be interim short-term finance as opposed to a permanent fixed component of the debtor's capital and partly because the finance is often very risky. The market jargon for this type of financing located midway between debt and equity is mezzanine debt—a term which, one must admit, hits the target.

(d) **Improved credit.** The debtor may wish to improve its balance sheet by enlarging the capital base ranking after senior creditors and thereby encouraging fresh senior credit.

(e) **Borrowing limits.** The debtor may wish to raise money without eroding the room available under borrowing restrictions in the debtor's loan agreements or constitutional documents. This may be achieved if the borrowing limit—providing that borrowings must not exceed a prescribed multiple of equity capital and reserves—defines equity capital as including subordinated debt.

(f) Work-outs. By subordinating debt, a borrower may seek to survive without going through a formal insolvency rehabilitation proceeding or going into liquidation. Typically, insiders or major suppliers might be persuaded to agree to subordinate their claims to induce bank creditors not to enforce their loans in the hope that the borrower will live to see better days. If the junior creditor is also a major shareholder as well as a creditor, subordination may be the only way of protecting his investment from total loss.

Comparison of subordinated debt and equity 1.4

Advantages. A simple way to subordinate an investor is for him to take shares, not debt. But subordinated debt may be preferable to equity for the following reasons:

— A debtor is usually entitled to deduct interest payable by it from gross profits in calculating its net profits on which the debtor pays tax. Dividends invariably are not deductible.
— Interest may not be subject to a withholding tax but dividends may be.
— The debtor may be liable to pay capital duty on the issue of shares, but not on the issue of loan capital. United Kingdom capital duty on the issue of shares has been abolished.
— The liability of a debtor to pay interest on debt is not dependent on the debtor's profits and is therefore mandatorily payable in full. The payment of dividends is usually dependent on profits. But even here junior debt can be very similar to preferred shares in economic substance if, for example, the debt is perpetual and non-payment of interest is not a default if the borrower is also not able to pay dividends.
— Some institutions cannot invest in equities (particularly unlisted shares) but may be able to invest in debt. This may be true of pension funds and insurance companies.
— A corporate debtor can repay debt without complying with legal restrictions on the ability of the company to reduce its share capital.
— The interest rate on debt is usually less than preferred share dividends because debt is higher in the pecking order and therefore less risky. Hence the debtor's cost of capital is reduced.
— If the subordination is achieved by a turnover by the junior creditor to the senior creditor of dividends on the junior debt, the senior creditor receives a double dividend and is hence in a better position then if the junior creditor were instead a holder of preferred shares: see the examples at paragraph 2.8.
— The double dividend resulting from a turnover subordination is a way of giving the senior creditor some security in a case where the debtor is prevented by a negative pledge in its credit agreements

from granting security or where the debtor does not wish to grant security on the ground that it might inhibit future trade or bank credit.

— Debt can be secured but equity cannot be. Hence a secured junior creditor can rank himself ahead of trade creditors.

— The debtor's shareholders may wish to exclude the subordinated investor from benefiting from an expected appreciation in the debtor's business and hence watering their equity. A similar result could of course be achieved by preference shares.

— Subordinated debt can be issued without disturbing shareholder class rights and without any need to satisfy preemption rights in favour of shareholders or to obtain the approval of shareholders to the issue of new shares.

Disadvantages. On the other hand, debt has the following disadvantages compared to equity:

— creditors have no right to vote and can control management only through covenants in the debt instrument;

— creditors do not share in profits. A right to share in profits may result in the debt being treated as equity on insolvency: paragraph 11.8;

— debt does not benefit from appreciations in the capital value of the debtor's business;

— trade creditors who do not benefit from the subordination as senior creditors may be less inclined to continue credit than if the junior debt were equity;

— subordinated debt under a turnover subordination should normally be treated as a liability in determining whether a debtor is insolvent and for the purposes of wrongful trading by the directors, but equity never is: paragraph 2.16.

1.5   Definition of senior debt

The senior debt may, for example, be the following:

(a) Senior debt may be all other debt except subordinated debt. This is typical of subordinated bond issues. A typical provision would be:

"*Senior debt*" means all present and future liabilities of the debtor other than those which by their terms or by law are subordinated to ordinary liabilities on the winding up or dissolution of the debtor.

(b) Senior debt may be debt of a particular creditor or class of creditors such as banks. This is typical of insider subordinations. A common formula would be:

"*Senior debt*" means all present and future liabilities of the debtor to the senior creditor, absolute, contingent or otherwise, whether or not matured, whether or not liquidated, and whether or not owed solely or jointly by the debtor or to the senior creditor solely or jointly, including without limitation (a) liabilities which the senior creditor acquires by purchase, security assignment or otherwise, (b) interest, (c) damages and claims for restitution and (d) costs.

In the case of senior debt arising out of a specific credit agreement, the definition might state (in outline):

"Senior debt" means all present and future liabilities of the debtor to the senior creditor under the credit agreement dated [   ] between the debtor and the senior creditor (including under all variations of and supplements to the credit agreement) together with:

    (a) any refinancings, refundings, novations, or extensions of any of those liabilities: paragraph 7.12;

    (b) additional principal up to £[   ] if lent by the senior creditor plus all interest thereon and fees and costs in connection therewith: paragraph 7.12;

    (c) any claim for damages or restitution in the event of rescission of any of those liabilities: paragraph 11.7;

    (d) any claim against the debtor flowing from any recovery by the debtor or its estate of a payment or discharge in respect of those liabilities on grounds of preference or otherwise: paragraph 9.9;

    (e) any amounts (such as post-insolvency interest) which would be included in any of the foregoing but for any discharge or non-provability or unenforceability of the same on any insolvency proceedings affecting the debtor: paragraph 9.8;

    (f) any liability arising in substitution or exchange for or on a modification of any of the foregoing in connection with any plan or arrangement relating to the debtor.

  (c) Senior debt may be a class of debt, such as borrowings or listed borrowings. Thus the definition of senior debt may be defined so as to exclude trade debt and hence apply only to borrowings, purchase price credits maturing more than 90 days after incurrence, liabilities under finance leases, and guarantees of these obligations. The object of the debtor would be to benefit financial creditors but not ordinary suppliers and hence improve access to financial credit.

The wider the definition, then the more deeply subordinated is the junior debt. Under a turnover subordination, the senior creditor's double dividend is diluted by inclusion of other creditors because the proceeds of the junior debt have to spread over a larger amount of senior debt. Hence a senior creditor will seek to narrow the scope of senior debt. But borrowers will wish to widen the definition of senior debt so as to enhance their ability to raise additional money on the strength of the subordinated cushion. In financings of leveraged bids, the senior debt may include not only debt under the senior credit agreement but also ancillary working capital loans under separate financings.

1.6   Definition of junior debt

The junior debt owed by the debtor to the junior creditor may be:

— all debt. This may be worded on the lines of the relevant definition of senior debt cited in paragraph 1.5 above.
— all debt incurred under a specific junior credit agreement. This would be typical of project finance or change of control financings. The definition should also include damages and other recoveries on rescission of the junior debt: paragraph 11.7.
— debt incurred to particular creditors prior to a specified date. This would be typical in work-outs. Thus a supplier agreeing to subordinate existing credits should be permitted to rank senior for future credits as an inducement to continued trading with the debtor.
— debt to a particular creditor up to a specified amount. The purpose here would be to maintain a maximum cushion of subordinated capital. The definition should make it clear whether the limit relates only to principal or whether it also includes interest, fees and costs.
— debt constituted by specific issue of debt securities, as in the case of a subordinated bond issue.

1.7   Identity of the debtor

In principle the subordination should apply to all debtors who may be liable for the junior debt, directly or by way of guarantee or otherwise.

Thus if the junior creditor makes a loan to a subsidiary under the guarantee of the parent and the guarantee is subordinated, the loan itself should also be subordinated. Otherwise the liquidator of the subsidiary might be able to claim from the parent-guarantor any on-lending of the loan by the subsidiary to the parent, and pay dividends out of the proceeds to the junior creditor as a creditor of the subsidiary who thereby side-steps the subordinated guarantee.

If the junior creditor obtains guarantees or security from other members of a corporate group, the senior creditor should obtain the same guarantees and security and the junior guarantees or security should be subordinated: paragraph 7.23.

1.8   *Pari passu* agreements compared

Subordination agreements may be compared with *pari passu* agreements. A subordination agreement ranks one creditor prior to another. A *pari passu* agreement ranks the creditors equally.

The most common forms of *pari passu* agreement are:

(a) *Pari passu* **security agreements** whereby secured creditors agree to rank their security equally and to share proceeds of realisation equally.

(b) *Pro rata* **sharing clauses** in syndicated loan agreements whereby the banks agree that, if one of them is paid (by set-off, realisation of security, proceeds of attachment, direct payment or otherwise) in a greater proportion than the other banks, the recovering bank must share the excess with the other banks so as to re-establish *pro rata* holdings. The recovering bank is expressly subrogated to the claims of the other banks to the extent it has paid those claims out of the excess receipt.

(c) **Loss-sharing clauses** in work-out agreements whereby the creditors typically agree to share receipts if the debtor is put into default. The sharing may be tiered in order to reflect the fact that, for example, some of the creditors may have had security prior to the work-out but others did not. The sharing is usually achieved by provisions for the proceeds of the security to be paid out by a common trustee of the security equally and for the making of intercreditor equalising payments for other receipts (such as set-offs) on the lines of a *pro rata* sharing clause.

CHAPTER 2

CLASSES OF SUBORDINATION

2.1 Complete and springing subordinations

A subordination may be a complete subordination or a springing subordination.

Under a complete subordination, the junior debt is postponed from the time of the subordination contract and may not be paid so long as the senior debt is outstanding.

Under a springing (or inchoate) subordination, the junior debt may be paid until a specified event happens, such as the insolvency of the debtor, the occurrence of an event of default under the senior credit agreement, or the breach by the debtor of a financial ratio. So long as all is well with the debtor, the subordination lies asleep. But when an event occurs indicating that the senior debt may be at risk, the subordination at once leaps up, pounces on the junior debt and holds it down. One disadvantage is that, unless the alarm rings early enough the pounce may come too late when the junior debt has escaped.

When these payment blockages should occur depends on the circumstances: see paragraphs 7.5 *et seq*.

In any event, all subordinations spring into effect on liquidation or insolvency proceedings because it is then that the subordination is essential so far as the senior creditor is concerned.

The timing of the spring may differentiate between categories of debt included in the junior debt. Thus the principal of the junior debt may be locked up from the beginning but payment of interest, fees and costs to the junior creditor may be allowed until some subsequent springing event such as an event of default under the senior credit agreement.

In insider subordinations, the following amounts payable to the junior creditor may be liberated until an event of default on the ground that they are proper payments for services or supplies:

— salaries and fringe benefits (if the junior creditor is an officer of the corporate debtor);
— reasonable payment for services or supplies provided by the junior creditor or rent payable to the junior creditor;

2.2 Initial and subsequent subordinations

A junior creditor may agree to subordinate the junior debt when the debt is initially incurred or he may subordinate it subsequently while the debt is outstanding.

An example of a subsequent subordination is the subordination of outstanding junior debt agreed in connection with work-outs where bank creditors prevail upon insiders or suppliers to subordinate their existing claims as a condition to the continuance of bank facilities. Initial subordinations are typical of subordinated bond issues or any transaction involving new loans.

A risk for the senior creditor is that a subordination may amount to a preference of the senior creditor by the junior creditor which is liable to be avoided on the junior creditor's insolvency. One difference between initial and subsequent subordinations is that this risk is usually remote in the case of initial subordinations: paragraph 4.4. Another risk is that if a junior creditor subsequently subordinates a guaranteed debt, then, on familiar principles of guarantee law, the guarantor may be released unless the guarantee permits this variation and weakening of the junior creditor's claim: paragraph 9.4.

A subordination may be agreed in relation to senior debt which is then outstanding or in relation to future senior debt or both. If the senior debt is outstanding and the senior creditor is not a party to the subordination, a risk for the senior creditor is that the junior creditor may be able to vary the subordination without the consent of the senior creditor: paragraph 7.20.

Methods of subordination generally   2.3

There are two basic methods of subordination—turnover subordinations and contractual subordinations. The technique used has a major impact on the efficiency of the subordination, the recoveries by the senior creditor and the risks run by the senior creditor. These techniques are primarily directed to subordinating the junior debt on the insolvency of the debtor: prior to a forced distribution of assets the subordination can largely be achieved by simple contractual prohibitions on the payment of the junior debt.

Turnover subordinations   2.4

In the case of a turnover subordination, on the insolvency of the debtor the junior creditor agrees to turn over to the senior creditor all recoveries received by the junior creditor in respect of the junior debt. This is the classic traditional form and the method which is most widely used. Indeed, it is apparently the only available method if the junior creditor is to be subordinated only to a single senior debt, or class of senior debt, as opposed to all other debt. There are two basic forms:

(a) Subordination trusts. Under a subordination trust, the junior creditor agrees to hold dividends, proceeds and other payments on the junior debt received by the junior creditor on trust for the senior creditor as property of the senior creditor for application towards the senior debt until the senior debt is paid in full. This is the most satisfactory method and confers on the senior creditor a proprietary claim against the junior creditor for recoveries on the junior debt. It will also usually prevent set-offs between the junior creditor and the debtor which might otherwise destroy the subordination: paragraph 6.5.

Legal aspects of subordination trusts include:

— whether the trust constitutes a security interest created by the junior creditor: Chapter 5;
— whether the trust will be recognised in jurisdictions inimical to the common law trust: paragraph 4.6;
— whether the transfer of proceeds must be perfected by special formalities in certain jurisdictions: paragraph 2.10;
— the application of the perpetuity rule: paragraph 11.4;
— the priority of the senior creditor as against assignees of the junior debt: paragraph 7.21;
— the validity of the claim of the senior creditor if the junior creditor becomes insolvent before the proceeds fall in: para 4.1;
— the standing of the senior creditor to vote on or prove for the junior debt: paragraphs 3.6 *et seq*;
— whether the subordination can be nullified without the senior creditor's consent: paragraph 7.20;

There is no objection to a trust for future persons provided that the beneficiaries of the trust can be ascertained with certainty when the trust property vests.[1]

As mentioned, a subordination in favour of a limited group of senior creditors, as opposed to all creditors, can evidently be achieved only by some sort of turnover obligation. Apart from debtor-creditor subordinations described below, this turnover must inevitably involve a transfer of property in the junior creditor's claim or its proceeds. It is immaterial whether one characterises this transfer as an assignment of proceeds, or a constructive trust, or an equitable lien, or as marshalling or as some species of subrogation, since, at the end of the day, the property of the junior creditor becomes the property of the senior creditor to the extent necessary: see also paragraph 3.3.

The junior creditor could go one step further and assign the junior debt to the senior creditor as collateral security for the senior debt. For the differences between a security assignment and a subordination trust, see paragraph 5.6.

(b) Debtor-creditor turnover subordinations. Under this (somewhat unusual) form, the junior creditor agrees to claim or prove for the junior debt on the insolvency of the debtor and to pay an amount equal to dividends or other payments received by him to the senior creditor. The main disadvantage is that the junior creditor is merely a debtor to the senior creditor to the extent of those recoveries and the senior creditor relies on the continued solvency of the junior creditor. The senior cred-

---

[1] Snell's *Principles of Equity* (28th ed.), pp. 114 *et seq*.

itor does not have a proprietary claim for those recoveries since the junior creditor does not transfer them to or hold them on trust for the senior creditor. Hence this method is suitable only where the junior creditor can be relied on not to become insolvent. But the technique has been used where there have been fears that a contractual subordination conflicts with a mandatory insolvency rule providing for *pari passu* payment of the insolvent's debts and that the conventional subordination trust may create a security interest.

In practice, even if the subordination is achieved by a trust of proceeds of the junior debt, this will usually be also accompanied by a back-stop debtor-creditor turnover obligation imposed on the junior creditor. Thus the junior creditor is obliged to pay to the senior creditor amounts equal to recoveries (instead of holding the recoveries on trust) in order to cover the following situations:

— the junior debt is discharged by a set-off. In this instance there is no recovery of an asset to turn over.
— the subordination trust is invalid, *e.g.* because it is an unregistered security interest (paragraph 5.2), or because the local jurisdiction does not recognise the trust (paragraph 4.6), or because the trust is an assignment requiring to be perfected by certain formalities which have not been complied with: paragraph 2.10.

Contractual or "contingent debt" subordinations 2.5

The junior creditor agrees with the debtor that, so long as the senior debt is outstanding, the junior debt is not payable unless and until the senior debt has been paid in full. If the debtor becomes subject to insolvency or dissolution proceedings, the liquidator is directed to pay the senior debt first.

The clause might read:

> "If the debtor becomes subject to any liquidation, dissolution, rehabilitation or insolvency proceeding or to any assignment for the benefit of its creditors or any other distribution of its assets, or any analogous event occurs the junior debt will rank in right of payment subordinate to and after the prior payment of the senior debt."

Because this formulation may conflict with a mandatory insolvency rule that unsecured debts are to be paid *pari passu* (paragraph 3.1), a contractual subordination is sometimes framed as a contingent debt subordination. This states that if the debtor goes into liquidation or becomes subject to a rehabilitation proceeding or any other insolvency proceedings, the junior debt is contingent or conditional on the debtor being able to pay the senior debt in full. If the debtor is insolvent, the senior creditor will not be paid in full. The junior creditor in effect renounces his junior debt in that event. If the debtor would be solvent if the junior debt were shaved down but not wholly wiped out, then the junior debt is diminished accordingly. If the debtor would still be insolvent even if the junior debt were completely wiped out, the junior debt is cancelled. Unhappily the drafting of the contingency can never be entirely satisfactory.

A sample clause might provide:

"(1) If the debtor becomes subject to any liquidation, dissolution or similar insolvency proceedings or to any assignment for the benefit of its creditors or any other distribution of its assets, the junior debt will be payable only on condition that the senior debt has been or is capable of being paid in full. Accordingly in any such event the junior debt will be reduced to such amount down to zero as is necessary to ensure that the debtor is able to pay the senior debt in full.

(2) The reduction of the junior debt will be applied first to costs and expenses, secondly to interest, and thirdly to principal of the junior debt."

Other English forms provide that on insolvency or dissolution proceedings, the junior debt is conditional on the debtor being solvent and that accordingly the junior debt is not payable except to the extent that the debtor could pay it and still be solvent after the payment. It is stated that the debtor is solvent if it is able to pay its provable debts as they fall due disregarding any debts which are subordinated to the senior debt. The objection to this formulation is that it requires a sophisticated definition of solvency which must reflect provability and which must also exclude liabilities which are subordinated debt (itself a slippery concept). One cuts through all these technicalities by providing that the junior debt is conditional on the debtor's ability to pay the senior debt in full.

The main feature of contractual or "contingent debt" subordinations is that the junior debtor is in effect subordinated to all creditors and not just to a particular senior loan or class of senior debt. The implications of this are illustrated at paragraph 2.8.

The contingency should apply only on forced distributions of the debtor's assets, as on liquidation. If the junior debt is shaved down merely if the debtor is insolvent, it will sometimes be uncertain whether this test is met. Further, if the junior debt is secured, the contingency may prevent recovery by the junior creditor even though the security is sufficient. Hence the contingency should not apply to the extent that the junior debt is recoverable out of the security: paragraph 8.16. The freeze on payments prior to forced distribution should be dealt with by a contractual freeze rather than a contingency.

2.6 Statutory subordinations

In some jurisdictions a statute provides for subordination of qualifying debt and the junior creditor agrees that his debt will be subordinated in accordance with the statute. In countries as diverse as Austria, Finland and Mexico the junior creditor can contract into the subordination statute in the case of issuers to whom the statute applies, e.g. banks. The efficacy of this type of subordination depends entirely upon the statute and its recognition abroad. In France, the French Company Law of 1966 was amended in 1985 to permit the issue of subordinated debt ranking after all other creditors: Article 339–7.

Other subordinations 2.7

Other somewhat idiosyncratic methods of subordination may be noted here:

(a) Preference shares. In some jurisdictions, a subordination can be achieved by the issue of preference shares by a parent company to a finance subsidiary which the finance subsidiary charges in favour of bondholders to secure an issue of bonds by the finance subsidiary matching the preference shares as to income and maturity. The preference shares are similar to a subordinated guarantee by the parent but in the meantime rank as share capital of the parent company, *e.g.* for the purposes of capital adequacy. Consideration should be given to any prohibitions on a subsidiary holding shares of its parent, even if they are preference shares only.

(b) Spanish *escritura publica*. Under Spanish law and the law of some Spanish-based jurisdictions (such as Panama) an unsecured creditor whose debt instrument is formalised as an *escritura publica* ranks ahead of unperfected creditors. The procedure generally involves the execution of the senior debt instrument before a notary and the payment of a significant documentary tax.

(c) Compulsory subordinations. A debt may be compulsorily subordinated by a rule of insolvency law: paragraph 11.8.

(d) Structural subordinations. A lender to a holding company is generally in a worse position than a lender to the operating subsidaries since the lender to the holding company looks only to the value of the shares in the subsidiaries, *i.e.* what is left after the creditors of the subsidiaries have been paid. Many effective "subordinations" are achieved in this way. But this structural subordination will be weakened if the holding company on-lends the proceeds of the "junior" loan to the subsidiary or is a creditor of the subsidiary since the holding company and its creditors will then effectively rank equally with the "senior" lenders to the subsidiaries—exactly in economic substance as if the junior creditor were ranking equally.

Comparison of recoveries according to method of subordination 2.8

If the debtor goes into insolvent liquidation, the recoveries of senior debt, junior debt and other debt vary markedly according to the method of subordination.

The chief distinction between a contractual subordination and a turnover subordination is that in the latter case the senior debt benefits from the turnover of dividends on the junior debt and hence receives a double dividend. The economic effect is as if the senior creditor had a charge over the junior debt. The value of this "collateral" or double dip is unpredictable because it depends upon the amount of the distribution in the bankruptcy of the debtor.

The recoveries of the junior claimant will also vary according to whether he is a subordinated creditor subject to a turnover subordination or a holder of preference shares.

The amount of the recoveries may be illustrated by two examples set out in detail below which assume three classes of debt on the debtor's bankruptcy, namely, senior debt, junior debt and other debt. The results of these examples may be summarised as follows:

1. In the case of a contractual subordination, other debt benefits even though other debt is not intended to rank as senior debt in relation to the junior debt. Hence contractual subordinations are suitable only where the junior debt is to be subordinated to all other debt. In the case of a turnover subordination, other debt is not benefited but recovers exactly the same amount as it would recover in the absence of a subordination.
2. If the debtor's assets are insufficient to pay both senior debt and other debt, then senior debt recovers more by virtue of the double dividend than would be the case if the junior claimant were contractually subordinated or if the junior claimant were a preference shareholder.
3. If the debtor's assets are sufficient to pay both senior debt and other debt, but not junior debt as well, then junior debt recovers more in the case of a turnover subordination than would be the case if the junior creditor were contractually subordinated or a preference shareholder.

The effect therefore is that under a turnover subordination, as opposed to a contractual subordination, the senior creditor is always better off, and the junior creditor can be better off.

Example 1

In this example the debtor's assets are sufficient to cover senior debt and other debt, but not junior debt as well.

Debtor's assets 400   Senior debt: 200
                        Junior debt: 200
                        Other debt: 100
                                      500

(a) Contractual subordination

The junior debt must be reduced to 100 so that the debtor is solvent. Therefore the recoveries are:

Senior: 200
Junior: 100
Other: 100
         400

So long as the assets are sufficient to cover both senior debt and other debt, other debt benefits from the subordination even though other debt is not intended to benefit from it and is not senior debt.

(b) Turnover subordination

Each creditor receives an 80 per cent. dividend.
Therefore the recoveries before turnover are:

Senior: 160
Junior: 160
Other: 80

The junior creditor must turn over 40 to the senior creditor to pay the senior debt in full.
Therefore the final recoveries are:

Senior: 200
Junior: 120
Other: 80

Other debt does not benefit from the subordination with the result that junior debt receives more than in the case of a contractual subordination.

(c) Junior claimant is preferred shareholder

The recoveries are:

Senior: 200
Junior: 100
Other: 100

The recoveries are the same as with a contractual subordination.

Example 2

In this example the debtor's assets are insufficient to cover any of the claims.

Debtor's assets: 100	Senior debt:	200
	Junior debt:	100
	Other debt:	100
		500

(a) Contractual subordination

The junior debt must be reduced to nil because the assets are insufficient to pay the senior debt. The dividend on senior debt and other debt is 33⅓ per cent.
Therefore the recoveries are:

Senior: 66⅔
Junior: Nil
Other: 33⅓

Other debt benefits from the subordination even though not designated as senior debt.

(b) Turnover subordination

Each creditor receives a 20 per cent. dividend on its full claim.
Therefore the recoveries before turnover are:

Senior: 40
Junior: 40
Other: 20

The junior creditor must turn over 40 to the senior creditor.
Therefore the final recoveries are:

Senior: 80
Junior: Nil
Other: 20

Other debt does not benefit from the subordination. But the senior creditor benefits from the double dividend and does better than with a contractual subordination.

(c) Junior claimant is preferred shareholder

The dividend payable to creditors (excluding the junior claimant as shareholder) is 33⅓ per cent.
Therefore the recoveries are:

Senior: 66⅔
Junior: Nil
Other: 33⅓

Both senior debt and other debt receive the same as with a contractual subordination. But the senior debt receives less than would be the case if the junior debt were subject to a turnover subordination.

2.9 Characteristics of transfers of proceeds

Most subordination trusts are trusts of proceeds of the junior debt.

A transfer or trust or assignment of the *proceeds* of a debt, as opposed to the debt itself, is a curious half-way house. The debt is not transferred, only its fruits.

In the context of subordinations, the transfer of proceeds as opposed to the debt itself gives rise to the following issues:

— whether set-off mutuality is destroyed between the junior creditor and the debtor: paragraph 6.5.
— whether a priority notice can be given to the debtor before the proceeds come into existence: paragraph 7.21.
— whether the proceeds as a future asset fall into the pool of the junior creditor's estate if he should become insolvent before the debtor: paragraph 4.1.
— whether the senior creditor is owner of the junior debt for the purposes of insolvency proof and voting: paragraphs 3.5 *et seq.*
— whether the trust of proceeds is a gift of a future asset which is revocable by the junior creditor before the asset comes into existence: paragraph 7.20.

The transfer of proceeds is often contingent on insolvency proceedings so that the junior creditor owns the junior debt until then. Examples are security assignments of insurance proceeds and of the proceeds of letters of credit: see Art. 55 of the Uniform Customs and Practice for Documentary Credits (1983 Revision).

Three cases show that restrictions on assignment do not prejudice an assignment of proceeds.

In *Re Turcan* (1888) 40 Ch.D. 5, it was held that a prohibition on assignments by express contract or law did not prevent a trust of proceeds of an insurance policy.

In *Glegg* v. *Bromley* [1912] 3 K.B. 474, Mrs. Glegg assigned to Mr. Glegg the proceeds of an action for slander against Lady Bromley. If she had assigned the claim for slander itself, the assignment would have been void on grounds of champerty. *Held*: the assignment was good on the grounds that proceeds had been assigned, not the claim itself. Parker J. said at 489, "The subject-matter assigned is money or other property which might thereafter be acquired by means of the pending action for slander. It is not an existing chose in action, but future property identified by reference to an existing chose in action."

In *Russell & Co. Ltd.* v. *Austin Fryers* (1909) 25 T.L.R. 414, a circus performer assigned to a moneylender all his rights under his contract to perform at a circus "and all moneys and payments receivable thereunder." *Held*: although a contract of personal service is not assignable, there was no objection to assigning the proceeds. The court relied on *Crouch* v. *Martin and Harris* (1707) 2 Vern. 595.

Another case validates an assignment of proceeds arising after the assignor's bankruptcy.

In *Re Irving, ex p. Brett* (1877) 7 Ch.D. 419, a Mr. Bushby wrote to his bank as follows: "I hereby undertake that I will, when and as received, pay over to you all dividends coming to me in respect of my proof upon the Estate of Mr. John Irving." Mr. Bushby became bankrupt and the bank gave notice of its claim to the trustees in the bankruptcy of Mr. Irving. *Held*: this was a good equitable assignment of the dividend and that the bank was entitled as against Mr. Bushby's trustee in bankruptcy. Bacon C.J. said at 422 that Bushby (the assignor) "binds himself to pay over to the bank those dividends when he receives them. He does not promise . . . that he will pay them out of an uncertain fund, but he undertakes to pay over the very fund itself . . . It is clear that Bushby, at the time of his bankruptcy, was entitled to this chose in action, but it was subject to a trust to hand it over to the bank when received . . . Bushby was the assignor to, and at the same time the trustee for, the bank of these dividends."

Finally it has been held that an assignee of proceeds takes subject to a defect affecting the debt itself.

In *The Litsion Pride* [1985] 1 Lloyd's Rep. 437, an insured assigned the proceeds of a marine insurance policy. A loss occurred and the assignor-insured made a post-loss fraudulent claim. *Held*: the assignee of the proceeds was debarred from recovery because the fraud avoided the policy. The assignee did not acquire a vested right to the proceeds on the loss occurring.

2.10   Perfection of Transfer

Whether the local jurisdiction will apply to turnovers its requirement for special formalities validating assignments is a matter for investigation. In countries such as France, Belgium, Luxembourg, Japan and Korea, an assignment is void against creditors of the assignor (the junior creditor) and on his insolvency unless the assignment is either consented to by the debtor or notified to the debtor in a formal manner prescribed by law. Thus in France, Article 1690 of the Civil Code requires the formal service of a translation of the assignment on the debtor by a *huissier* (bailiff) or the debtor's acceptance or acknowledgment of the transfer by an *acte authentique*. Article 467 of the Japanese Civil Code is to similar effect: the notice of consent must be in writing as a notarial act (*kakuteihizuke*). Whether these formalities would apply to transfers of proceeds, as opposed to the junior debt itself, should be considered: see Chapter 12.

These formalities are not required in England to validate the transfer as against creditors of the junior creditor as transferor. In England an assignment of a specific debt without notice to the debtor is effective against judgment creditors of the assignor who attempt to garnish the assigned debt (see, for example, *Pickering* v. *Ilfracombe Ry.* (1868) L.R. 3 C.P. 235) and is also effective on the assignor's subsequent insolvency. Notice to the debtor merely affects such matters as priority between successive assignees, who the debtor pays, and set-off.

2.11   Scope of turnover obligation: recoveries from all sources

Under a turnover subordination, the turnover obligation should ideally apply to all recoveries on the junior debt, from whatever source, even if not from the debtor. Examples are:

— payments under guarantees of the junior debt;
— proceeds of security given by a third party for the junior debt;
— turnover from creditors who are themselves subordinated to the junior debt, as where there are multiple layers of subordinated debt;
— receipts by the junior creditor from other syndicate members under a *pro rata* sharing clause in a syndicated credit agreement;
— evasive payments by a third party to the junior creditor out of money provided by the debtor.

If the junior debt is guaranteed and it is not intended that payments on the guarantee should be turned over, the intercreditor agreement between the junior and senior creditor should so provide. From the point of view of the junior creditor the guarantor should remain liable to pay the junior creditor until the junior creditor has recovered the full junior debt for its own benefit and all its turnover obligations have been satisfied.

Recoveries in kind   **2.12**

The turnover obligation should also apply to distributions in kind on the junior debt as well as payments in cash. Thus the junior debt may be "paid" by an issue of debt or equity securities in a bankruptcy rehabilitation proceeding. From the point of view of the senior creditor, the intercreditor agreement should provide that the senior creditor may realise distributions in kind as it sees fit and that these distributions do not reduce the senior debt until their realised proceeds are actually received by the senior creditor. If this was not the case, there might be difficult problems of valuation and consequent uncertainty as to whether the junior creditor's turnover obligation is completely fulfilled.

However as an exception, it is sometimes provided under the so-called "X clause" that the turnover will not apply to securities issued to the junior creditor on a reorganisation of the debtor if those securities are subordinated to the senior debt or if securities are issued to the senior creditors on terms no less protective of the senior creditors than the original subordination.

As to currencies, the agreement could provide that, if turnover proceeds are received by the senior creditor in a currency different to the senior debt, the senior debt is discharged only when the proceeds, converted by the senior creditor at a market rate of exchange, are applied to the senior debt. If the junior debt is in a currency different from the currency of the debtor's country of incorporation, liquidation dividends will usually be payable in local currency since most commercial jurisdictions convert foreign currency debts into local currency for the purposes of an insolvency proof: see, for example, the Insolvency Act Rules 1986, r. 4.91. Similar rules prevail in Austria, Germany, France, Italy, Brazil, Argentina and the Netherlands.[2]

Events diminishing the turnover   **2.13**

The amount which is in fact turned over will be affected by such factors as:

— the validity of the junior debt. If the junior debt is invalid or non–provable (such as post-insolvency interest), there is nothing to recover which can be turned over;
— the validity of any security for the junior debt. If the security is invalid or loses priority, the turnover to the senior creditor will be diminished;
— whether the junior debt is convertible into equity. Once the junior debt has been converted, there would be no recoveries on the insolvency of the debtor to turn over: paragraph 11.5;
— the width of senior debt. A wide class of senior creditor will dilute the turnover to a particular senior creditor;

[2] Mann, *The Legal Aspect of Money* (4th ed. 1983) 337.

— the compulsory subordination of the junior debt on bankruptcy, *e.g.* on the basis of the United States equitable subordination of the claims of those who interfere in the management of the debtor or on the basis of a statutory rule that debts receiving interest varying with profits or receiving a share of profits are subordinated to all other creditors: paragraph 11.8. If the junior creditor cannot claim until all other creditors are paid, he again has nothing to turn over to the senior creditor. The senior creditor as transferee of the junior creditor should not be in a better position than the junior creditor.

2.14   Acceleration of senior debt on turnover

The senior creditor should have the right to accelerate part of his debt on the receipt of an unexpected turnover prior to bankruptcy so that there is an accrued claim eligible for payment by the turnover. If the payment by turnover results in a breakage cost suffered by the senior creditor, this should be payable by the debtor under the senior credit agreement. A breakage cost arises where the rate of interest at which the lender can relend the prepaid money is less than the rate of interest the lender is paying on a term deposit borrowed to fund the loan. Alternatively it may be provided that the turnover is to be held by the senior creditor until the next payment date on the senior debt.

2.15   Circular subordinations

If C subordinates to B who subordinates to A who subordinates to C, the subordination is circular. A, who should be he most senior creditor, has subordinated himself to C who is the most junior creditor. The turnover would go round and round infinitely.

This puzzle usually arises because of drafting error. For example, A may be senior to B and C and then subordinate his debt to all other creditors, forgetting that he should have added "all other creditors except B and C." Or B may subordinate to "all other creditors except creditors who agree to be subordinated to other creditors," forgetting that some creditors are subordinated by law: paragraph 11.8. Many solutions to this conundrum have been attempted but the solution is likely to be determined largely by the terms of each subordination (which may be very different) and whether one subordination is to a specific creditor and another to all creditors: it is pointless to set up cardboard figures of theoretical problems without facts.

A useful approach is an elegant solution proposed by Gilmore in *Security Interests in Personal Property* (1965) at p. 1021 which unhappily only resolves one particular situation.

In the end, it may be necessary to breach the circle, *e.g.* by not compelling a junior creditor to turn over dividends received from a turnover to him, but only dividends received from the debtor on his own claim.

Subordination, insolvency tests and wrongful trading   **2.16**

An important question is whether subordinated debt counts as a liability for the purposes of determining the insolvency of the debtor in relation to winding-up petitions, wrongful trading and the commencement of the preference suspect period.

Section 123 of the Insolvency Act 1986 adopts, in the alternative, both the cash-flow test of insolvency (inability to pay debts as they fall due) and the balance sheet test ("the value of the company's assets is less than the amount of its liabilities, taking into account its contingent and prospective liabilities").

Where payment of the junior debt is postponed, then plainly the junior debt will not count as regards the cash-flow test of inability to pay debts as they fall due.

Where the test is excess of liabilities over assets, the junior debt will count as a liability in the case of a turnover subordination because, as between the debtor and the junior creditor, the junior debt is unconditionally payable and the turnover is purely an arrangement between the junior and the senior creditor.

In the case of contractual or contingent debt subordinations where the payment of the junior debt is conditional upon payment of the senior debt or upon the solvency of the debtor, the application of the balance sheet test depends upon a construction of the subordination agreement and the particular issue in question.

As regards wrongful trading, section 214 of the Insolvency Act 1986 provides that a director is potentially liable to contribute to the assets of the company if the company has gone into insolvent liquidation (meaning "goes into liquidation at a time when its assets are insufficient for the payment of its debts and other liabilities and the expenses of the winding up") and the director "knew or ought to have concluded that there was no reasonable prospect that the company would avoid going into insolvent liquidation", subject to a "best efforts" defence. If the effect of the subordination contract is that, at the time that the winding up order is made or resolution passed, the junior creditor has renounced his claim to the extent necessary to ensure solvency, it is suggested that the directors ought to be entitled to disregard the junior debt as a liability in determining whether the company would avoid going into insolvent liquidation. This should be the case if, for example, the junior creditor is deemed to be in the position of a shareholder if the company goes into liquidation or if payment of the junior debt is conditional on prior payment of all other creditors or conditional on the solvency of the company both before and after payment. If this is correct, then these forms of subordination allow the directors to continue trading longer than would be the case with ordinary debt and in this respect the junior debt performs a similar function to equity.

As regards fraudulent trading, section 213 of the Insolvency Act 1986 provides that if in the course of a winding up it appears that any business of the company has been carried on with intent to defraud creditors of the company, the court may order that persons knowingly parties to the fraud are to be liable to contribute to the company's assets. One effect of this is that, if the directors incur debts when they know that there is little prospect of those debts being paid, the directors are potentially liable to contribute to the company's assets. In determining whether a new creditor will be paid, the directors ought to be able to take into account the fact that junior debt will be subordinated to the creditor.

Nevertheless these issues deserve careful consideration in the context of the particular circumstances and the underlying policies informing insolvency law in this area, namely, the protection of creditors from abuse. Thus the deliberate wiping out of the junior debt by reckless trading might conceivably amount to a fraud within fraudulent trading rules such as section 213.

A provision that, on insolvent liquidation, the junior creditor must convert into preferred shares is undesirable since a company may not be able to issue shares once it is in liquidation: see, for example, section 88 of the Insolvency Act 1986. It is preferable to state that in that event the junior creditor is deemed to have converted immediately prior to the liquidation.

As regards the availability of a winding-up or administration petition based on insolvency in the sense of negative net assets, the test of whether the junior debt is to be counted as a liability ought to be determined according to whether, at the time of petition, the junior debt has been effectively renounced. A similar principle should apply as regards the commencement of the suspect period for preference and the like.

CHAPTER 3

SUBORDINATION AND THE DEBTOR'S BANKRUPTCY

Mandatory *pari passu* rules   3.1

The better view is that an arrangement between junior creditor and the debtor that the junior creditor is to be contractually subordinated should not in principle conflict with English insolvency rules that liabilities of the insolvent are to be paid *pari passu*, but the matter is undecided in England. The problem arises because the provision for the payment of ordinary debts *pari passu* is expressed to be mandatory and the courts may give it literal effect as a matter of strict statutory construction, regardless of whether such a result is required by the policy of the insolvency statute. As will be seen, however, it is usually possible to avoid this statutory difficulty.

Section 107 of the Insolvency Act 1986 provides that, subject to the priority of preferential debts, "the company's property in a voluntary winding up *shall* on the winding up be applied in satisfaction of the company's liabilities *pari passu* . . . " (emphasis added). Rule 4.181(1) of the Insolvency Rules 1986 as amended provides: "Debts other than preferential debts rank equally between themselves in the winding up." This provision applies whether or not the company is unable pay its debts: see rule 4.181(2). Provisions to a similar effect are found in the insolvency law of many English-based jurisdictions.

Apart from the question of statutory language, the policy of these provisions should not be infringed where one creditor agrees to be paid after another creditor since the object of the *pari passu* rule is to ensure that a creditor is not paid ahead of the general body of creditors rather than that one creditor agrees to be deferred. No policy of the insolvency laws is offended. It was held in an Australian case that a deferment of debt which does not prejudice the equal ranking of other creditors is not prohibited by the terms of equivalent provisions in Australian insolvency legislation: *Horne* v. *Chester & Fein Property Developments Pty. Ltd.* [1987] A.C.L.R. 245.[1]

In this case, an agreement provided that "all moneys advanced to [G] shall be accepted by it as loans" and "shall rank equally in order of

---

[1] See also *Re Walker Construction Co. Ltd.* [960] N.Z.L.R. 523; *Re Marlborough Construction Co.* [1978] A.C.L.C. 29, 487 (Australia)—although this case involved a scheme of arrangement sanctioned by the court; *Re Industrial Welding Co. Pty. Ltd.* (1977–1978) A.C.L.R. 30, 168 (Australia) obiter; *Re NBT Builders Pty. Ltd.* [1984] 8 A.C.L.R. 724, 727–8 (obiter).

23

priority as to repayment by [G]." There was a proviso that if any creditor made an "additional loan" to G, such amounts should be repaid before any other repayment of loans to other creditors. Two creditors had made "additional loans" to G.

Held:

(1) Section 440 of the Companies (Vic.) Code does not require that in all cases a liquidator must distribute assets *pari passu* amongst creditors. He may distribute in accordance with an agreement between the parties where to do so could not adversely affect any creditor not a party to the agreement. Section 440 provides:

> "440. Except as otherwise provided by this Code, all debts proved in a winding up rank equally and, if the property of the company is insufficient to meet them in full, they shall be paid proportionately."

(2) It is a general principle of insolvency law that the whole of a debtor's estate should be available for distribution to all creditors and that no one creditor or group of creditors can lawfully contract in such a manner as to defeat other creditors not parties to the contract. However, this principle is not contravened where the performance of an agreement between various parties can in no way affect the entitlement of creditors not a party to that agreement.

In *Re Walker Construction Co. Ltd. (in liq.)* [1960] N.Z.L.R. 523, a company called a meeting of creditors, at which it was resolved that liabilities for goods supplied after a certain date be treated as preferred, and prior liabilities should be deferred. Later a deed of arrangement was executed by most creditors, pursuant to which the moratorium was preserved. Later again, a scheme of arrangement was submitted to meetings of creditors. Section 293 of the New Zealand Companies Act 1955 provides that a company's debts shall be paid *pari passu*.
Held: the deferment should be upheld. F. B. Adams J. said at 536–537:

> "It would be unconscionable in the extreme to permit any deferred creditor who assented to the arrangement, and whose assent was acted on, to prove in competition with the current creditors . . . it seems to me that the statutory requirement of *pari passu* payment does not rest on considerations of public policy, but is a matter of private right . . . the statutory right of a creditor who is entitled to prove . . . in a winding up is within the rule, and may be qualified or renounced as the creditor thinks fit: and, to the extent to which he may have chosen to waive or qualify his right to *pari passu* payment, the liquidator's duty to him will be affected accordingly. . . . But where it is binding by contract or on equitable grounds, I cannot believe that the court having jurisdiction in the winding up is bound to ignore it, or unable to give due effect to it in the winding up. . . . I am not prepared to hold that the court is powerless in such circumstances. . . . In my opinion, the deferred creditors who assented to the arrangement in this case are bound by the arrangement in such a way that it would be grossly inequitable if they are permitted to insist on a distribution contrary thereto."

It is considered that the *obiter dicta* to the contrary in *Re Orion Sound Ltd.* [1979] 2 N.Z.L.R 574 would not be followed in England: that case appears to have been influenced by an overwide interpretation of the *British Eagle* case discussed below.

Further the English courts have been content to subordinate a claim on grounds that the creditor and the bankrupt are quasi-partners even though this was not sanctioned by statute: see the cases where a loan by a mistress to her lover for the purposes of the lover's business were postponed on the lover's insolvency: *Re Beale* (1876) 4 Ch.D. 246; *Re Meade* [1951] Ch. 774. However in these cases the mistress was treated as not being a creditor at all, rather than as a deferred creditor.

In *British Eagle International Airlines Ltd.* v. *Air France* [1975] 2 All E.R. 390, H.L., there were dicta that the *pari passu* rule is mandatory. But this case concerned a contract to take away an asset of the insolvent after petition without having a charge over the asset. The insolvent was owed a vested debt which, by clearing house rules, was snatched away after petition. All that the case decided was the routine proposition that a creditor cannot, after the insolvency, walk into the insolvent's house and help himself to the furniture—a proposition as ancient as the bankruptcy laws themselves. The case was strictly a decision on post-petition disposals, not *pari passu* payment of debts.

In *National Westminster Bank Ltd.* v. *Halesowen Presswork and Assemblies Ltd.* [1972] A.C. 785, H.L., the House of Lords held by a majority that parties could not contract out of the insolvency set-off clause because the section stated that there "shall" be a set-off and therefore this was mandatory as a matter of strict statutory construction. But it is suggested that the mandatory nature of insolvency set-off is backed by a strong policy. This is the sensible policy that a creditor will almost invariably be benefited by a set-off on insolvency even though he preferred to exclude set-off by contract prior to insolvency, *e.g.* to maintain cash-flow. If the section were not mandatory, there would be questions as to whether a contract excluding solvency set-off continued into insolvency and some unexpected results from creditors: the result would often be to defeat legitimate expectations as has been found in American cases on the non-mandatory nature of United States insolvency set-off.[2] Further the mandatory nature of the section was clearly signalled by the specific alteration of the permissive "may" to "shall" in the 1869 version of the clause.

The only policy which might be involved in preventing subordinations is that the liquidator should not be concerned with the extra work of reflecting priority agreements or be concerned with arrangements between creditors—a point which was debated in the United States before the United States courts, very sensibly, accepted contractual subordinations: paragraph 3.2. The answer to this is that the liquidator takes the insolvent as he finds him and that there is nothing new in the duty to pay claims in hierarchy or to value contingent debts. This "convenience" argument in favour of *pari passu* payment was rejected in *Horne* v. *Chester and Fein Property Developments Pty. Ltd.* [1987] A.C.L.R. 245.

A similar point arises in relation to registration statutes which prescribe that security "shall" rank according to time of registration: paragraph 8.2.

In any event, the rule will not be infringed by a subordination trust or a

---

[2] See the author's *English and International Set-off* (1989) para. 24–111.

debtor-creditor turnover subordination because in both cases the junior creditor claims the full amount of the junior debt on the insolvency of the debtor *pari passu* with all other general creditors, including the senior creditor. The turnover obligation, which achieves the subordination, is purely a relationship between the junior creditor and the senior creditor.

The *pari passu* rule should also not be infringed by a contingent debt subordination (whereby the junior debt is contingent on the debtor's solvency) because the junior debt is inherently contingent and is hence provable only in its contingent amount. In English corporate insolvencies contingent liabilities are provable by statute in their valued amount: see rule 4.86 of the Insolvency Rules 1986. If the debtor is insolvent and the junior debt is conditional on solvency, the provable amount will usually be nil.

It is considered most unlikely that a court would regard the contingency as not a real contingency but as an attempt to circumvent a mandatory *pari passu* rule.

3.2   United States law

This problem (if there is one) of mandatory *pari passu* payment does not arise under United States insolvency law. The Bankruptcy Code of 1978 codifies previous law by providing in section 510(a) as follows:

> "A subordination agreement is enforceable in a case under this title to the same extent that such agreement is enforceable under applicable nonbankruptcy law."

Prior to the enactment of section 510(a), United States courts generally gave effect to subordination agreements, with only limited exceptions, on the basis of at least six separate theories, depending largely on the form of the subordination and the issue to be decided.[3]

(a) Equitable lien. Some cases held that the holder of the junior debt intended that the senior creditor should have first call on any payments made from the borrower's assets in liquidation and, although this did not constitute a legally enforceable security assignment, the subordination agreement gave rise to an equitable lien upon the assets as against the junior creditor.[4]

(b) Equitable assignment. Under this theory, it was held that the effect of the subordination was that the junior creditor agreed equitably to assign its claims to the senior creditor in the event of the bankruptcy of the debtor.[5]

---

[3] This summary is based mainly upon the summary by C. Edward Dobbs "Debt Subordination," Chapter 13 in Ruda (ed.) *Asset Based Financing: A Transactional Guide*, Matthew Bender 1988. The cases make sense and there seems no reason why similar results should not be reached in other common law jurisdictions on the same facts.

[4] *Searle* v. *Mechanics' Loan & Trust Co.*, 249 Fed. 942 (9th Cir. 1918); *In re George P. Schinzel & Son*, 16 F. 2d 289 (S.D.N.Y. 1926); *Bank of America* v. *Engleman*, 101 Ca.App. 2d 390, 225 P2d 597 (1950).

[5] See *In re Handy-Andy Community Stores*, 2 F.Supp. 97 (WD La 1932); *In re Itemlab, Inc.*, 197 F.Supp. 194 (E.D.N.Y. 1961).

(c) Constructive trust. Under this theory it was held that the junior creditor was a constructive trustee of his claim against the debtor for the benefit of the senior creditor.

In *Re Dodge-Freedman Poultry Company*, 148 F. Supp. 647 (D.N.H. 1956) affd. *sub nom.* *Dodge-Freedman Poultry Co. v. Delaware Mills Inc.* 244 F. 2d 314 (1st Cir. 1957), the junior creditor, who was the president and principal shareholder of the borrower, sought to defeat the senior creditor's right to receive distributions allowable on the junior debt in the borrower's Chapter IX case by waiving his claim against the borrower. *Held*: the waiver was tantamount to the junior creditor returning to the borrower money to which the senior creditor was equitably entitled. The junior creditor could not give effect to the waiver since he was constructive trustee of the money for the senior creditor.

(d) Estoppel. Under this theory if it could be shown that the senior creditor incurred his debt in reliance upon the junior debt, the junior creditor was equitably estopped from claiming parity with the senior creditor in a distribution from the insolvent debtor's assets: see *Lodner* v. *Pearlman*, 129 App. Div. 93, 113 N.Y.S. 420 (1908). However if the senior debt was incurred prior to the subordination or after but without knowledge of the subordination, then the senior creditor could not show reliance and hence could not rely on the estoppel.[6]

(e) Third-party beneficiary. Under this doctrine the United States courts have sometimes found that the junior creditor holds the benefit of the subordination agreement for the senior creditor as a third-party beneficiary.[7]

(f) Subordination contract enforced. More recently the United States courts have abandoned the above theories of enforcing subordination agreements and have instead simply given effect to them as ordinary contracts.[8]

Distribution by liquidator to senior creditor 3.3

Subordinations commonly direct the liquidator, trustee in bankruptcy or other insolvency representative to pay dividends on the junior debt direct to the senior creditor until the senior debt is paid. The advantage of this is that it short-circuits the double procedure of payment to the junior creditor who then hands over the payment to the senior creditor. It also avoids the necessity for the senior creditor to seek out the junior creditor (difficult or impracticable in the case of issues of junior debt securities not constituted by a trust deed) and it avoids the risk that the junior creditor might divert the proceeds.

---

[6] *In re Joe Newcomer Fin. Co.*, 226 F.Supp. 387 (D.Colo. 1964); *In re Temple of Music, Inc.*, 114 F.Supp. 759 (E.D.N.Y. 1953) *affd.* 220 F2d 749 (2d Cir. 1955).

[7] *In Re National Discount Corp.*, 212 F.Supp. 929 (W.D.S.C.), *affd. sub nom. Austin* v. *National Discount Corp.*, 322 F2d 928 (4th Cir. 1963).

[8] See, *e.g. First National Bank* v. *Am. Foam Rubber Corp.*, 530 F2d 450 (2nd Cir. 1976), *cert. denied sub nom. Buchman* v. *Am. Foam Rubber Corp.* 429 U.S. 858 (1976); *In re Credit Indust. Corp.*, 366 F2d 402 (2d Cir. 1966); *In re Bird & Sons Sales Corp.*, 78 F2d 371 (8th Cir. 1935); *In re Eaton Factors Co., Inc.* 3 B.R. 20 (B.C., S.D.N.Y. 1980); *New York Stock Exch.* v. *Pickard & Co., Inc.*, 296 A2d 143 (Del. 1972).

Other forms involving a trustee for the junior debt direct the trustee to pay dividends on the junior debt back to the liquidator on trust to pay them to the senior creditor first, *i.e.* the liquidator is constituted a trustee. It is thought that a liquidator should normally accept a trusteeship which is beneficial to creditors: if not, equity does not want for a trustee.

It is important to note that in the case of subordination trusts, the direction to pay the liquidator is pure mechanics of channelling the payment through a nominee for convenience and does not obscure the fact that the junior creditor transfers beneficial ownership of the junior debt or its proceeds to the senior creditor.

Under the United States Bankruptcy Code 1978 there appears to be no objection to imposing this duty on the trustee in bankruptcy: see section 510(a) cited at paragraph 3.1.

Under English insolvency law, it also seems that a liquidator can be required to pay dividends to the assignee of those dividends under a turnover subordination trust.

Rule 11.11(1) of the Insolvency Rules 1986 provides:

> "If a person entitled to a dividend gives notice to the responsible insolvency practitioner that he wishes the dividend to be paid to another person, or that he has assigned his entitlement to another person, the insolvency practitioner shall pay the dividend to that other accordingly."

This rule apparently contemplates that the assignor is the proving creditor who subsequently assigns the benefit of his proof, as opposed to an assigneee of dividends granted prior to the liquidation. Further the notice must evidently come from the junior creditor. However it has been held that, although a bankruptcy court has no jurisdiction to order the trustee in bankruptcy to pay dividends to an assignee of a proof, the court can enable the assignee to file a proof in substitution for the assignor's proof.[9]

In the case of debtor-creditor turnover subordinations, the question does not arise because distributions are payable to the junior creditor for his own benefit: he merely has to pay the senior creditor amounts equal to those distributions.

In the case of contractual subordinations drafted as a contingent debt, there is no turnover of distributions and the liquidator pays the junior creditor only if the contingency is satisfied, *e.g.* the senior debt has been paid. But it is often provided that, if the junior creditor receives a payment on the junior debt which he is not entitled to receive, he holds it on trust and must pay it over to the debtor's estate.

3.4   Insolvency reorganisations

It is essential that the subordination should stand up in the event of insolvency reorganisation proceedings as well as on a final liquidation leading to dissolution.

A common thread of rehabilitation proceedings is that a plan may be

---

[9] *Re Frost* [1899] 2 Q.B. 50; *Re Iliff* (1902) 51 W.R. 80; *Re Hills* (1913) 107 L.T. 95 (equitable assignment).

proposed for the survival of the debtor as a going concern. Examples are the United States Chapter 11 proceedings and the British administration order or voluntary arrangement under the Insolvency Act 1986.

In principle any such plan should not unfairly discriminate between classes of creditors. There is an unfair discrimination test in section 1129(b)(i) of the United States Bankruptcy Code of 1978 and an "unfair prejudice" test in section 27 of the British Insolvency Act 1986 in relation to administrations. The language of section 27 is not altogether apt to cover discrimination between creditors but the better view is that such an application could be made if the proposals approved by creditor majorities do not honour the subordination. It should be noted that, unlike voluntary arrangements under the Insolvency Act 1986, majority creditor resolutions in relation to administrations do not expressly bind dissentient creditors.

If the main creditors are trade debt, senior bank debt and junior insider debt and if the junior debt is subordinated only to the senior bank debt under a turnover subordination, the entitlement of the senior bank debt under the plan or proposal should reflect the fact that the senior debt is entitled to the dividends on the junior debt. The trade debt should not be entitled to benefit from the dividend since the junior debt is not subordinated to the trade debt. This is not true if the junior debt is contractually subordinated, because, as has been seen, contractual subordinations also benefit debt other than senior debt; paragraph 2.8.

If the plan provides for a degree of debt forgiveness, junior debt should be reduced before senior debt in order to reflect the subordination.

One would expect similar principles to apply in the case of schemes of arrangement under the formal procedures in the Companies Act 1985, ss.425 *et seq.* These arrangements can bind dissentient creditors, but must be sanctioned by the court.

A subordination agreement may provide that on a reorganisation honouring the subordination, *e.g.* by giving the junior creditor a lower class of equity security then the senior creditor or a debt security subordinated to the senior debt on terms no less protective of the senior creditors than the original subordination, the junior creditor may keep the reorganisation distribution without turning it over since the status quo is maintained. This is the so-called "X clause."

Proof and voting on junior debt generally   3.5

Where the subordination is achieved by a turnover subordination, whether a subordination trust or a debtor-creditor turnover subordination so that the senior creditor relies on the benefit of distributions on the junior debt, it could be important to the senior creditor on the insolvency of the debtor that he has the ability either to prove for the junior debt himself or to compel the junior creditor to prove for the junior debt and that the senior creditor can control the vote on the junior debt.

Turnover subordination contracts commonly contain express provisions to cover these situations. In the case of subordination trusts it is uncertain whether the senior creditor, as transferee of the proceeds of the junior debt, is the "creditor" for the purposes of proof and voting and hence entitled to prove for and vote on the junior debt. This is because his rights do not spring up until the proceeds come into existence. Further, the whole of the junior debt may not have to be turned over to cover the senior debt, but only part of it: the entitlement of the senior creditor and the balance left to the junior creditor will only be known when the insolvent estate is fully realised. But if there is no doubt as to the extent of the beneficial interest vested in the senior creditors (as where the debtor is so hopelessly insolvent that all the dividends on the junior debt will clearly be insufficient to cover the senior debt), it is suggested that the senior creditors ought, as vested beneficiaries, to be entitled to put an end to the trust and call upon the junior creditor as trustee to transfer the trust property to them, a rule which has been in force since at least *Smith* v. *Wheeler* (1669) 1 Mod.Rep. 16: see the summary in *Stephenson* v. *Barclays Bank* [1975] 1 All E.R. 625, 637.

3.6   **Proof on junior debt.** It is often provided the junior creditor must file a proof of claim and, if he fails to do so within good time, *e.g.* 14 days before the expiry date for proofs, the senior creditor has power of attorney to do so on his behalf. If the junior creditor did not claim the junior debt, the junior debt would of course not compete with the senior debt, but the senior creditor would not have the advantage of the double dividend.

3.7   **Voting the junior debt.** The agreement may provide that the senior creditor may vote on the junior creditor's claim in insolvency proceedings and has power of attorney to do so. Control of voting may be crucial in relation to such matters as the appointment of an insolvency representative, the approval of transactions by the insolvency representative and more particularly the approval of a reorganisation plan. A vote protecting junior creditors may not protect senior creditors.

Since control of voting may confer too much power on the senior creditor, the provision may allow the junior creditor to vote but state that the junior creditor will not vote the junior debt so as to impair the subordination. This is a vague formula and may be resisted on the ground that the junior creditors do not know what they are obliged to do with sufficient certainty. But it is a compromise.

In practice, the exercise by the senior creditor of these rights may be hindered because of the risk of liability to the junior creditor for wrongfully depleting the junior creditor's claim.

Whether the junior creditor may grant a power of attorney or proxy to a senior creditor to vote his claim (assuming that the senior creditor is not a transferee of the full junior debt) depends upon applicable bankruptcy law. In the case of English administration orders and voluntary arrangements, the Insolvency Rules 1986 provide that it is the "creditor" who votes: rules 2.22 *et seq.* and 1.17 respectively. Rule 8 of the Insolvency Rules provides for the appointment of individual proxies and for representation by companies. The United States Bankruptcy Code of 1978 provides in s.1126(a) that the "holder" of a claim may vote to accept or reject a plan. The junior creditor should, as a back-stop, be obliged to vote as the senior creditor directs.

If both junior and senior debt are payable to a trustee by a parallel covenant in favour of the trustee for both classes of debt, the trustee ought to be the creditor entitled to vote: paragraph 10.4.

Generally a secured creditor can vote only for the unsecured balance of his claim: see rule 4.67 of the Insolvency Rules 1986.

United States cases are divided on whether the senior creditor may vote the junior debt if not expressly authorised to do so. These cases illustrate the equivocal approach of the law to transfers of proceeds.

In *Re Alda Commercial Corp.*, 300 F.Supp. 294 (S.D.N.Y. 1969) the subordination agreement did not expressly authorise the senior creditor to vote on the junior debt. *Held*: the senior creditor was not entitled to vote the claim of the junior creditor in the election of a trustee in a straight bankruptcy case. The reason was that the bankruptcy laws entitle all creditors to vote in the election of a trustee, regardless of whether their claims may be subordinated as to eventual payment.

On the other hand in *In re Itemland, Inc.* 197 F.Supp. 194 (E.D.N.Y. 1961), a senior creditor challenged the acceptance of a Chapter IX plan of arrangement by the junior creditor on the ground that the senior creditor, by virtue of the subordination, had the exclusive right to vote the junior debt. The subordination agreement did not expressly authorise the senior creditor to vote on the junior debt. *Held*: the senior creditor was entitled to vote on this issue. The reason was that the vote attached to the claim as the only means of determining how and when the claim was to be enforced and the terms of its payment. If the senior creditor was not entitled to vote then the junior creditor had the power to use his vote to determine how the senior creditor should collect a claim in which the junior creditor no longer had any interest. The effective transfer of the claim carried control of the claim via voting.

The voting provisions in relation to British administration orders do not divide creditors into classes (except for the exclusion of secured creditors). But section 1122(a) of the United States Bankruptcy Code of 1978 provides that a "plan may place a claim or an interest in a particular class only if such claim or interest is substantially similar to the other claims or interests of such class."

International bankruptcies   3.8

The senior creditor needs to be sure that the subordination will work in all jurisdictions where the debtor has assets or where bankruptcy proceedings may be brought. Multiple concurrent bankruptcies are not uncommon. The foreign forum, away from the place of incorporation, may not recognise:

— a contractual subordination (because it conflicts with a mandatory *pari passu* rule): paragraph 3.1;
— a transfer of the proceeds of the junior debt to the senior creditor because it has not been properly perfected as an assignment (paragraph 2.10) or because the transfer is treated as an unregistered security interest: paragraph 5.2;
— a statutory subordination provided for by a statute of the home

forum (see paragraph 2.6) because the ranking of debt is typically a matter for the law where the bankruptcy proceedings are brought which may not be the home country.

One solution for junior Eurobond issues is to limit the claims of the junior creditor to petitioning for liquidation only in the home jurisdiction of the debtor. The disadvantages of this include:

— the junior creditor loses the opportunity to participate in bankruptcy proceedings elsewhere;
— because the junior creditor has to go to the home forum, he loses any insulation against local exchange controls and the like achieved by a choice of external governing law and forum.

Under the insolvency law of many jurisdictions, including English law, a creditor who receives a larger dividend in a foreign insolvency proceeding than he would be entitled to receive in the home insolvency by reason of a mandatory insolvency rule in the home country (as opposed to differences in available assets), must account for the excess before he can receive dividends in the home insolvency, *i.e.* he cannot receive dividends until the dividends received by other creditors have levelled them up to his prior receipt: see Dicey & Morris, *The Conflict of Laws*, 11th ed., p. 1110. Accordingly if the junior creditor avoids the subordination in a foreign proceeding, he ought to be subject to this hotchpotch if he proves locally.

3.9   Junior creditor as preferential creditor

The junior creditor may be a preferential creditor on the insolvency of the debtor, as where the junior creditor is a bank which finances the payment of the wages of the debtor's employees and hence steps into the shoes of the employees by way of subrogation to their preferential status: see the Insolvency Act 1986, Schedule 6, para. 11.

In the case of a turnover subordination, the senior creditor will enjoy the benefit of the enhanced preferential dividend payable to the senior creditor.

Where the junior creditor has agreed to be subordinated to all other creditors of the debtor company on terms that the junior debt is contingent on other debts being paid, the contract might override his statutory entitlement to subrogation and preference, but this does not appear to have been decided.

CHAPTER 4

SUBORDINATION AND THE JUNIOR CREDITOR'S INSOLVENCY

The efficacy of the subordination should be tested in the event of the junior creditor's bankruptcy as well as that of the debtor.

This question is likely to be more important in relation to insider subordinations and issues of subordinated notes to small investors than to mezzanine debt held by major institutions. Nevertheless bankruptcy is blind and strikes down the big as well as the small.

Assets of the junior creditor's estate   4.1

Where a *subordination trust* springs up to grasp payments on the junior debt paid by the debtor after the junior creditor's insolvency, under English insolvency law the proceeds of the junior debt would not fall into the junior creditor's insolvent estate. The trust would bite on to the proceeds as soon as they come into existence even though this is after the insolvency.[1] In *Re Lind* [1915] 2 Ch. 345 it was held that a pre-insolvency assignment of a future debt which came into existence after the assignor's insolvency was effective to vest the debt in the assignee. The proceeds belong to the assignor's estate only if the liquidator of the assignor has to earn those proceeds after the insolvency, *e.g.* by completing works.[2] In any event it is doubtful whether a trust of proceeds flowing from an existing debt should be treated as a future debt for this purpose. The problem would not arise if the trust were over the junior debt itself, not just its proceeds.

In the case of a *contractual subordination*, the main question will be whether a contractual diminution of the junior debt coming into effect after the insolvency of the junior creditor removes an asset of the estate of the junior creditor after his insolvency contrary to the fundamental *pari passu* principle of insolvency law that creditors may not take assets of the insolvent for themselves unless they have a charge over them. It is considered that, where the diminution of the claim is not sparked off by the junior creditor's insolvency but rather by the debtor's insolvency, the junior creditor has merely a limited or conditional asset from the start and

---

[1] See *Re Irving, ex p. Brett* (1877) 7 Ch.D. 419 (facts at para. 2.9); *Re Lind* [1915] 2 Ch. 345. See also *Re Davis & Co., ex p. Rawlings* (1889) 22 Q.B.D. 193, C.A. (future instalments of hire); *Re Tout & Finch Ltd.* [1954] 1 All E.R. 127 (building employer's retention moneys for work done pre-insolvency but payable after insolvency. The contrary case of *Collyer* v. *Isaacs* (1881) 19 Ch.D. 347, C.A., is considered to be wrong.

[2] *Re Jones, ex p. Nichols* (1883) 22 Ch.D. 782, C.A.; *Wilmot* v. *Alton* [1897] 1 Q.B. 17, C.A.

no violation of the prohibition on divestment of the assets of an insolvent would be involved.

In the case of a *debtor-creditor turnover subordination* where the junior creditor must pay to the senior creditor amounts equal to recoveries on the junior debt, the senior creditor would take the risk of the junior creditor's insolvency and would be left merely with a right to prove in the junior creditor's insolvency for dividends measured by reference to distributions on the junior debt. If the debtor were not insolvent the senior creditor's claim against the junior creditor would be a contingent claim provable at its valued amount: see Insolvency Rules 1986, r. 4.86.

4.2   Preference of senior creditor by junior creditor generally

Subordinations may be subject to preference rules in the junior creditor's insolvency. If a junior creditor agrees during the junior creditor's suspect period to subordinate his debt to a specified senior creditor, this may constitute a voidable preference of that senior creditor or a voidable transaction at an undervalue. The effect of the subordination is to improve the senior creditor's position and potentially to diminish the assets of the insolvent junior creditor.

The concept of the returnable preference is universal in insolvency law. An insolvent should not be able to prefer some creditors at the expense of others and thereby disturb the *pari passu* principle. The payment of creditors should come before charity. A debtor should not be able deliberately to defeat creditors by putting assets beyond their reach. The principle preserves fairness amongst creditors and also discourages scrambles by creditors which will oppress the debtor and result in his early demise.

By reason of tougher rules for connected persons, such as related companies and directors, the rules are particularly important for insider subordinations where the debtor is in financial difficulties.

The main English preference sections are summarised below.

4.3   Transactions at an undervalue

The Insolvency Act 1986, s.238 (which applies to companies and is paralleled by s.339 in relation to individuals) applies where in summary:

(a) the debtor is insolvent (as defined by s.123—companies; s.341(3) —individuals). There is a rebuttable presumption of insolvency in the case of transactions with a "connected person" which by section 249 includes (*inter alia*) directors and related companies;

(b) the debtor makes a gift to a person or otherwise enters into a transaction with that person on terms that provide for the debtor to receive no consideration or the debtor enters into a transaction with that person for a consideration the value of which, in money or money's worth, is significantly less than the value, in money or money's worth, of the consideration provided by the debtor;

(c) an administration or bankruptcy order is made or the company goes into liquidation within the applicable time period, namely two years for companies and five years for individuals; and

(d) (in the case of a company) there is no "good faith" and "benefit to the company" defence within section 238(5) which excludes transactions at an undervalue if the court is satisfied

"(a) that the company which carried out the transaction did so in good faith and for the purpose of carrying on its business; and

(b) that at the time it did so there were reasonable grounds for believing that the transaction would benefit the company."

This defence does not apply in the case of individuals.

On the application of the relevant insolvency representative, the court "shall . . . make such order as it thinks fit for restoring the position to what it would have been" if the debtor had not entered into the transaction: section 238(3). I.A. 1986, ss.240 (companies) and 342 (individuals) set out the various orders which may be made for recovery of the property transferred or for the restoration of the original position.

Plainly a turnover subordination of an existing debt in the suspect period could be set aside if there is an element of undervalue and if there is no defence within (d). A contractual subordination may have a similar effect.

Preferences   4.4

The Insolvency Act 1986, s.239 (which applies to companies and is paralleled by s.340 in relation to individuals) applies where in summary:

(a) a debtor is insolvent (as defined by s.123—companies; s.34(3)—individuals); and

(b) the debtor does anything or suffers anything to be done which has the effect of putting one of the debtor's creditors or a surety or guarantor for any of the debtor's liabilities into a position which, in the event of the debtor going into insolvent liquidation or bankruptcy, will be better than the position he would have been in if that thing had not been done;

(c) the debtor which gave the preference was influenced in deciding to give it by a desire to produce the effect mentioned in (b); and

(d) an administration or bankruptcy order is made or the company goes into liquidation within the applicable time period, ranging generally from six months to two years (for connected persons which term includes directors and related companies—see s.249).

On application of the relevant insolvency representative, the court "shall . . . make such order as it thinks fit for restoring the position to what it would have been" if the debtor had not given the preference. See the Insolvency Act 1986, ss.240 and 342 for the various orders that may be made.

Again a turnover subordination could be preferential if entered into during the suspect period and *one* of the motives was to prefer the senior creditor. It is irrelevant that the senior creditor did not know of the preferential motive. A contractual subordination could also be preferential even though the junior creditor does not turn over proceeds to the senior creditor. This is because the contract improves the position of the senior creditor. But in each case the precise facts would have to be considered.

The mere purchase by an investor of a junior security, such as a subordinated bond, should rarely constitute a preference by the junior creditor of the senior creditor. The reason is that the investor will not usually intend to prefer the senior creditors and further the improvement in position should relate back to the initial issue not the subsequent purchase. The preference rules are more likely to affect subordination of existing debts than subordinations of new debt at the time they are incurred.

4.5   Transactions defrauding creditors

The Insolvency Act 1986, s.423 (which applies to both companies and individuals) applies in summary where:

(a) a person makes a gift to another or otherwise enters into a transaction with the other on terms that provide for him to receive no consideration or he enters into a transaction with the other for a consideration the value of which, in money or money's worth, is significantly less than the value, in money or money's worth, of the consideration provided by himself; and

(b) he entered into the transaction for the purpose of putting assets beyond the reach of a claimant or prospective claimant or of otherwise prejudicing the interests of such a claimant.

An application to the court may be made by (amongst others) the relevant insolvency representative or by a victim of the transaction. The court may make such order as it thinks fit for "restoring the position to what it would have been if the transaction had not been entered into" and "protecting the interest of persons who are victims of the transaction." Unlike the sections relating to transactions at an undervalue and preferences, the section technically does not only apply on insolvency nor need the person entering into the transaction be insolvent at the time. The section is drafted in wide terms and is effectively limited only by the "purpose" test. It is undecided whether the stated purpose must be the only purpose of the transaction.

4.6   Recognition of subordination trusts

If the junior creditor is insolvent and has declared a subordination trust of recoveries on the junior debt, then the trust will fail if it is not recognised by the local bankruptcy jurisdiction applicable to the junior creditor.

It is undoubtedly much too sweeping to parrot the old adage that civil code jurisdictions recognise only absolute ownership and not the trust. A subordination trust merely amounts to a transfer of recoveries by the junior creditor to the senior creditor and it would be surprising if a mature civil jurisdiction declined to recognise what is in substance an assignment of proceeds. In exceptional cases, consideration should be given to any local implementation of the Hague Convention on the Law Applicable to Trusts and on their Recognition, absorbed into United Kingdom law (with modifications) by the Recognition of Trusts Act 1987: paragraph 10.5.

But special formalities may be required in some jurisdictions, *e.g.* France, Belgium, Luxembourg, Japan and Korea, to perfect a transfer of proceeds if it is to be effective on the junior creditor's insolvency: paragraph 2.10.

CHAPTER 5

SUBORDINATION TRUSTS AS SECURITY INTERESTS

5.1 Generally

A subordination trust is in economic substance a collateral charge by the junior creditor over the junior creditor's debt or the proceeds of that debt to secure the senior debt, but without imposing any personal liability on the junior creditor to pay the senior debt himself. The question is whether the transfer of proceeds is in law a security interest.

5.2 Consequences of security

If the trust does in law constitute security then the consequences listed below may ensue.

(a) Registration. Registration or filing requirements may be attracted. If the security is not duly perfected, then it may be void on the insolvency of the junior creditor or void against attaching creditors. Because of doubts, sometimes the senior creditor registers in English-based jurisdictions as a precautionary measure. But in a particular case, a senior creditor may be prepared to take a view that the junior creditor is unlikely to become insolvent or to transfer the proceeds to a third party, *e.g.* if the junior creditor is a major bank.

English-based corporate registration systems commonly require registration of charges created by a company over its "book debts": see section 396 of the Companies Act 1985 as amended by the Companies Act 1989.[1] If the trust is only over recoveries on liquidation of the debtor, the better view is that a liquidation dividend is not a "book debt" within these registration requirements but this is undecided. If (as is commonly the case) the subordination trust is over proceeds of the junior debt as opposed to the junior debt itself, there may be a further question as to whether those proceeds constitute a book debt of the junior creditor: the proceeds of the debt are not the debt itself. Book debts have been judicially defined as "debts arising in a business . . . which ought to be entered in the company's books": *per* Lord Esher M.R. in *Official Receiver* v. *Tailby* (1886)18 Q.B.D. 25, 29, affirmed (1888) 13 A.C. 523.[2] Consider whether an alternative registration head applies, *e.g.* a charge

---

[1] Amendment not in force at time of writing.

[2] See also *Paul & Frank* v. *Discount Bank (Overseas) Ltd.* [1967] Ch. 348; *Watson* v. *Parapara Coal Co. Ltd.* (1915) 17 C.L.R. 791; *Re Stevens* (1883) W.N. 110; *Re Brightlife Ltd.* [1986] 3 All E.R. 673.

to secure an issue of debentures which may apply if the senior debt is evidenced by an issue of debt securities.

If the charge is not duly registered, then the company and its officers are liable to a fine and (more importantly) the charge is void against an administrator and liquidator of the company and against persons who for value acquire an interest in or right over the property subject to the charge even if they have notice of the charge, subject to exceptions: section 399 of the Companies Act 1985 as about to be amended.

Under a subsequent addition to the Uniform Commercial Code discussed below, subordination trusts do not attract Article 9 filing requirements in those U.S. states which have adopted the provision and, perhaps, even if they have not.

(b) Negative pledges. The charge may conflict with negative pledges granted by the junior creditor.

(c) Regulatory prohibitions. Creditors which are banks or other institutions (such as insurance companies) may be inhibited by law, official guidelines or internal policy from creating charges.

(d) Secured creditor on insolvency. The senior creditor would be a secured creditor on the *junior creditor's* insolvency and might therefore be excluded from proof or voting to the extent he is secured: see rule 488 of the Insolvency Rules 1986. The same may apply on rehabilitation proceedings. Thus a secured creditor cannot vote in relation to a voluntary arrangement or an administration under the British Insolvency Act 1986: see rules 1.19(3)(b) and 2.24 of the Insolvency Rules 1986. But the senior creditors should not be excluded from voting and proof where the insolvency proceedings relate to the debtor, as opposed to the junior creditor, since the security is not given by the debtor (see the definition of secured creditor in section 248 of the Insolvency Act 1986), but this is not altogether clear in the case of voluntary arrangements because of the language of rule 1.19(3)(b) of the Insolvency Rules 1986.

(e) Junior creditor's administration. If an administration order is made in relation to the junior creditor, the enforcement of the charge may become subject to the freeze and to the administrator's prior rights of realisation prescribed by the Insolvency Act 1986.

Absolute transfers and security 5.3

The better view is that a properly drafted subordination trust of proceeds should not create a security interest under English law but the matter is undecided and, in light of the potentially disastrous consequences if this view is wrong, a doubt must be recorded.

The distinction between a transfer which destructs when the senior debt is paid and an equity of redemption can be a fine one. The economic effect of a subordination trust and a security interest is the same because in both cases the senior creditor cannot claim the junior debt in excess of the amount of the senior debt. Still, a purchaser of subordinated debt securities would be very surprised to be told he is buying a debt security which is subject to a charge created by the initial holder over the proceeds of the debt security in favour of senior creditors.

Whether or not a transfer is framed as an absolute transfer or as a trust, the true test of a security interest is that the grantor has an equity of redemption, *i.e.* a right to the return of the asset over which the security is granted when the secured debt is paid. A trust of receipts by the junior creditor in favour of the senior creditor *up to an amount equal to* the senior debt leaves no equity of redemption since the junior creditor never transfers more than is required to pay the senior debt: there is no surplus to swing back.[3] The beneficial ownership in the proceeds is split.

A similar point arises in relation to retention of title in contracts for the sale of goods: when the buyer resells the goods it should be possible to provide that the proceeds are split into two amounts, the first equal to the unpaid price due to the original seller which he holds in trust for the original seller and the second equal to the rest which the buyer keeps for himself. The trust should not create a charge: see the retention of title case *Clough Mill Ltd.* v. *Martin* [1984] 3 All E.R. 982, C.A., where Robert Goff L.J. suggested this solution at p. 988.

By contrast, a security assignment of the junior debt by the junior creditor to the senior creditor is a security assignment of the *whole* of the junior debt or its proceeds to secure the junior debt. The junior creditor has an equity of redemption for the surplus if recoveries on the junior debt exceed the unpaid amount of the senior debt.

It follows that the junior creditor's liability should be to pay over amounts up to the senior debt, and not all proceeds received on terms that any surplus is handed back.

It may also be material that the transfer of proceeds is often contingent on the insolvency of the debtor or that the trust is a transfer for a limited duration which terminates on the happening of a future event, namely the payment of the senior debt: see, for example, *Re Laye* [1913] 1 Ch. 298.

This distinction between an ownership interest and a security interest is well precedented in financial leasing, recourse factoring of debts, sale and repurchase, sale and lease-back and retention of title. English law is on the whole slow to treat a transfer of property as a security interest unless the parties ignore the legal effect (in which event the transaction is a sham) or unless the transferor in effect has an equity of redemption, *i.e.* a right to have his property back once the "secured" debt is paid.

5.4   Subordination trust constituted by trust deed

To overcome doubts as to whether a subordination trust amounts to a security interest, perhaps a subordination trust may be constituted by a

---

[3] The leading cases include *Re George Inglefield Ltd.* [1933] 1 Ch. 1; *Ashby Warner & Co. Ltd.* v. *Simmons* [1936] 2 All E.R. 697 and *Siebe Gorman & Co. Ltd.* v. *Barclays Bank Ltd.* [1979] 2 Lloyd's L.R. 142. Consider the building contract retention money cases of *Re Tout & Finch Ltd.* [1954] 1 All E.R. 127; *Re Arthur Sanders Ltd.* (1981) 17 Build.L.R. 125; *Gericevich & Contracting Pty. Ltd.* v. *Sabemo (W.A.) Pty. Ltd.* (1984) 9 A.C.L.R. 452 (W. Australia S.Ct.).

trust deed under which the junior debt is payable to a trustee who holds the recoveries for the benefit first of the senior creditor and then the junior creditor. The covenant in favour of the trustee may be a covenant parallel to the obligation of the debtor to pay the junior creditors, *e.g.* by virtue of their holding of subordinated bonds. The debtor is authorised to pay the bondholders direct until an event of default in which event the debtor must pay the trustee.

The rationale would be that the trustee is not creating a charge because the trustee has no property of its own to charge. The beneficiaries are not charging their beneficial interests because they do not convey any proprietary interest to the senior creditors: they are merely taking a limited interest under the trust. But the matter has not been decided.

United States: U.C.C. Art. 1–209   5.5

As to the United States, a new section 1–209 was recommended for inclusion in the Uniform Commercial Code in 1966 as follows:

> "An obligation may be issued as subordinated to payment of another obligation of the person obligated, or a creditor may subordinate his right to payment of an obligation by agreement with either the person obligated or another creditor of the person obligated. Such a subordination does not create a security interest as against either the common debtor or a subordinated creditor."

This stemmed from the doubts provoked by section 9–102(1)(a) of the Uniform Commercial Code which provides that Article 9 applies to any transaction "which is *intended* to create a security interest in personal property." The Official Comment to the new section states that Article 9 was never intended to cover debt subordination agreements although nothing in the section prevents the creation of a security interest in a case where the parties to the agreement so intend. Hence the problem has gone away in those U.S. states that have adopted the new section 1–209— including financially important states such as New York, California and Illinois.

Security assignments of junior debt   5.6

The subordination is improved if the junior creditor assigns the junior debt to the senior creditor by way of collateral security for the payment of the senior debt. A security assignment may give the senior creditor as assignee enhanced power to prove for and vote on the junior debt: paragraph 3.5. It will also circumvent potential problems (if any) of post-insolvency proceeds received by the junior creditor falling into his estate free of a turnover obligation (paragraph 4.1) or of the trust not being recognised in jurisdictions mystified by the trust: paragraph 4.6. A security assignment of the whole debt avoids the curiosities of assignments of proceeds only: paragraph 2.9.

On the other hand a security assignment may require registration (or filing) and infringe negative pledges binding on the junior creditor.

If the junior creditor is to be entitled to scheduled payments on the junior debt until the subordination crystallises, it would be for consideration whether the security would be treated as a floating charge. Fortunately, this is not a question which this book seeks to answer, except to note that some jurisdictions, e.g. Norway, may disregard a charge over receivables if the charger controls the receivable until a default.

5.7   Other contractual inhibitions

Other potential inhibitions on subordinations by a junior creditor should be considered:

(a) If the subordination is constituted by a subordination trust, the transfer of proceeds might conflict with a restriction in the junior creditor's loan agreements on disposals of assets of the junior creditor.

(b) If the subordination is a debtor-creditor turnover subordination (whereby the junior creditor agrees to pay the senior creditor amounts equal to recoveries on the junior debt until the senior debt is paid), the contingent debt liability may be counted towards indebtedness of the junior creditor under financial ratios or restrictions on liabilities in its credit agreements or constitutional documents or for the purposes of supervision by regulatory authorities of the financial condition of the junior creditor.

(c) The junior debt may be non-assignable, *e.g.* because there is an express restriction on assignments. A prohibition on assignments may not however restrict a trust of proceeds since the law construes limitations on free dispositions narrowly: see, for example, *Re Turcan* (1888) 40 Ch.D. 5.

CHAPTER 6

SUBORDINATIONS AND SET-OFF[1]

Set-off defeats subordination **6.1**

If a junior creditor can set off the junior debt against a debt owed by the junior creditor to the debtor, this will defeat the subordination: the junior creditor gets paid by his set-off. The same would apply where the debtor exercises the set-off. The question may arise (a) prior to insolvency, or (b) when either the debtor or the junior creditor becomes an insolvent.

Questions of set-off will often arise. For example, in the case of mezzanine finance for a leveraged bid, the junior creditors may be banks owing deposits to the borrower potentially eligible for set-off against the junior debt. In the case of insider subordinations a junior parent company may have trading relationships with its subsidiary giving rise to claims by the subsidiary against the parent. A junior creditor may attempt to evade the subordination by taking a deposit from the debtor eligible for set-off.

Pre-insolvency contracts against set-off **6.2**

Under English law an agreement by the debtor or the junior creditor not to exercise a set-off is effective as between themselves prior to the insolvency of either and overrides the policies of judicial economy requiring cross-claims to be litigated in the same proceedings.[2]

In other words sanctity of contract overtops the policy of the avoidance of multiplicity of proceedings. Accordingly both the debtor and the junior creditor should agree with the senior creditor not to raise set-offs which operate as a discharge of the junior debt except to the extent that the terms of the subordination permit the junior debt to be paid. Note that both parties should agree not to set off, since both may be debtor-creditors and generally each debtor-creditor has a reciprocal right of set-off.

In the case of a subordination trust, the debtor could not set off, against the senior creditor's claim for the proceeds, a cross-claim owed by the

---

[1] Citation for the propositions in this Chapter will be found in the author's *English & International Set-Off* (1989) Sweet & Maxwell, referred to as *English and International Set-Off*.

[2] *English and International Set-Off*, paras. 12–13 *et seq*. See, for example, *Hong Kong and Shanghai Banking Corpn.* v. *Kloeckner & Co. A.G.*, Q.B.D., April 24, 1989 (Hirst J.); *First National Bank of Chicago* v. *Moorgate Properties Ltd.* (1975) *The Times*, October 25, 1975, C.A.; *Mottram Consultants* v. *Bernard Sunley Ltd.* [1975] 2 Lloyd's L.R. 197, H.L.

junior creditor to the debtor if the debtor has agreed in the junior debt instrument not to raise set-offs against transferees: paragraph 6.5 (b).

A solvent set-off may in any event be prevented by the terms of the subordination. Thus:

(a) If the subordination postpones payment of the junior debt, a solvent set-off may be defeated by the fact that set-off requires both cross-claims to have matured due and payable.[3]

(b) A solvent set-off may be prevented if the junior debt and the claim owed by the junior creditor to the debtor are not mutual as in the case of certain subordination trusts: see below.

(c) Usually a debtor on a negotiable instrument cannot set off, against the first payee of the instrument, a cross-claim owed by the payee to the debtor.[4]

In an Alberta case a holder of subordinated notes was held disentitled to use the notes as a cross-claim for set-off on the ground that only the trustee of the notes could sue for them. This reasoning seems doubtful since the availability of set-off depends on beneficial ownership not procedural ability to sue.[5] But the result of the decision was correct.

In *Atlantic Acceptance Corpn Ltd.* v. *Burns & Dutton Construction (1962) Ltd.* (1971) 1 W.W.R. 84 (Alberta S.Ct.), a company as assignee of a debt owed by a debtor sued for the assigned debt. The debtor held subordinated notes of the assignee. By the terms of these notes, once an event of default has occurred (which it had), only the trustee for the noteholders could sue and there was a turnover of receipts to the holders of senior debt. *Held*: no set-off. The debtor did not have an enforceable claim which he could sue for. A better explanation would have been that the subordination, by establishing a subordination trust of the junior claim in favour of the senior creditors, destroyed mutuality between the debtor and the company

6.3   Junior debt is secured: solvent set-off

A solvent set-off may impliedly be prohibited by the terms of the ranking of security if the junior creditor has agreed not to accept payment before the senior creditor.

In *H. Wilkins & Elkington Ltd.* v. *Milton* (1916) 32 T.L.R., H the holder of second mortgage debentures agreed with the issuing company that the second mortgage debentures would not be entitled to payment until the first debentures were redeemed. H appointed a receiver of the second debentures which accordingly became due. A debt from H to the company on a bill of exchange became due the following day. On that day a receiver (apparently at the request of the first debenture-holders) was appointed by the court. *Held*: H could not set off the second debenture debt against the bill of exchange debt. H had agreed that the second debentures were to be postponed to the first debenture and the effect of allowing the set-off would be to give the second debentureholder H preference to the first debentures contrary to the agreement.

But the mere fact that a junior creditor's security is expressed to rank

---

[3] *English and International Set-Off*, paras. 2–131 *et seq.*

[4] *English and International Set-Off*, para. 12–68.

[5] *English and International Set-Off*, para. 14–40.

after the senior security (as opposed to the debt itself) may not amount to an agreement not to set off.

In *Nelson & Co. Ltd.* v. *Faber & Co.* [1903] 2 K.B. 367, Joyce J. said at 377:
"In my view, it is immaterial that the debentures held by the defendants are expressed to be subsequent to the existing issue of prior debentures. This only had reference to the order of priority of the debentures considered as charges, and does not preclude the defendants from obtaining payment of their debentures in cash or by setting off the amount."

Whether insolvency set-off is mandatory   6.4

Most developed commercial jurisdictions allow insolvency set-off, including British Commonwealth countries, the United States, Scandinavia, Germany, Switzerland, the Netherlands, Italy, Japan, Korea, Thailand and many others. Exceptions are states basing their bankruptcy law on French ideas such as France, Belgium, Luxembourg, Spain, Greece and many Latin American states. In England and many other common law jurisdictions basing the insolvency law on the English model (such as Australia, New Zealand, Bermuda, Hong Kong and Singapore) insolvency set-off is mandatory and it is not possible to contract out.[6] Insolvency set-off is probably not mandatory in Canada (because section. 97(3) of the Bankruptcy Act simply applies the "law of set-off" without making it mandatory) or under section 553 of the United States Bankruptcy Code of 1978—although there are likely to be variations in state law: see *Collier Bankruptcy Manual*, (3rd ed.), para. 553.10.

The English insolvency set-off clause is contained in section 323 of the Insolvency Act 1989 (for individuals) and in r. 4.90 of the Insolvency Rules 1986 (for companies).

If the set-off is mandatory, methods of precluding the set-off need to be explored.

Subordination trusts and insolvency set-off   6.5

(a) **Junior creditor owes cross-claim to debtor.** A subordination trust of the entire junior claim should destroy the mutuality necessary for insolvency set-off between the junior debt and another debt owed by the junior creditor to the debtor. Under the doctrine of set-off mutuality, one person's money must not be used to pay another's debt.[6a] In the result, there must be only two debtor-creditors, each of whom is beneficial owner of the claim owed to him (regardless of who is the titular or nominal owner and regardless of who has the procedural right to sue) and each must be personally liable for the debt owed by him.

A teasing question is whether mutuality is destroyed if the trust is over liquidation dividends only or proceeds only, as opposed to the junior debt itself. As mentioned at paragraph 2.9, case law distinguishes between the

---

[6] See for example, *National Westminster Bank Ltd* v. *Halesowen Pressworks & Assemblies Ltd* [1972] A.C. 785; *Re The Paddington Town Hall Centre Ltd.* [1979] 4 A.C.L.R. 673 (Australia); *Rendell* v. *Doors & Doors Ltd.* [1975] 2 N.Z.L.R. 191 (New Zealand).

[6a] *English and International Set-Off*, paras. 14–1 *et seq.*

claim and its proceeds and it is possible to assign the proceeds of a claim but not the claim itself: see, for example, *Glegg* v. *Bromley* [1912] 3 K.B. 474; *Re Irving, ex p. Brett* (1877) 7 Ch.D. 419. The better view is that the set-off would be precluded on grounds of lack of mutuality because the set-off would lead to the junior creditor using the senior creditor's ulti-mate asset (the proceeds of the junior debt) to pay the junior creditor's debt (his liability to the debtor) contrary to the principle on which mutuality is based. Thus if the junior creditor owes a deposit to the debtor, there should be no mutuality between that deposit and the junior debt whose proceeds have been transferred to the senior creditor.

If there is a clear ascertained surplus of the junior debt over the amount to be turned over to the senior creditor, the surplus belonging absolutely to the junior creditor would be eligible for set-off against a cross-claim owed by the junior creditor to the debtor. The junior debt is split between the turnover amount belonging to the senior creditor and the surplus belonging to the junior creditor. But the amount of the surplus must be clear: hence the question could only arise in practice when the debtor is in insolvent liquidation so that the amount for turnover can finally be worked out.

> *Example* The junior debt is 100. Out of this 40 must be turned over to the senior debt. Accordingly the surplus of 60 belongs to the junior creditor. This 60 is eligible for set-off against a debt, such as a deposit, owed by the junior creditor to the debtor.[7]

It does not matter that the junior creditor's reacquisition of the surplus is after the insolvency date since the compulsory re-establishment of mutuality after the insolvency date satisfies the mutuality rule even though there was no mutuality on the insolvency date, provided that there was mutuality between the junior creditor and debtor pre-insolvency.[8]

(b) Debtor's set-off against senior creditor of cross-claim owed by junior debtor. The junior debtor may owe a cross-claim to the debtor and the debtor may seek to set this off against the senior creditor's claim for the proceeds of the junior debt. For example, the junior debtor may be a bank owing a cross-claim for a deposit to the debtor.

A contract by the debtor not to set off, as against the senior creditor as assignee of proceeds, a cross-claim owed by the junior creditor to the debtor is effective. This situation has arisen most commonly in relation to marketable debentures which are expressed to be transferable free of "equities."[9] In the absence of contract, the ability of the debtor to set-off the cross-claim is complex and depends upon the class of set-off, the

---

[7] For English case law on the splitting of claims, see paras. 14–48 *et seq*; paras. 21–127 *et seq*.

[8] See, *e.g. Bolland* v. *Nash* (1828) 8 B. & C. 105; *Re Wise, ex p. Staddon* (1843) 3 M.D. & D. 256; *English and International Set-Off*, paras. 14–21 *et seq*.

[9] See, for example, *Re Blakely Ordnance Co.* [1867] L.R. 3 Ch.App. 154; *English and International Set-Off*, paras. 16–135 *et seq*.

characteristics of the junior debt and the cross-claim, and the timing of notice to the debtor of the subordination.[10]

(c) Senior creditor owes cross-claim to debtor. Where the senior creditor owes a cross-claim, such as a deposit, to the debtor, this cross-claim is potentially eligible for set-off against either the senior debt or the junior debt. In principle, the senior creditor could set off against the junior debt (if at all) only if the senior creditor has clear ascertained title to the junior debt as transferee which could happen only if the subordination had crystallised and the amount of the turnover was fully ascertained.[11] Nobody is harmed by such a set-off since the proceeds belong to the senior creditor and he is simply paid by set-off what is owed to him.

Debtor-creditor turnover subordinations and insolvency set-off   6.6

If the subordination is a debtor-creditor subordination whereby the junior creditor agrees to pay the senior creditor amounts equal to receipts on the junior debt, there would be an insolvency set-off between the junior debt and an eligible debt owed by the junior creditor to the debtor if either the debtor or the junior creditor were insolvent.

There would be no objection to the set-off on the grounds of lack of mutuality because the junior creditor is beneficial owner of the junior debt and does not transfer any property in the junior debt to the senior creditor.

The junior creditor should agree to pay to the senior creditor amounts equal to any discharge of the junior debt by set-off.

Contractual subordinations and insolvency set-off   6.7

In the case of contractual subordinations, there is no transfer of proceeds to the senior creditor and hence no destruction of mutuality defeating the set-off.

If the junior debt is treated as a contingent debt and the debtor is insolvent, the amount of the junior debt eligible for insolvency set-off will be the valued amount of the contingent junior debt.[12]

If, again, the subordination treats the junior debt as contingent and if the junior creditor is insolvent but the debtor is not, the junior debt might be eligible for set-off under English insolvency law, but probably only if the amount of the junior debt becomes fixed and ascertained during the course of the insolvency proceedings.[13]

If the contractual subordination expressly states that the junior creditor renounces the junior debt to the extent necessary to ensure that the debtor is solvent and the senior debt is paid, then the result ought to be

---

[10] *English and International Set-Off*, paras. 16–10 *et seq.*
[11] *English and International Set-Off*, paras. 16–170 *et seq.*; 16–186 *et seq.* As to the appropriation of set-offs, see *English and International Set-Off*, paras. 2–199 *et seq.*, paras. 16–163 *et seq.*
[12] *English and International Set-Off*, paras. 7–71 *et seq.*
[13] *English and International Set-Off*, paras. 10–56 *et seq.*

the same as stated above where the junior debt is contingent. Thus if the debtor is hopelessly insolvent and there would be no dividend on the junior debt, the junior creditor has no provable claim and hence nothing to set off. For a case where a renounced claim was held ineligible for insolvency set-off, see *Kitchen's Trustee* v. *Madders* [1950] Ch. 134, C.A. Note that, although a creditor may not contract out of insolvency set-off, he can prevent the set-off by in effect cancelling his claim.

If the subordination merely states that the junior debt is subordinated on liquidation to all other creditors without characterising the junior debt as contingent or renounced, the courts ought to arrive at the same result as is stated above. But in relation to the subordination of loans under the Partnership Act 1890, s.3 where the interest varies with the profits, there is a dictum in *ex p. Sheil* (1877) 4 Ch.D. 789, 791 *per* James L.J. in the course of argument that the lender might be entitled to set off: "What is there in [Bovill's Act—the precursor to s.3] to prevent the lender from availing himself of a right of set-off, if he had one, under Section 39 of the Bankruptcy Act 1869 [the then insolvency set-off clause]?" In the United States case of *Texas Bank & Trust* v. *US (In re Sound Emporium, Inc.)*, 17 C.B.C. 2d 253 (W.D. Tex. 1987), it was held that a subordinated claim can be used as a set-off under section 553 of the Bankruptcy Code of 1978, even though the subordinated claim could not itself share in the dividends of the estate.

Notwithstanding this, the proper view is that a subordinated creditor who is not entitled to be paid ought not to have a set-off. This is supported by *Badeley* v. *Consolidated Bank* (1888) 38 Ch.D. 238 where Cotton L.J. said at 254 that the corresponding section in Bovill's Act "only means that the lender shall not come in and rank with other creditors in the bankruptcy. . . . " No proof, no set-off.

6.8   Junior debt is secured: insolvency set-off

Where the junior debt is secured and the debtor is insolvent, the secured junior creditor has no right of proof except for the unsecured balance (unless he surrenders his security)[14] and, if he has no proof, he ought not to have a set-off. A contrary decision in *Re Moseley Green Coal & Coke Co., Barrett's Case* (1864) 4 De G.H. & S.; 34 L.J. (N.S.) Bcy. 41, is considered incorrect on this point.[15] An unsecured balance of a secured debt is eligible for set-off (*Clark* v. *Cort* [1840] Cr. & Ph. 154) but the set-off may be prevented by the rules discussed in preceding paragraphs.

If a secured creditor is insolvent, the secured debt owed to him is eligible for set-off: *Re Deveze, ex p. Barnett* (1874) L.R. 9 Ch. 293. But again the set-off may be prevented by the subordination.

6.9   Junior creditor to pay amounts equal to set-offs

The junior creditor should agree to pay the senior creditor amounts

---

[14] See the Insolvency Rules 1986, rr. 4.88, 4.95 *et seq*; 6.109, 6.115 *et seq*.
[15] See generally *English and International Set-Off*, paras. 7–204 *et seq*.

equal to any discharge of the junior debt by reason of a set-off. The weaknesses of the claim are:

— the junior creditor's liability will be a debt claim and hence irrecoverable in full if the junior creditor is insolvent
— if there are numerous or anonymous junior creditors, as in the case of subordinated bond issues, the senior creditors may face practical difficulties in claiming from the junior creditors.

CHAPTER 7

TERMS OF SUBORDINATION AGREEMENTS

7.1   Documents

The terms of the subordination may be contained in

— the junior debt instrument between the debtor and the junior creditor, such as a bearer bond and trust deed. The senior creditors are not parties and may therefore not be able to control changes to the subordination: paragraph 7.20;
— an intercreditor agreement between the junior and senior creditors. The debtor should also be a party so that the debtor may give appropriate undertakings on the lines described in paragraph 7.2;

It is usually necessary for a trustee to be appointed in the case of junior debt issues and in the case of secured debt: paragraph 10.1.

7.2   Undertakings of debtor: summary

Typically the debtor would agree as follows:

(a) The debtor will not pay or prepay any of the junior debt in cash or in kind and not purchase or otherwise acquire any of the junior debt (or permit any of its subsidiaries to do so) except as permitted by the terms of the agreement, *e.g.* permitted payments of interest prior to a default (paragraphs 7.5 *et seq.*), or required distributions on liquidation proceedings so as to give rise to proceeds for turnover to the senior creditor. As to prepayments, it is generally provided that prepayments may be made with the consent of the senior creditor. The language should be wide enough to cover "defeasing" payments made by the debtor to the junior creditor on terms that the junior creditor agrees not to sue or claim for the junior debt but does not renounce it;
(b) The debtor will not discharge any of the junior debt by set-off to the extent that the junior debt is permitted to be paid by the terms of the agreement prior to any insolvency proceedings;
(c) The debtor will not amend the terms applicable to the junior debt so as to prejudice the subordination or will not amend certain key clauses: paragraph 7.20;
(d) The debtor will not create or permit to exist any security for the junior debt or permit any of its subsidiaries to do so: paragraph 7.21.

(e) The debtor will not take or omit any action whereby the sub-ordination may be prejudiced. This is a sweeping-up clause to cover situations one cannot think of now. But one can think of various forms of direct or indirect defeasance payments.

Pari passu covenant in subordinated bond issues 7.3

Subordinated bond issues often provide that the issuer is to ensure that other subordinated issues are to rank equally. A hierarchy of subordinations or stacked subordinations have the following disadvantages (amongst others):

— confusion in the minds of investors presented with issues of varying ranking;
— complex contribution and subrogation problems;
— risk of circular subordination, as where A subordinates to B who subordinates to C who subordinates to A: paragraph 2.15.

Undertakings of junior creditor: summary 7.4

The scope of the junior creditor's undertakings depends on the type of subordination, but, to indicate the range of protections available, these might include covenants that, so long as the senior debt is outstanding, the junior creditor will:

— not demand or receive any payment or distribution in cash or kind in respect of the junior debt except as permitted by the terms of the subordination;
— not set off the junior debt except to the extent payments of the junior debt are permitted: paragraph 6.2;
— prove for the junior debt on the insolvency of the debtor so as to produce dividends for turnover: paragraphs 3.5 *et seq.*;
— not vote the junior debt so as to prejudice the subordination: paragraphs 3.5 *et seq.*;
— not enforce the junior debt by suit or execution or otherwise, nor accelerate the junior debt, nor invoke or support insolvency pro-ceedings in relation to the debtor except as permitted by the terms of the subordination: paragraphs 7.15 *et seq.*;
— not vary the terms of the junior debt or certain key provisions: paragraph 7.20;
— not waive or release the junior debt (so as to preserve the turnover to the senior creditor);
— not assign or novate the junior debt unless the assignee or trans-feree agrees to be bound by the subordination terms: paragraph 7.21;
— not permit to subsist any security over the junior debt unless the secured party agrees to be bound by the subordination terms: paragraph 7.21;
— not subordinate the junior debt to any other debt. Another sub-ordination would dilute the turnover to the senior creditors and

potentially give rise to priority problems: paragraph 7.21. There is also the risk of circular subordination as where A subordinates to B who subordinates to A; paragraph 2.15;

— (sometimes) not convert the junior debt into shares of the debtor: paragraph 11.5;
— not receive any security for the junior debt or, if any security is allowed, maintain the security: paragraph 8.16;
— not permit the junior debt to be evidenced by a negotiable instrument unless the instrument is legended with the subordination or is deposited with the senior creditor: paragraph 7.20;
— give details to the senior creditor of the amount and nature of the junior debt on request from time to time;
— notify the senior creditor of events of default in the junior debt instrument.

7.5 Springing subordinations and payment freezes generally

As mentioned at paragraph 2.1, a subordination may be a complete subordination in the sense that the junior creditor may not retain any payments on the junior debt so long as the senior debt is outstanding, or it may be a springing (or inchoate) subordination in which event the junior creditor may receive payments until certain events happen. The object is to block payments on the junior debt when an event occurs which indicates that the senior debt is at risk.

More strictly, in springing turnover subordinations, the block on payments on the junior debt only applies prior to insolvency proceedings against the debtor. If a payment is in fact received by the junior creditor, *e.g.* from some other source such as a guarantor, that payment must be turned over so that the senior debt is prepaid. However once the debtor becomes subject to insolvency proceedings, payments on the junior debt are not merely liberated but must compulsorily be claimed so that they can be turned over to the senior creditor who thereby has the benefit of the double dividend.

In summary, therefore, prior to insolvency proceedings payments of the junior debt are blocked on the prescribed events. After insolvency proceedings, payments are unblocked, must be claimed and must be turned over.

The events which crystallise the freeze or blockage depend on the circumstances, notably whether the subordination is:

— an insider subordination
— a subordinated bond issue
— mezzanine debt for a leveraged bid or other change of control financing.

7.6 Payments freezes: insider subordinations.
Where an insider of the debtor, such as a parent, affiliate, shareholder or officer, is subordinated to bank loans, the subordination is often complete and the junior creditor has no rights to any payment so long as the senior debt is outstanding.

One purpose of this is to ensure that the senior creditor's loans are used in the borrower's business and not to repay the insider's debt. Another is to ensure that undue strain is not put on the borrower's resources in having to repay both junior and senior debt. A third is to control the possible temptation of insiders to engineer a payment before the springing event: insiders who also manage the borrower are likely to have advance knowledge of the borrower's financial deterioration and of a looming springing event.

Even in the case of complete subordinations the junior creditor may be permitted to recover if, say, a specified financial test is met by the debtor indicating a margin of solvency, or if at the time of payment an auditor's certificate shows that the debtor is solvent and would be solvent after the payment.

Payment freezes: junior bond issues. At the other extreme are sub-   **7.7**
ordinations which spring only on bankruptcy of the debtor. These springing subordinations are typical of subordinated bond issues. Under a common eurobond form for issues by banks intended to qualify as capital for capital adequacy purposes, the remedies of the junior bondholders are limited to liquidating the issuing debtor. It is provided further that the subordination comes into effect on liquidation. To enhance control of the junior creditors the subordinated debt is payable to a trustee for the junior creditors and the trust deed contains a "no-action" clause whereby only the trustee is authorised to enforce the bonds.

Springing subordinations in mezzanine debt: generally. The above   **7.8**
extremes are not usually appropriate in leveraged finance for acquisitions, management buy-outs and other change of control financings comprising layers of senior and junior debt. In the first place, the junior lenders commonly lend short-term in order to finance the transaction and the junior debt is not intended as part of the borrower's long-term capital structure. Secondly, the junior creditors are often institutional investors or banks who should legitimately be paid current principal and interest so long as the debtor is in good financial health: they are prepared only to invest in performing assets. The senior creditors on the other hand will wish to stop payments on the junior debt if the safety of the senior debt is threatened. Thirdly, mezzanine debt is often very risky—hence the term "junk bonds." As a result the junior debt holders look for greater protections than in, say, capital issues by banks.

Mezzanine debt: scheduled payments of junior debt   **7.9**

It is usually agreed that the junior creditor may be paid scheduled payments until a prescribed event occurs.

The scheduled payments on the junior debt should exclude voluntary prepayments and accelerated payments. Ideally the scheduled repayment instalments of the junior debt should be staggered so as to follow, say, three to six months after the senior debt repayment instalments so as to avoid the possibility that the debtor pays off the more expensive junior debt without leaving enough to pay the senior debt. The delay also gives the senior creditors time to organise a cure for the default if they do not receive a scheduled instalment. Alternatively the junior repayments might be limited to interest, with principal being payable in restricted circumstances.

Junior bridge finance. Where the junior debt is short-term bridge finance for an acquisition, which is to be refinanced by longer-term debt arranged by the junior creditor (such as by an issue of medium-term debt securities issued to a broader group of investors) the senior creditors will be prejudiced if the junior bridge debt matures without the longer-term refinancing having been arranged. The bridge is often very short, *e.g.* six months. Methods of improving the certainty of the roll-over into the longer-term debt include:

— the bridge lenders underwrite a portion of the long-term debt
— the conditions precedent to this underwriting (such as no-default, no material adverse change in the debtor's financial condition) are watered down or eliminated.

All kinds of other tactics have been attempted in the United States to slow the racing maturity of the bridge loan, including drafting it as a long-term issue of debt securities with an earlier acceleration right if a registration statement covering the junior debt is not filed with the S.E.C. within the bridge period (so that the bridge lender has to take affirmative action to accelerate, an action which will freeze further payments on the bridge), ratcheting up the interest rate (so that the junior creditors are compensated for the absence of greater marketability on registration or listing), removing the more onerous convenants in the bridge loan automatically at the end of the bridge period and replacing them by the slim covenant protections typical of long-term debt issues (so that the bridge lender must either refinance as contemplated or live with lesser protections as if he had), and restricting the rights of the bridge lender to sell off or subparticipate the bridge loan (so as to encourage the refinancing, to ensure that the senior lenders continue to deal with a known sophisticated institution free of the pressure of sharks and to preserve the bridge lender's voting control of the bridge loan).

Where a selling shareholder subordinates the balance of his selling price which is not paid in cash, the shareholder will generally be content with lesser covenant protections and with a long maturity.

7.10 Mezzanine debt: springing events

The definition of the events which should unleash the catch on the spring in mezzanine finance for change of control financings is a matter for negotiation. The senior creditor must aim to freeze the junior debt before it is too late. The junior creditor will rise to ensure that payment of the junior debt is not to be frozen for trivial defaults but only when there is a real probability that the senior debt is being eroded. On the other hand the junior creditor will be more trigger-happy than the senior creditor because the senior creditor has the cushion of the junior debt.

The following are examples of negotiated compromises:

— A payment default on the senior debt blocks payments on the junior debt because the junior creditors should never be paid while the senior debt is due but unpaid. Defaulted interest on the senior debt may give rise to a temporary block on the junior debt.

— Insolvency events, such as liquidation, always block payments which the junior creditors are entitled to keep since the debtor has stopped payment on all debt. But in this case the junior creditor must prove and turn over receipts to the senior creditor.

— An acceleration by the junior creditors will often also be a blocking event—mainly as a disincentive to acceleration, if otherwise permitted.

The negotiation tends to centre upon other events of default, notably breach of warranty, breach of covenant, creditors executions and other processes and the cross-default with a view to defining when the red light comes on.

Various methods have been resorted to in order to balance the competing interests.

Payment blockage period. One method is to limit the period of the payment blockage on the junior debt to, say, 90 to 360 days. The payment blockage period commences on the service of a notice by the agent for the senior creditor that an event of default has occurred under the senior credit agreement. This period is commonly referred to in the United States as a "fish-or-cut-bait" period. At the end of the payment blockage period of, say, 180 days or any earlier curing or waiving of the default, scheduled payments on the junior debt (including missed payments) may be resumed on the basis that the senior creditors are content to continue or are not promoting a restructuring of the borrower's liabilities and business. During the payment blockage period the debtor should have a breathing-space to get its house in order and hence ideally the junior creditors should be prohibited from (a) accelerating the junior debt (because this will almost certainly render the debtor insolvent in the sense of being unable to pay its debts as they fall due and hence prevent management from continuing to trade—although a restraint on acceleration is often not acceptable), (b) obtaining judgment and levying execution for the junior debt, and (c) initiating rehabilitation or insolvency proceedings.

Unless the debtor can cure the default during the payment blockage period or unless the senior creditors have the power and the time to restructure the debtor and to compel the junior creditors to accept a work-out plan, *e.g.* by overriding restrictive covenants in the junior credit agreement (see paragraph 7.14), the payment blockage merely delays the collapse of the debtor. The hand of the senior creditors will be forced at the end of that period—they must either accelerate and enforce so as to spring a complete subordination or allow the junior creditors to be paid the missed scheduled payments. The senior creditors may be pressured into advancing fresh money to pay off the default. On the other hand junior creditors may argue that the suspension should not go on indefinitely and that the senior lenders should act diligently in resolving the default—or else accelerate themselves. It might incidentally be remarked that 90 days will usually be much too short a period for the senior creditors to arrange a rescheduling or a work-out. If the period is too short, the senior lenders may be panicked into an over-hasty restructuring.

It is usually provided that only one block can be initiated in every 365-day period on the basis of defaults existing at the time of the original block so as to prevent the senior creditors using old defaults for a series of successive blocks.

A payment block on the junior debt may result in a default on the junior debt and hence confer on the junior creditors a right to accelerate: as to restraints on this right, see paragraph 7.16.

If there are several classes of senior debt, *e.g.* the main senior financing debt and also senior working capital loans, the principal senior lenders have an interest in ensuring that the other senior lenders are restrained from using up payment blockages or from blocking payments on the junior debt which result in a default on the junior debt and hence a junior acceleration right. The rights to serve notice could be limited to senior creditors holding more than a threshold amount of debt.

7.11   Restrictions on rights of junior creditor generally

An important question from the point of view of the senior creditor is the extent to which he has freedom of action in the management of the senior debt, particularly if the debtor gets into financial difficulties, and the extent of the junior creditor's ability to rock the boat, *e.g.* by precipitating a liquidation of the debtor at an inopportune time. If the junior creditor has too much power to block a work-out of the debtor sponsored by the senior creditor or can force the senior creditor into springing the subordination by liquidating the debtor, the junior creditor might harass the senior creditor into paying out the junior creditor and thereby, commercially, to turn the subordination upside down. In change of control financings, sharks or spoilers might buy up the junior debt specifically with a view to extracting more money from the company debtor under threat of exploding the transaction, liquidating the debtor or vetoing routine changes to the financing agreements to accommodate sensible changes of plan.

The main points to be considered include:

— the advance of new money by the senior creditor
— variations of the senior debt
— the borrower's covenants in the junior credit agreement
— events of default and acceleration rights in the junior credit agreement and other remedies of the junior creditor.

The scope of the restrictions on the rights of the junior creditor depend fundamentally on the particular transaction, *e.g.* whether the junior debt is insider debt, or is a junior bond issue or is institutional finance for a change of control transaction.

The scope of the protections is also influenced by the ability of the senior creditors to negotiate with the junior creditors if there is a downturn in the debtor's business. Junior creditors who are banks or institutional lenders financing a leveraged bid may be granted greater protections because the senior creditors can generally negotiate with them as a sophisticated club of creditors and because the junior creditors have greater bargaining power. This is not true of junior bond issues unless the junior debt is held by a trustee and under applicable law the trust deed confers wide powers on bondholder meetings to alter the terms of the bonds—the ability to do so is highly restricted in the United States by the Trustee Indenture Act of 1939. In any event negotiation by bondholder meetings is cumbersome and formal and, if the bondholders are small investors, the cut-off of payments by the senior creditors may attract unfavourable publicity and pressure from official sources. As a result the protections of junior creditors in junior debt issues are generally very slim.

A junior creditor entitled to convert the debt into equity will often tolerate lesser protections since he may view his debt as transitional only and substantially intended to be equity in due course. Commercially, the conversion privilege sweetens the debt.

Advance of new money by senior creditor   7.12

If the debtor gets into financial difficulties, new money for working capital will almost invariably be required and the question will be whether new money lent by the senior creditor will rank ahead of the junior debt.

In insider subordinations, the senior creditor should have freedom to add on as much senior debt as he wishes. If the insider controls the debtor, he can in any event control whether the debtor will increase senior borrowings from the senior creditor. As to the position in respect of senior secured debt, see paragraph 8.5.

In junior bond issues subordinated to all other debt, including future debt, the question does not arise.

In purchase price financings, such as leveraged bids, many compromises are possible, *e.g.* the senior debt may be increased by a specified amount over the originally contemplated commitments in the senior credit agreement less any actual repayments of the senior debt. The senior creditors ought to be able to tide the debtor over a difficult patch or to finance unexpected cash-flow deficits without a veto from the junior creditors.

The senior creditors ought also to be entitled to defer payments of the senior debt and to increase the interest rate without prejudicing the subordination.

The definition of senior debt should cover refinancings or refundings of the senior debt in order to facilitate restructurings and to enable the senior creditors to arrange take-out finance. This is especially true of transaction finance for leveraged acquisitions which is intended to be bridge finance and to be taken out by ordinary debt and longer-term money at more realistic interest rates.

It is not usual to provide that, if the senior creditors extend a payment date, the junior creditors will similarly extend. Nor is it usual to establish that if the senior creditors convert into equity, *e.g.* on a work-out, the junior creditors must convert into a lower-ranking class of equity. The reason is that it is too complicated to legislate in advance and too difficult to impose those requirements ahead of the actual facts: one has to leave them to work-out negotiations or to the operation of a rehabilitation plan in bankruptcy proceedings.

7.13   Variations of senior debt

Apart from variations of payments, such as deferments and changes in the interest rate, the senior creditor will seek to have a free hand in varying other terms of the senior credit agreement, such as the covenants and events of default and in giving consents and waivers. The rationale is that the junior creditor should not be entitled to veto a sensible change or a variation to accommodate an unforeseen change in the debtor's business plan.

In turnover subordinations, a variation of the senior debt not agreed by the junior creditor may prejudice the subordination unless otherwise agreed in advance: paragraph 9.4.

7.14   Covenants in junior debt agreement

The covenants in the junior debt agreement have three main repercussions:

— breach generally entitles the junior creditor to refuse to lend further advances under a conditions precedent clause in the junior credit agreement, thereby removing the expected cushion and turnover of proceeds to the senior creditor. Because of this, in mezzanine finance the junior loans should be advanced at the outset of the transaction or pro rata with the senior loans, and should not be revolving.

— breach will usually be an event of default empowering the junior creditor to accelerate. This is discussed in paragraph 7.16 below.

— the junior creditor can enjoin the debtor or the senior creditor from entering into a transaction, as on a work-out, which infringes a covenant. Any violation resulting from a transaction with the senior creditor may render the senior creditor liable to the junior debtor for the tort of inducing a breach of contract. In practice the ability of the junior creditor to enjoin a transaction is a more powerful weapon than the sanction of acceleration. This is because an acceleration is likely to put the debtor out of business and will crystallise the subordination on the resulting insolvency or under an express term freezing junior payments on an acceleration by the junior creditor. A veto does not of itself bring about this cataclysm.

In short-term change of control financings, junior lenders naturally seek greater covenant protection than is appropriate for insider subordinations and junior bond issues. The object of the senior creditor is to denude the junior creditors of as much as possible of their covenant protection so as to prevent the junior creditors holding the senior creditors to ransom. The junior creditors on the other hand will seek to protect their debt by normal credit covenants, so that they can accelerate and enforce before the debtor's financial condition deteriorates so as to prejudice the junior debt.

Nobody is likely to object to routine covenants of the debtor in the junior credit agreement, such as the provision of financial information and compliance certificates, the maintenance of consents for the finance, the maintenance of corporate existence and of insurances, the prompt payment of taxes, a restriction on dividends and a prohibition on mergers or consolidations.

The more sensitive covenants in the junior debt instrument for mezzanine finance include:

— *Negative pledge.* A negative pledge prohibits the grant of security by the debtor. Normally the senior creditors will resist a negative pledge in the junior debt instrument. But if such a clause is included, it should be modified. The debtor should be entitled to secure the senior debt since the junior creditor is benefited. There should equally be no objection to the grant of security to the senior creditor if the junior creditor is secured on the same assets in a junior position and on the basis that the rights of the junior creditor are restricted along the lines indicated in Chapter 8. Many work-outs involve the grant of new or additional security.

— *Financial covenants and ratios.* If any are negotiated in the junior credit agreement, they should be light, allow much headroom and crystallise only in the event of the virtual collapse of the debtor.

— *Restriction on substantial disposals.* Senior creditors should resist an anti-disposal covenant in the junior debt instrument. Work-outs or adverse conditions may necessitate a disposal programme. Further, senior bank loans for leveraged bids are often made in the expectaction of significant disposals of assets of the acquired company in order to repay the senior loans quickly. If a disposal covenant is included, it should apply only to major disposals and should exclude cumulative disposals and ordinary course of business transactions. The senior creditors should have power to consent to disposals by the debtor (and to override any contrary covenants in the junior credit agreement) if the disposal is at fair value and the proceeds are applied in reducing the senior debt. Disposals up to a specified cumulative amount for specified

periods should be considered, as should disposals where the debtor invests the proceeds in other long-term producing assets.
— *Restriction on changes in business.* A period of difficulty may necessitate a slimming down of the debtor's lines of business.
— *Borrowing limits.* These may restrict new money—see paragraph 7.12 above. Any borrowing limit in the junior credit agreement should allow massive headroom. Borrowings in excess of the limit should be allowed if they are used to repay the senior debt within a specified period. Care should be taken to ensure that, if the senior credit agreement is revolving or contemplates staged drawdowns, the future senior advances are not stopped by the fact that the borrowing limit in the junior credit agreement would be breached.

As a matter of drafting, one technique is to permit extensive covenants in the junior credit agreement and to provide in an intercreditor agreement that the senior creditors can compel the junior creditors to waive their covenants except for those which are agreed to be entrenched. This technique maintains the junior covenants if the senior debt should be paid off leaving the junior debt intact. If the junior covenants are slight, there is no need for compulsory parallel waivers.

Certainly it should be possible in mezzanine finance for the majority junior creditors to waive covenants since this will facilitate the ability of the senior creditors to obtain a waiver. But it needs to be recognised that, if the debtor's position becomes parlous, the existence of any significant covenants in the junior debt instrument is likely seriously to hamper the senior creditors. Hence a watering down of the junior covenants will tend to assist the senior creditor only in the case of routine changes to a business plan.

In *insider subordinations*, there are either negligible covenants in the junior debt instrument (since the insiders commonly control the debtor) or, in the rare case that there are any, the senior creditor should have complete freedom to override the debtor's covenants given to the junior debtor.

In *junior eurobond issues*, particularly debt issues by banks, the bondholders' covenant protection is generally non-existent apart from a very light negative pledge applying only to listed subordinated debt. They are treated almost as preferred equity, though without a vote or the ability to participate in profits or capital appreciations.

7.15   Remedies of junior creditor generally

The main remedies of the junior creditor on an event of default are to accelerate the junior debt, to enforce a judgment by execution against assets of the debtor, and to initiate insolvency proceedings. The exercise of any of these remedies could prejudice the senior creditor's efforts to see the debtor through a downturn in its fortunes if there is a light at the end of the tunnel. A junior creditor is likely to be quicker to exercise remedies to prevent further erosion of the junior debt by further trading at a loss.

In insider subordinations, the junior creditor is generally barred from exercising any of these remedies.

In junior bond issues, the events of default are commonly very light and in some extreme forms (particularly junior bond issues by banks qualifying as capital for capital adequacy purposes (see paragraph 11.1) the remedies of the junior bondholders are limited to liquidating the debtor—a nuclear bomb they are not likely to drop if the only result is that they are so deeply subordinated to all other creditors that they will receive nothing.

The more complicated controls on the junior creditor's remedies in mezzanine finance are discussed below.

Mezzanine debt: acceleration by junior creditor   **7.16**

In junior purchase price financings it is desirable from the senior creditor's point of view to prevent accelerations of the junior debt altogether until the onset of insolvency proceedings. This is because an acceleration usually would render the debtor insolvent in the sense that it is not able to pay its debts as they fall due. In that event the directors of the debtor must cease trading in case they incur personal liability for wrongful or fraudulent trading. Any new security granted to the senior creditors to encourage them to lend new money might, to the extent it secures old debt, be vulnerable to be set aside by a preference made in the suspect period—which commonly commences when the debtor is insolvent. In the result the junior creditor has the power to bring the house down—a strong bargaining chip, although it is substantially weakened by the risk that the debtor will be put into bankruptcy with little or no return to the junior creditor and by any contractual freeze on further payments to the junior creditor.

In mezzanine finance, the mezzanine creditor's events of default can be emasculated by the usual techniques of long grace periods, materiality tests, exclusion of subsidiaries other than major subsidiaries, high thresholds and high acceleration majorities. Non-payment of junior interest could be excluded as a default if the debtor has insufficient net earnings and is not paying dividends. But these will not normally be enough to neuter the events of default altogether. Only if the events of default are very slight and if there are no significant covenants and no cross-default can the senior lender be reasonably secure.

A complete freeze on acceleration rights can be difficult to negotiate. But many intermediate positions are possible. An acceleration by the junior creditor could spark off the senior creditor's right to initiate a payment blockage period of the type discussed at paragraph 7.10. Any accelerated debt could be subject to turnover by the junior creditor to the senior creditor. Both of these would act as a disincentive to an untimely acceleration by the junior creditor. Acceleration rights could be stayed during a standstill period during which the default could be cured. The senior creditors might be able to pay off the default in the standstill period—not always an attractive solution. Of course any acceleration by the junior creditor will normally entitle the senior creditor to accelerate under a cross-default clause in the senior credit agreement and hence enforce a clause providing for complete blockages on payments of the junior debt so long as there is a payment default on the senior debt: paragraph 7.10. But the need to initiate a cataclysm of this sort introduces a fragility into the financing.

Similarly, the senior creditor will endeavour to exclude the other remedies of the junior creditor—to levy execution or to initiate insolvency proceedings—at least during a standstill period. But junior creditors may legitimately be permitted to petition for a reorganisation or a liquidation if the debtor is insolvent. In that event the junior creditors stand to lose the most and hence are more likely to support a rehabilitation plan.

7.17 Mezzanine debt: cross-default in junior credit agreement

Most term credit agreements contain a cross-default by the terms of which the acceleration or non-payment of other borrowings is an event of default. This is the leading anticipatory event of default and is designed to ensure that all creditors have a sufficient sanction to get them to the negotiating table if one creditor accelerates. It is also designed to prevent one creditor from being paid out in priority and hence is, commercially, a *pari passu* clause.

As a minimum, the cross-default in the junior debt instrument should spark off only if other defined debt is actually accelerated, *i.e.* a cross-acceleration clause. If it crystallises on the mere occurrence of an event of default or inchoate event of default in another debt instrument, the junior creditors will effectively piggy-back on to all the defaults and covenants in the senior credit agreement since the occurrence of a default in the senior credit agreement will be a cross-default in the junior agreement. If a payment default on the senior debt is within the junior cross-default, the senior creditors should seek a high amount threshold and a long grace period.

A sample cross-default in the junior credit agreement might read:

"Any borrowings of the Debtor exceeding £[ ] in total are declared prematurely payable by reason of an event of default and a period of [ ] days has elapsed without the declaration being rescinded or guarantees given by the Debtor of borrowings exceeding £[ ] in total are not paid within [ ] days of the due date."

If the threshold is high enough, it might catch only the debt under the senior credit agreement which the senior lenders can control.

7.18 Poison pills

Some junior agreements and junior bond issues contain a poison pill, namely an event of default or mandatory prepayment event if there is a change in control of the debtor, *e.g.* on a bid or private sale (together with, sometimes, a downgrading in the credit rating of the debtor or the particular issue by a rating agency). The term "poison pill" is a felicitous piece of market slang to describe the impact which such a clause might have upon a bidder for the debtor company.

In junior debt issues, the reason for the clause is that the position of bondholders lending to a private company is usually worse, both commercially and legally, from those lending to a public company regulated by stricter company law, stock exchange and investor standards. In charge of control financings, the junior creditors may be willing to lend to a company under a particular management but not under some other management. They may not favour giving the benefits of the subordination to companies other than the company for whom it was intended.

A premature acceleration under such a clause should be a subordinating event. The clause should be cross-defaulted in the senior credit agreement.

Representations and warranties   7.19

The purpose of representations and warranties by the junior creditor and debtor in a subordination agreement are:

— to spark off an event of default in the senior creditor agreement if they are incorrect;
— to flush out disclosure in advance; and
— to ground an action for damages.

Consideration should be given to usual warranties covering the debtor, the junior debtor, the junior debt instrument and any intercreditor agreement, including warranties as to status, powers, authorisations, validity, official consents, and non-conflict with laws, constitutional documents or contracts.

In insider subordinations where the senior creditor is relying on the turnover of distributions on the junior debt, there might be warranties by the junior creditor in favour of the senior creditor that:

— the amount of the junior debt is as disclosed
— the junior creditor is the sole owner of the junior debt
— the junior debt is unsecured except as disclosed and any security for the junior debt is valid and enjoys the contemplated priority: paragraph 8.16.
— the junior debt has not been subordinated in favour of any other creditor: paragraph 7.20.
— the junior debt is not subject to any set-off or defence by the debtor: paragraph 6.1.

As a matter of market practice, representations would not normally be found in a subordinated eurobond issue or in any other junior debt issues.

Variations of junior debt and desubordinations   7.20

In the case of subordinations where the senior creditor is a party, the debtor and the junior creditor will typically agree with the senior creditor not to amend key provisions in the junior credit agreement, including:

— the definition of junior debt
— the subordination clauses
— the amount and time of payment of principal and interest of the junior debt (so as, for example, to ensure that senior debt matures before the junior debt if the junior payments are allowed prior to an event of default)
— the covenants, events of default and acceleration rights (including majorities) in the junior debt instrument (so that the junior creditors do not enhance their ability to bring the house down)
— the currency of the junior debt.

In the case of subordinated bond issues where the senior creditors are not parties, the senior creditors are vulnerable if the debtor and the junior creditor can, between themselves, agree to de-subordinate the junior debt without the consent of the senior creditor.

On the other hand, in the case of junior debt issues subordinated to all other debt, it might be dangerous for both debtor and junior creditor to render the junior debt completely unalterable since it would in practice be impossible to obtain the agreement of all senior creditors to a sensible change. In England the ability of the courts to vary a trust under the Variation of Trusts Act 1958 is very limited since the Act is mainly intended to permit variation of trusts in favour of infants and future unascertained persons. It is not unreasonable that the junior debt instrument should contain provisions enabling some latitude for amendments in an appropriate case by junior creditor meetings without the consent of senior creditors, provided that the subordination is not impaired or terminated.

In civil code countries, statutes frequently provide for the establishment of communities of bondholders and the terms which can be altered by specified majorities: paragraph 10.16. These powers may be regarded as exhaustive, as in Switzerland and Luxembourg. Whether the legislator inadvertently inserted a power to desubordinate subordinations is a matter for the microscopic examination of the relevant statute, but plainly the junior bondholders are advantaged by such a variation.

In any event the senior creditor could object to a variation only if some nexus between him and the junior creditor can be established. For example:

(a) Beneficiary under trust If the senior creditor is a vested beneficiary of existing property under a subordination trust the trust may not be altered or abrogated without his consent. But a subordination trust might be alterable without the consent of the senior creditor if the trust is over future assets. This is because a volunteer (the senior creditor) cannot enforce an imperfectly constituted trust, such as a trust over a future asset, unless he has given value for the asset. The underlying principle is that if a donor gifts future property to a donee, the donor can change his mind until he has actually handed over the property to the donee. Executing the gift under seal is not sufficient.[1]

Junior debt issues subordinated to all other debt commonly crystallise the subordination only on liquidation of the debtor in which event the question might arise whether dividends on liquidation are a future asset or are an existing asset. This is another aspect of the mysteries of assignments of proceeds, as opposed to the debt itself: paragraph 2.9. The common sense view is that a trust of future proceeds of an existing debt should not be regarded as a trust of a future asset subject to revocability and that the cases relating to the revocation of trusts of future expectancies under wills should have no application. This view is supported by a dictum in *Glegg* v. *Bromley* [1912] 3 K.B. 474, C.A., where Vaughan Williams L.J. said at 484 in relation to the assignment of the proceeds of an action: "It has been said that this is an assignment of an expectancy within the meaning of the rule laid down in *In re Ellenborough* [1903] 1 Ch. 697. I think this was an assignment of property, and not an expectancy." See also the cases cited in paragraph 7.21 in relation to assignments of future debts. But plainly the subordination of a debt not yet in existence would be a future asset.

Even if the assignment is of existing property, the "gift" is revocable unless the donor has done everything necessary to transfer the property: As to the vexed question as to what is necessary to achieve this result, see Chitty on Contracts (26th edn), Vol I, para. 1407.

A subordination trust will be alterable without the senior creditor's consent if the trust deed expressly allows alterations, *e.g.* by bondholder majorities. The senior creditor contracts on the basis of the power of alteration. If the senior creditor wishes to inflict a sanction against desubordination, he should require the debtor in the senior credit agreement not to desubordinate.

(b) Contracting party. If the senior creditor is a party to the subordination agreement he can prevent variations as a contracting party. Unhappily it is impracticable for the senior creditors to be parties in the case of the subordinations to all other debt. In the case of junior bond issues, the senior creditors may not even be aware of subordination and their credits may not arise until well after the issue of the bonds.

But if there is a provision in the subordination agreement whereby the junior creditor offers to maintain the subordination on the basis that the senior creditor can accept the offer by lending senior debt to the debtor, the senior creditor may become a party to the contract by accepting the offer in accordance with its terms on the basis of the engaging case of *Carlill* v. *Carbolic Smoke Ball Co.* [1893] 1 Q.B. 256.

(c) Representation leading to estoppel. If the senior creditor can show that the junior creditor collaterally warranted to the senior creditor that the junior creditor would remain subordinated and in reliance on this the senior creditor subsequently contracted his debt or changed his position,

---

[1] *Re Ellenborough* [1903] 1 Ch 697; *Meek* v. *Kettlewell* (1843) 1 Hare 464; *Re Tilt* (1896) 74 LT 163.]

e.g. by agreeing not to enforce his debt, the junior creditor may be estopped from varying the subordination on usual principles of promissory estoppel. There would probably have to be some affirmative representation by the junior creditor to the senior creditor in order to set up an estoppel.

Whether the publicity achieved by the recording of the subordination in the debtor's accounts or the filing of the subordination with a credit rating agency would be enough to invite reliance should depend on the circumstances.

Some subordination agreements may specifically invite reliance as follows:

> "The junior creditor agrees that this subordination is an inducement and consideration to each senior creditor to give or continue credit to the debtor or to acquire senior debt. The senior creditor may accept the benefit of this subordination by giving or continuing credit to the debtor or acquiring senior debt. The junior creditor waives reliance and notice of acceptance."

Language similar to this was held in a United States decision to constitute a waiver by the junior creditor of the defence of reliance: *In re Discon Corp.*, 346 F.Supp. 839 (S.D. Fla. 1971).

7.21   Transfers of rights to junior debt and priorities

If a junior creditor transfers his debt, will the assignee take free of the subordination?

Simple debts. Where the junior debt is an ordinary loan or other simple debt, a term of the junior debt that it is non-assignable relies on a first-instance (and not wholly watertight) English decision to the effect that assignments in breach of a prohibition on assignments are totally void: *Helstan Securities Ltd.* v. *Hertfordshire County Council* (1978) 3 All E.R. 262. Of course junior debt is often intended to be fully marketable, such as subordinated bond issues and institutional loans for change of control transactions.

In the case of subordination trusts, the junior creditor might create a subordination trust of proceeds of the same debt in favour of another creditor or might transfer the junior debt without disclosing to the assignee the presence of the intercreditor agreement under which the junior creditor transfers the proceeds of the debt to the senior creditor if the subordination crystallises. The English priorities between assignees depend primarily on who is the first to give notice to the debtor. A subsequent assignee would take free of a prior assignment if he did not know of the prior assignment when he took his assignment and he is the first to give notice to the debtor. Priority does not depend upon taking a legal assignment for value without actual or constructive notice of the trust, but depends upon notice to the debtor: *E. Pfeiffer Weinkellerei-Weinenkauf GmbH & Co.* v. *Arbuthnot Factors Ltd.* [1988] 1 W.L.R. 150. Whether notice to the debtor of an assignment of proceeds has the same effect as an assignment of the debt itself is unclear. The sensible solution is that the senior creditor ought to be able to protect his priority by notice to the debtor because an assignment of proceeds carries with it the entire commercial value of the claim. If this is incorrect, there would seem to be no full-proof method of protecting the priority.

A possible obstacle is that English case law suggests that notice to the debtor to protect the priority of an assignment of a future claim cannot be given until the claim comes into existence: see, for example, *Re Dallas* [1904] 2 Ch. 385, C.A.; *Roxburghe* v. *Cox* (1881) 17 Ch.D. 520. A contrary view has been taken in Ontario: *L.F. Dommerich & Co. Inc.* v. *Canadian Admiral Corp. Inc.* (1962) O.R. 902. It is considered that the proceeds of an existing debt are not a future claim for this purpose since the proceeds are the fruits of an existing claim.[2]

It is considered incidentally that the special rules relating to priorities between successive assignments of interests under trusts do not apply to trusts of proceeds. Trusts of proceeds are in substance assignments by reason of the fact that they establish bare trusts and it would make no sense for notices to be served on the junior creditor as nominal trustee of those proceeds.

If the junior creditor receives the proceeds which he is to hold on trust but then diverts the proceeds, the senior creditor has a right to trace. The right to trace is lost if, for example, the proceeds are paid into an overdrawn account of the junior creditor at a bank which does not know that the moneys are trust moneys at the time of payment and has given value before notice: *Thomson* v. *Clydesdale Bank Ltd.* [1893] A.C. 282, H.L.

An intercreditor agreement may restrict the various potential forms of disposal as follows:

"So long as any senior debt is outstanding, the junior creditor will not
    (a) create or permit to subsist any security in favour of any person over any of the junior debt or its proceeds or any interest in the junior debt or its proceeds;
    (b) assign or otherwise dispose of any of the junior debt or its proceeds or any interest in the junior debt or its proceeds to any person;
    (c) transfer by novation any of its rights or obligations in respect of the junior debt to any person; or
    (d) subordinate any of the junior debt or its proceeds to any other person unless in each case that person agrees with the senior creditor that he is bound by all the terms of this subordination in manner satisfactory to the senior creditor or by the execution of an accession agreement in the form set out in the schedule hereto."

---

[2] For cases on future debts, see: *Shepherd* v. *Commonwealth of Australia Taxation Comr.* (1965) 113 C.R.L. 384 (future patent royalties under existing agreement is existing debt); *Hughes* v. *Pump House Hotel Co. Ltd.* (1902) 2 K.B. 190, C.A. (future sums payable under existing building contract are existing debts); *Walker* v. *Bradford Old Bank* (1884) 12 Q.B.D. 511; D.C. (future credit balance on death under existing bank account is existing debt); *Norman* v. *Federal Taxation Comr.* (1963) 109 C.L.R. 9 (interest payable in the future on an existing loan is a mere expectancy—an extreme decision); *N.W. Robbie & Co. Ltd.* v. *Witney Warehouse Co. Ltd.* [1963] 3 All E.R. 613; [1963] 1 W.L.R. 1324 at 1329, C.A.; *Williams* v. *Commissioner of Inland Revenue* [1965] N.Z.L.R. 395 (assignment of "the first £500 of the net income which shall accrue to the assignor" from an existing life interest under a trust fund—a mere expectancy).

Negotiable instruments. If the junior debt is evidenced by a negotiable instrument not recording the subordination, then a holder in due course of the negotiable instrument should take free of the subordination on usual principles of bills of exchange. It is unclear whether under English law an express subordination provision in a promissory note itself would destroy its strict negotiability: the position may depend upon the terms of the subordination, *e.g.* as to whether the note is conditional. But there ought to be no objection to referring to the subordination effected by the intercreditor agreement on the face of the instrument so as to notify it to holders provided that this does not qualify the obligation to pay: consider the Bills of Exchange Act 1882, s.3(3).

In the United States, a holder of a negotiable instrument takes subject to a subordination stated on the instrument: see U.C.C. ss.3–302 and 3–306.

The senior creditor should if possible in a private subordination take possession of any negotiable instruments evidencing the junior debt. The agreement may provide that if any junior debt is subsequently evidenced by a negotiable instrument, the instrument will be deposited with the senior creditor.

Subordination of a bearer bond (either directly or by virtue of a trust deed for bondholders) does not destroy negotiability because negotiability of bearer bonds is sanctioned by commercial usage which (unlike bills of exchange legislation) does not insist on unconditionality. The bond is negotiable if the market treats it as negotiable: *London Joint Stock Bank* v. *Simmons* [1892] A.C. 201.

A purchaser of a subordinated debenture or negotiable bond will plainly be on notice of a subordination noted on the instrument. In the United States, section 202(1) of the U.C.C. will render a purchase of an investment security subject to a subordination noted on or referred to in the security.

7.22   Transfers of obligations: marketable junior debt

In the case of a debtor-creditor turnover subordination whereby the junior creditor agrees to pay to the senior creditor amounts equal to his receipts, any transferee of the junior creditor must, in order to bind him to the turnover, undertake the same obligation by express agreement with the senior creditor.

In the case of turnover subordination trusts, it may be necessary to bind assignees to positive covenants in the subordination agreement and to establish privity between assignees and the senior creditor, *e.g.* in relation to covenants to pay amounts equal to set-offs realised by the junior creditor and covenants not to accelerate or vary the junior debt. Further, the transferring junior creditor will wish to be released from liability to the senior creditor for breaches by the assignee.

It ought not be be necessary for an assignee of a debt subject to a trust of its proceeds to re-declare a trust in favour of the senior creditor. An assignee who knows of the prior trust ought to take subject to the trust in the same way that any assignee of a beneficial interest takes subject to known previous trusts of or assignments affecting that interest. If the assignee received the trust property, he ought to be treated as a constructive trustee and be obliged to hand it over to the beneficiary.

Because of these considerations, the subordination agreement should establish that the junior creditor may not transfer the junior debt unless the transferee agrees with the senior creditors that he will be bound by the terms of the subordination or intercreditor agreement.

If the junior debt is not an issue of bearer bonds or other securities but it is intended that the debt should be marketable by way of private placement amongst sophisticated institutions, the intercreditor agreement could set up a procedure for novations on a transfer. Where the senior and junior debt are syndicated bank loans, one possibility would be for the agent for the senior creditors to be appointed irrevocable agent on behalf of all parties to accept an incoming junior creditor on a novation in accordance with a prescribed form of accession agreement. An alternative would be for all parties to agree in the intercreditor agreement to hold an offer open to incoming junior creditors who can accept by executing a prescribed form of novation and despatching it to the agent for the senior creditors on terms that, when the agent countersigns, the new junior creditor takes the place of the outgoing junior creditor. Similar procedures could be adopted for cases where a senior creditor novates its portion of the senior debt.

If the junior debt is secured, then the security must be held by a trustee if the novation procedure is to work: paragraph 10.1.

Securities laws might be relevant to the above, notably the Financial Services Act 1986 and the United States Securities Act of 1933.

Accession of new debtors   7.23

In leveraged bids, the banks and other institutions financing the offeror generally require that, if the bid is successful, the offeror company will procure that the target company and its subsidiaries will guarantee the loans made to the offeror company and create fixed and floating security over all their assets to secure those guarantees.

Since these guarantees and security would constitute unlawful financial assistance by the target and its subsidiaries for the purpose of paying back the loans to acquire the shares of the target contrary to section 151 of the Companies Act 1986, the usual procedure is for the offeror to be required to convert the target from a public company into a private company under section 53 of the Act (since private companies can give financial assistance in limited circumstances) and then for special resolutions to be passed by the members of the companies concerned approving the financial assistance under sections 155 *et seq.* of the Act. In order to secure the necessary resolutions the bidder must in practice have gained control of 75 per cent. of the shares and the directors must make a statutory declaration of solvency in the prescribed form backed up by an auditor's report.

The intercreditor agreement should contain provisions for the accession of the target and its subsidiaries to the subordination provisions. This can conveniently be achieved by setting out a form of deed of accession.

7.24   Attachments of junior debt

If a judgment creditor of the junior creditor garnishes the junior debt under R.S.C., Ord. 49 before proceeds are paid on the junior debt which are held in trust for the senior creditor, it is suggested that the garnishing creditor should not be entitled to those proceeds provided that the subordination trust was declared and notified to the senior creditor before the service on the junior creditor of the garnishee order nisi: see *Glegg* v. *Bromley* [1912] 3 K.B. 474 (where however the garnishment was served after the proceeds came into existence).[3] Further, moneys held by the judgment debtor in trust for another are not attachable: see, for example, *Harrods Ltd.* v. *Tester* (1937) 157 L.T. 7, C.A. Similar principles should apply to all forms of execution. Liquidation dividends are not usually attachable: see *The Supreme Court Practice 1988*, Vol. 1, p. 739.

7.25   Pro rata sharing clauses

Where the junior debt is a syndicated loan, it may contain a pro rata sharing clause whereby the creditors agree to share recoveries so that they are paid pro rata. These clauses commonly provide that if, for instance, one syndicate member is paid by a set-off in a larger proportionate amount than other members of the syndicate, he must pay an amount equal to the excess to the other syndicate members so as to establish pro rata recoveries and is subrogated to the claims which are so paid. In order to avoid delays and confusion, perhaps the turnover of proceeds under a subordination of the junior syndicated loan should come into effect before the operation of the pro rata sharing clause so that the turnover applies to the initial receipt by the receiving creditor, *e.g.* by set-off, and not to receipts recovered by each other junior creditor from the receiving creditor under the sharing clause. But one would need to consider the detail of the particular clause.

7.26   Default events in senior credit agreement

A number of additional events of default may be appropriate in the senior credit agreement. These include:

— non-compliance by the junior creditor or the debtor with the terms of the subordination agreement;
— breach of representation or warranty by the junior creditor or the debtor in the subordination agreement: paragraph 7.19;

---

[3] See the cases where a garnishing creditor did not succeed in attaching a debt which had already been assigned: *Pickering* v. *Ilfracombe Ry* (1868) L.R. 3 C.P. 235; *Robinson* v. *Nesbitt* (1868) L.R. 3 C.P. 264; *Holt* v. *Heatherfield Trust Ltd.* [1942] 2 K.B. 1.

— inefficacy or termination of the subordination agreement for any reason;

— occurrence of an event of default under any agreement evidencing junior debt and entitling the junior creditor to accelerate the junior debt.

— occurrence of any other event allowing premature acceleration of the junior debt, *e.g.* under a "poison pill" clause (paragraph 7.18) or an illegality clause.

The occurrence of one of these defaults should normally by the terms of the subordination agreement freeze any further permitted payments by the debtor to the junior creditor, either permanently until cured or during a payment blockage period: paragraph 7.10.

Preservation of junior debt   7.27

Intercreditor agreements commonly provide that, notwithstanding the postponement of the claims or any provisions suspending payment of the junior debt by virtue of the subordination, the junior debt, as between the debtor and the junior creditor, remains due and owing and payable in accordance with the terms of the junior debt instrument.

The provision is designed to cover the following:

— the debtor must pay default interest on overdue payments which are overdue because they are blocked by a springing subordination, such as a blockage notice from the senior creditor.

— missed payments must be made when a payment freeze is lifted

— the junior creditor is entitled to accelerate for a non-payment default on the junior debt even though the payment is blocked by the senior creditor or by virtue of the subordination having sprung, *i.e.* as between debtor and junior creditor, the debtor is in default

— a blocked payment is still due and payable for the purposes of the enforcement of security.

The preservation of the maturity of the debt as between debtor and junior creditor has the result that non-payment may be a default within a cross-default clause in other credit agreements of third party creditors. Consider whether the junior debt would be due and payable for the purposes of insolvency definitions based on inability to pay debts as they fall due (and hence the applicability of any suspect periods for preferences and the like): paragraph 2.16.

CHAPTER 8

SECURED SENIOR AND JUNIOR DEBT

8.1 Generally

If both the senior and the junior debt are secured, the subordination of the junior creditor is effectively achieved by the junior priority of his security. Subordination of the debt as well as the security remains desirable for the following reasons:

— the security may be insufficient, in which event both claims would be unsecured and would rank equally on the bankruptcy of the debtor unless the junior creditor had agreed to be subordinated;
— the security for the senior debt may turn out to be invalid;

In any event an intercreditor agreement is highly desirable to regulate the rights of the creditors as secured creditors in order to protect the senior creditor.

8.2 Variation of law of priorities

In the absence of a mandatory statute, secured creditors can agree between themselves to vary the priorities between successive security interests which would otherwise apply, e.g. the first in time rule, or the rule that the first to get the legal (namely, the best) estate for value without notice ranks ahead. There is much English case law on conduct by a mortgagee leading to a loss of a priority he would otherwise have, e.g. if he leaves the title deeds with the mortgagor. If a mortgagee can lose priority by conduct, he can lose it by agreement.

However, a registration statute may provide that the securities rank according to the order of registration—particularly registration regimes for assets (as opposed to registration by mortgagor)—such as those applicable to land, ships and aircraft. For example British ship mortgages rank according to the time of registration: Merchant Shipping Act 1894, s.33. It is not possible to vary this order by a note on the register. Aircraft mortgages rank according to the order of registration: Mortgaging of Aircraft Order 1972, Article 14(2). The Land Registration Act, s.29, provides that registered charges on the same land "shall as between themselves rank according to the date in which they are entered on the register" but for once this is "subject to any entry to the contrary on the register."

The easiest solution here is to register the senior security first and then the junior. Another solution is to vest the security in a common trustee. If neither route is possible, as where the subordination post-dates the grant of security and it is undesirable for preservation of priority or other reasons to release and re-create the prior security, it will be a matter of construction whether the statute permits contracting-out or is mandatory. If it is mandatory, it is considered that this should affect third parties only and not a different ranking agreed between mortgages. Indeed in the case of land, ships and aircraft, the first mortgagee can be postponed as regards a new advance voluntarily made after he has notice of a second mortgage. It would be astonishing if the junior creditor (who is statutorily the senior creditor) could not transfer his rights to proceeds to the agreed senior creditor. It would also be astonishing if the creditors could not also vary the other incidents of ranking, such as marshalling or the priority of the ability to sell, take possession or appoint a receiver. But if the junior creditor transfers his secured debt and the security has first-ranking by statute, the transferee might take free of the de-prioritisation unless he knows of it.

Section 9–316 of the U.C.C. comes to the rescue by providing that nothing in Article 9 "prevents subordination by agreement by any person entitled to priority." The re-ordering of priorities will be upheld on a United States bankruptcy. Section 510(c) of the Bankruptcy Code of 1978 provides that, "A subordination agreement is enforceable in a case under this title to the same extent that such agreement is enforceable under applicable non-bankruptcy law." It is thought that this applies to the subordination of security as well as to unsecured debts.

In the case of security over receivables, the security assignee who is the first to give notice to the debtor generally ranks prior. The debtor on the receivable should be entitled and bound to pay that assignee first. If notices are given in the wrong order, either the junior assignee ranking first by notice should hold receipts in trust for the agreed senior assignee or the assignee who ranks first by notice should direct the debtor to pay the assignee who is to be senior by the agreement.

In the case of insurances, the junior and senior creditor should arrange for the notices of assignments to the insurers, for the brokers undertakings and for noting of interests on the policies to reflect the agreed ranking.

Common trustee 8.3

The security may be given to each creditor separately or ideally granted to a common trustee for both sets of creditors. The usual advantages of a common trustee are set out at paragraph 10.1.

Restrictions on rights of junior secured creditor generally 8.4

An intercreditor agreement between the secured creditors should regulate the matters discussed at paragraphs 7.11 *et seq.*, such as permission for the senior creditor to add new money qualifying as senior debt, controls on the covenants in the junior debt agreement, and restrictions on the junior creditor's rights of enforcement. These and certain other matters require further discussion.

It needs to be emphasised again that the scope of the senior creditor's protections depends fundamentally on the class of transaction. In insider subordinations, the junior creditor can expect to have no, or very few, rights. His security is there only to put him ahead of trade creditors but otherwise the senior creditor is to have complete freedom in the management of the security and as to whether to add new money.

However in transaction finance involving secured mezzanine debt, the junior creditor commonly requires greater protections for the reasons given at paragraph 7.8.

8.5   New money advanced by senior creditor

As indicated at paragraph 7.12, the intercreditor agreement should permit the senior creditor to add additional debt to his security ranking prior to the junior debt since otherwise the junior creditor might block a work-out and, further, revolving advances under the senior credit agreement might not rank ahead as a matter of law. Normally a first mortgagee cannot add on further senior advances after he has notice of a second mortgage.

But under English law a first mortgagee has the right to add further advances ranking ahead of a second mortgagee if (amongst other cases) he is obliged to make further advances: see the Law of Property Act 1925, s.94, and the Land Registration Act 1925, s.30 (as amended). The weaknesses of these statutory rights are:

— the senior creditor must be under an obligation to make further advances. Sometimes in practice the senior creditor will not be under a strict obligation under a term loan agreement to lend more money by reason of some trivial breach of a warranty or covenant. Most term loan agreements will make the lender's obligations to advance a loan subject to the fulfilment of the condition precedent that all the warranties are true on an up-dated basis (including no material adverse change, no material litigation, no material contractual default) and that no event of default or inchoate event of default has occurred. If the events of default are particularly fine-trigger, the senior creditor may not even know that he is not obliged to lend, *e.g.* if the cross-default covers non-payment of all debt when due including trade debt.

— the sections might not catch situations where the mortgagee is a trustee for the senior creditor since the sections require that the "*mortgagee*" or the "*proprietor of a charge*" is obliged to make the further advances. The trustee as nominal mortgagee is not so obliged—only the beneficiary. This would be an absurd result and careful attention should be paid to the statutory definitions to see whether this would in any event be an arguable construction of the sections.

— the sections appear to relate only to mortgages of land (see, for example, L.P.A. 1925, s.94(4))).

If the senior creditor is permitted to advance senior-ranking new money up to a limit only, then any excess over the limit should be expressed to rank after the junior creditor who should be limited as to the amount of the junior debt.

Enforcement rights of junior creditor generally   8.6

Under English security law, the junior creditor has virtually the same rights of enforcement as the senior creditor—namely, rights to sue for the debt, to foreclose, to sell, to appoint a receiver and to take possession. If the senior creditor is to have any peace, these rights should be severely curtailed by the intercreditor agreement lest the senior creditor be forced into an inopportune realisation or the bargaining power of the junior creditor be disproportionately enhanced on a work-out or change of business plan. In relation to mezzanine transactional finance, see paragraphs 7.10 and 7.16 for suggested negotiating positions.

The powers of enforcement are commonly conferred by the security instrument itself, but, if not, they are generally available by virtue of the statutory powers in the Law of Property Act 1925 (if the mortgage is by deed) or, if not, by court order, subject to various qualifications.

Foreclosure[1]   8.7

By a foreclosure order, the court orders the transfer of the mortgaged property to the mortgagee. Such orders are rare and the court will generally order a sale instead at the request of the first or second mortgagee or the mortgagor under section 91(2) of the Law of Property Act 1925.

If in the exceptional case foreclosure is ordered, the second mortgagee becomes owner of the property, subject to prior incumbrances.

If the first mortgagee forecloses, the second mortgagee is left with a choice of either paying off the first mortgage or losing his security, unless he successfully applies to the court for a sale instead. This theoretically places the junior creditor in the unfortunate position of having to take out the senior creditor. It does not seem unreasonable that both junior and senior creditor should agree not to apply for foreclosure. Probably this restriction should apply only to land since, in the case of charges over receivables, it has always been possible for the chargee to collect the receivables on enforcement and to apply them in reduction of the secured debt even though the chargee technically takes over the receivables for himself. Nobody ever seems to have objected that this is a foreclosure requiring a court order, and the reason is obvious: the receipts have a certain monetary value and therefore there is no danger of the mortgagee taking over property worth more than the mortgage debt. Applying the

---

[1] See generally *Fisher and Lightwood's Law of Mortgages* (10 ed.), Chapter 21.

fruits of receivables without selling them is no more harmful than applying the monetary proceeds of realisation of land.

The remedy of foreclosure has been abolished in the Republic of
Ireland.

If foreclosure is sought and the court orders a sale instead, a disadvantage for the senior creditor is that the court may grant the conduct of
the sale to the mortgagor or the most junior mortgagee since they have
the most interest in obtaining a good price.[2] This is a further reason from
the senior creditor's point of view to abrogate foreclosure.

8.8   Sale

A junior mortgagee can exercise the powers of sale conferred on him
by his mortgage, by statute or by the court. He does not have to obtain the
concurrence of the first mortgagee if he sells subject to the prior mortgage
(*Manser* v. *Dix* (1857) 8 De G.M. & G. 703) but of course he can only sell
subject to the first mortgage and in practice purchasers may be reluctant
to buy on these terms. If the second mortgagee wishes to sell free of the
first mortgage on terms that the proceeds are paid first to the prior
mortgagor, he must obtain the concurrence of the first mortgagee or a
court order.

A junior mortgagee of land can in effect force a sale on the senior
mortgagee. Under the Law of Property Act 1925, s.50, the court can
order a sale of mortgaged land at the behest of a second mortgagee if
sufficient money is paid into court so that in effect the court compels the
payment off of the first mortgagee.

The ability of the second mortgagee to force a sale should be restricted
by the intercreditor agreement along the lines suggested at paragraphs
7.15 *et seq.*

In addition, the second mortgagee should be obliged to release his
security in the event of a private sale at fair value by the first mortgagee or
by the mortgagor with the consent of the first mortgagee. The first
mortgagee should be given power of attorney to release if the second
mortgagor fails to do so. The purpose of this is:

— to prevent the second mortgagee from blocking a private sale by
   the mortgagor at the insistence of the first mortgagee in those
   jurisdictions where only judicial sales or sale by public auction are
   permitted
— to forestall the necessity for applications to the court if the second
   mortgagee refuses to comply or delays the sale
— to allow the first mortgagee to persuade the mortgagor to sell if the
   position is hopeless, instead of compelling the mortgagee to be put
   to the trouble and expense of a forced sale.

---

[2] See *Fisher & Lightwood's Law of Mortgages* (10th ed.), p. 412.

Possession   **8.9**

A second mortgagee has power to take possession of the mortgaged property. But as there cannot be two persons in possession, he cannot do so if the first mortgagee is in possession or has appointed a receiver.[3]

The taking of possession is unusual for land since mortgagees are not equipped to run businesses, because it is easier to appoint a professional receiver, because possession exposes the mortgagee to liability to the mortgagor for "wilful default" in not realising sufficient profits or looking after the property, because the mortgage has the liabilities of an owner to third parties, because he may be liable for an occupation rent (*Marriott* v. *Anchor Reversionary Co.* (1861) 3 De G.F. & J. 177, 193) and because he has a (somewhat limited) liability to keep in repair.

The remedy however is useful in relation to ships, aircraft and other large mobile chattels since it enables the mortgagee to remove the asset to a favourable enforcement location, *e.g.* where prior liens are limited, where court proceedings are effective and quick, where there is *in rem* jurisdiction, where a judicial sale can be made in U.S. dollars, where there are no exchange controls restricting exportation of the sale proceeds, where there are no significant bonding costs, and where charterers can be wiped off. The right of possession is unusual in civil code jurisdictions.

The second mortgagee in possession must apply receipts to payment of interest on the first mortgage but consider whether he must do so in the unlikely event that the first mortgage debt is not due.

Besides restricting the timing of the exercise by the junior creditor of its rights of possession, the intercreditor agreement should as a minimum compel the junior creditor to give up possession if the senior creditor wishes to take possession or to exercise any other remedy, *e.g.* sale.

Appointment of a receiver   **8.10**

A second mortgagee can appoint a receiver if he has the power by the mortgage or by statute and if the first mortgagee has not already done so. The court may appoint in suitable cases.[4] In practice, apart from sale, this is the most commonly exercised power and is the remedy almost exclusively exercised where the security comprises a floating charge.

The Insolvency Act 1986 introduces the concept of an administrative receiver who by section 29(2) is:

> "a receiver or manager of the whole (or substantially the whole) of a company's property appointed by or on behalf of the holders of any debentures of the company secured by a charge which, as created, was a floating charge, or by such a charge and one or more other securities."

Apart from the ability of a receiver to run the business as a going concern

---

[3] See generally *Fisher & Lightwood's Law of Mortgages* (10th ed.), Chapter 19.
[4] See generally *Fisher & Lightwood's Law of Mortgages* (10th ed.), Chapter 18.

and to do so as agent of the company, not the chargee, the prime advantages of an administrative receiver are:

(1) his appointment before the making of an administration order (arehabilitation procedure under the Insolvency Act 1986) blocks the appointment of an administrator. An administration order can be highly prejudicial to secured creditors because

    (a) the administrator can (amongst other things) paralyse the sale of fixed assets subject to fixed security and sell in his own time (section 15(2));

    (b) he can deal with property subject to a floating charge as if it were not subject to the charge (section 15(1));

    (c) attachments and the like are frozen (sections 10 and 11);

    (d) the rehabilitation plan may be much less protective of secured creditors than a private receivership where the secured creditor is effectively in charge through his receiver.

(2) By section 43 an administrative receiver can in certain circumstances by order of court dispose of property subject to security having priority over his appointor's security if the court is satisfied that the disposal (with or without other assets) is likely to promote a more advantageous realisation of the company's assets than would otherwise be effected, provided that net proceeds of sale are applied in discharge of the prior security plus any make-up for a deficiency below market value. The object is to enable an administrative receiver to sell the whole business without being blocked by a prior mortgage of, say, the factory.

In order to appoint an administrative receiver and hence to block an administrator, the chargee must have security over all or substantially all the company's property *and* the security must include a floating charge. This explains the presence of comprehensive "featherweight floaters" to back up fixed security which might otherwise be prejudiced by an administration order.

It would be a matter for negotiation whether the intercreditor agreement should prevent the junior creditor from appointing an administrative receiver if the senior creditor decides not to do so in order to block an administration. In unusual circumstances a senior creditor may prefer to let the company go into administration rather than appoint an administrator, *e.g.* because

— the senior debt is small compared to the assets

— the senior creditor has unsecured loans which it wishes to protect and believes that this can best be achieved by an administration

— there are overseas assets and the court appointment of an administrator may carry more weight or stand a better chance of being accorded foreign recognition

— the administrator has enhanced control over assets which the company has taken on hire purchase, chattel lease, retention of title or conditional sale (sections 10, 11, 15(5))

— there are prior floating charges

— the administration freezes winding-up orders and resolutions (sections 10 and 11). These are a danger to receivers because they cease to be agents of the company after liquidation and hence incur personal liability (which in effect is usually passed on to the chargee under an indemnity agreement).

From the point of view of the junior creditor, an administrator could severely prejudice his position as a floating chargee because (amongst other things)

— the administrator can deal with the property charged as if it were not subject to the security (section 15) and the administrator may trade at a loss
— although the priority of the charge traces through (somewhat unpredictably) to property directly or indirectly representing the charged property if disposed of (section 15(4)), the administrator is not bound to make up any deficiency on a sale below market value, subject to an "unfair prejudice" application by the junior creditor under section 27 of the Insolvency Act 1986.

Senior creditor's responsibilities to junior creditor   **8.11**

In the case of subordinated debt, the junior creditor has an interest in ensuring that the senior creditor preserves and maximises the security. The less that the senior creditor receives out of the security, the greater is the turnover obligation of the junior creditor to the senior creditor and the smaller are the proceeds available to the junior creditor.

With insider subordinations, the insider can expect no reassurance from the senior creditor. But with transaction finance, such as loans to finance a bid, the position is different. Amongst the protections a junior creditor might seek one may include:

— a duty on the senior creditor to perfect his security by registration or filing
— a duty on the senior creditor not to release any security and not to release a floating charge (which is necessary to block an administrator, see paragraph 8.10)
— a duty on the senior creditor to maintain deposited title deeds and the like in safe custody
— a duty on the senior creditor to maximise proceeds of enforcement
— a duty on the senior creditor to exercise whatever contractual provisions it may have to call for additional security from subsidiaries of the borrower, e.g. after a successful takeover of a target and subject to privatising the target so as to implement the procedures in sections 155 et seq of the Companies Act: paragraph 7.23.
— a duty to preserve priorities against third parties by the giving of notices and the like.

Most of these duties would normally not be acceptable to a senior creditor except perhaps in very watered down form. If the security is given to a trustee, the trustee will normally expect elaborate exculpatory language, although this is cut down by law: paragraph 10.8.

If the junior creditor has separate security, the senior creditor also has an interest in ensuring the validity of the junior security since the junior security enhances the turnover to the senior creditor: paragraph 8.16.

8.12   Consolidation of securities

A junior mortgagee could be prejudiced if the senior mortgagee has a right to consolidate securities.

Under the doctrine of consolidation a mortgagor who holds several distinct mortgages from the same mortgagor may within certain limits insist that the mortgagor redeem them all and not only one of them if the date for redemption has passed. The object is to ensure that the mortgagor does not pay off one mortgage leaving the mortgagee with the risk of a deficiency on the other.[5]

Although section 93 of the Law of Property Act 1925 abolished this right of consolidation, it can be expressly preserved in the mortgage and commonly is.

If the senior creditor could insist on the debtor paying off some private mortgage as well as the senior mortgage, the ability of the second mortgagee to ensure that the prior debt is retired is prejudiced—almost as if the senior creditor could take on new senior debt.

The case law on the ability of a first mortgagor to consolidate against a second mortgagor is in conflict. *Andrews* v. *City Permanent Benefit Building Society* (1881) 44 L.T. 641 allowed the first mortgagee to do so, but *Hughes* v. *Britannia Permanent Building Society* [1906] 2 Ch. 607 (in which the *Andrews* case was not cited) refused the right. The case of *Bird* v. *Wenn* (1886) 33 Ch.D. 215 considers the effect on consolidation of a consent by the second mortgagee to the first mortgagee making further advances in priority to himself.

Because of the uncertainty in the law the intercreditor agreement should specifically deal with the question of whether the senior creditor should be entitled to consolidate.

8.13   Application of insurance proceeds

The intercreditor agreement should normally exclude any right the junior mortgagee may have to insist that insurance policy moneys be applied in reinstatement of the mortgaged property.

As to fire, under the Fires Prevention (Metropolis) Act 1774, s.83, any person interested in any building burned down or damaged by fire may give notice to the insurers calling upon them to expend the insurance moneys upon reinstating the premises. The Act is of general application and does not apply just to London: it has been held to apply in Ontario, British Columbia (but not Saskatchewan), Western Australia, New Zealand and Hong Kong, but not Ireland and probably not Scotland. The Act

---

[5] *Fisher & Lightwood's Law of Mortgages* (10th ed.), Chapter 27.

probably does not apply to insurance through Lloyds: *Portavon Cinema Co. Ltd.* v. *Price & Century Insurance Co. Ltd.* [1939] 4 All E.R. 601, 607–608 (*obiter*).

Both mortgagor and mortgagee are persons interested: *Sinnott* v. *Bowden* [1912] 2 Ch. 414; *Portavon Cinema Co. Ltd.* v. *Price & Century Insurance Co. Ltd.* [1939] 4 All E.R. 601, 607. But in *Westminster Fire Office* v. *Glasgow Provident Investment Society* (1888) 13 App.Cas. 699, 714, the Earl of Selbourne doubted that a postponed bondholder could call upon the insurer of a prior bondholder to lay out the insurance payable to the prior bondholder in reinstatement when each bondholder had insured his own interest and clearly had no claim on the other's insurance.

The senior creditor may in the event decide that the insurance moneys should be used to pay back the loan so that he does not have the delay of a new project, or the fuss of having to sell the property plus the insurance proceeds, or the exposure if the insurance is insufficient. It has been held that section 83 is not mandatory and contracting out is possible. Hence a contract may prevent the second mortgagee from giving notice to the insurers: *Reynard* v. *Arnold* (1875) L.R. 10 Ch.App. 386.

As it happens most fire insurance policies give the insurer the option to reinstate (partly as a disincentive to fraud or arson) and hence a senior mortgagee should negotiate a policy without this option, if possible. As to other powers to require application of proceeds to reinstatement, see section 108(3) of the Law of Property Act 1925.[6]

Recovery of receivables and set-off   **8.14**

If the junior creditor is a bank holding the debtor's operating bank account into which the debtor's receivables are paid, then, as discussed in Chapter 6, the bank should be prohibited from setting off the junior debt against credit balances on the accounts and should be obliged to pay to the senior creditor an amount equal to any set-off made.

If a deposit owed by the junior creditor to the debtor is covered by a floating charge in favour of the senior creditor, the junior creditor's right of set-off is not affected (in the absence of a prohibition) so long as the floating charge has not crystallised: *Biggerstaff* v. *Rowatt's Wharf Ltd.* [1896] 2 Ch. 93; *Nelson & Co. Ltd.* v. *Faber & Co.* [1903] 2 K.B. 367. However once the charge crystallises, *e.g.* on the appointment of a receiver, the crystallisation would operate as a fixed assignment of the deposit to the senior creditor having the consequences set out at paragraph 6.5(b): see, for example, *Business Computers Ltd.* v. *Anglo African Leasing Ltd.* [1977] 2 All E.R. 741. The same would apply if the deposit is initially subject to a fixed charge in favour of the senior creditor.

---

[6] For a detailed study of reinstatement requirements, see *McGillivray & Parkinson on Insurance Law* (7th ed., 1981) Sweet & Maxwell, Chapter 21.

8.15 Marshalling

The junior creditor should waive marshalling. Marshalling typically applies where a secured creditor has security over two assets of the same mortgagor and another creditor has a second ranking security over only one of those assets. If the senior secured creditor resorts to the doubly secured asset first, then the junior creditor is entitled to take over the senior creditor's sole security by marshalling so that the junior creditor is not disappointed.

One object of the waiver is to prevent the junior creditor from acquiring rights by subrogation in the single security. So far as English law is concerned there is no need to prevent the junior creditor from insisting that the senior creditor look to the sole security first because the senior secured creditor would not be compelled to resort to the sole asset first.[7] However, in some United States cases the court has compelled the senior creditor to look first to his own sole security and has also obliged the senior creditor to account to the junior secured creditor if the senior creditor releases the single security after notice of the rights of the junior creditor.[8]

8.16 Only junior debt is secured

If only the junior debt is secured and the subordination is achieved by a turnover subordination, the senior creditor in effect has the benefit of the junior's security by virtue of the turnover of proceeds in the senior's favour. But it is generally important for the senior creditor to be secured in seniority on the same assets since, if only the junior debt is secured, then

— the turnover of the security to the senior creditor is limited to the amount of the junior debt which is secured;
— the junior creditor might release the security;
— the senior creditor becomes involves in checking the validity, perfection, priority and continuity of the junior creditor's security. In particular, security for existing insider debt may be subject to long suspect periods for the purposes of preference rules;
— unless controlled by an intercreditor agreement, realisation by the junior creditor over assets of the debtor could seriously prejudice the debtor's business and hence the senior creditor's chances of recovery.

In the case of contractual subordinations, security only for the junior debt would be curious but possible. Under one form of contractual subordination the junior debt is reduced to the extent necessary to ensure

---

[7] See the discussion in Meagher, Gummow & Lehane, *Equity, Doctrines and Remedies* (2nd ed, 1984) Butterworths, Chapter 11.
[8] See, for example, *Burnham* v. *Citizens Bank of Emporia* (1895) 40 P. 912; *First National Bank of Boston* v. *Proctor* (1930) 40 F. (2d) 841.

that the senior debt is paid. The junior debt should not be contingent to the extent that the junior debt is covered by the security. The debtor might be hopelessly insolvent but the security may still be sufficient to cover both the senior and the junior debt in which event the junior debt should be a full unflawed claim not conditional on the debtor's solvency. Otherwise the junior creditor would not have the benefit of the security.

In cases where a lender's claim is subordinated to all other creditors under the Partnership Act 1890, s.3, *e.g.* because interest varies with the profits, it has been held that the statutory subordination does not affect the right of the lender to enforce his security: *ex p. Sheil* (1877) 4 Ch.D. 789; *Badeley* v. *Consolidated Bank* (1888) 38 Ch.D. 238. The section does not apply only to partnerships but is of general application and can affect loans to companies.

Registration of intercreditor agreements   8.17

An intercreditor agreement which simply re-orders the priority of security and which does not of itself create security does not have to be registered in England under the provisions for the registration of company charges. Only charges have to be registered. But under section 401 of the Companies Act 1985, as about to be amended, any variation of the registered particulars of a charge should be registered.

There is provision for the registration of priority for further advances in charges relating to registered land: Land Registration Act 1925, s.30.

In the United States, no U.C.C. filing of these intercreditor agreements is required, although some states permit a creditor to subordinate his security by filing a U.C.C. amendment statement (commonly known as a U.C.C.–2 or U.C.C.–3) indicating an intent to subordinate.

Invalidity of security for senior debt   8.18

Normally where secured creditors rank their priorities, the junior creditor moves up if the senior security is invalid, *e.g.* because the senior creditor fails to register or perfect his security or because it is set aside on the insolvency of the debtor.

But in the case of subordinations, the junior creditor agrees to be junior in such circumstances to the senior creditor: hence the need to subordinate the junior debt as well as the junior security. In a United States case the court forced a subordinating secured lender to remain subordinated where the senior security failed for lack of perfection. The court inferred an intention from the priority agreement that the debt was subordinated as well as the security: *General Electric Credit Corp.* v. *Pennsylvania Bank & Trust Co.*, 11 U.C.C. Rep. 858 (Pa. 1972).

Preferential creditors   8.19

Preferential creditors, such as certain taxes and employee remuneration, must be paid in priority to the claims of a floating chargee: Insolvency Act 1986, ss.40(1), 175(2)(b), 251. But a fixed charge is not subordinated to preferential creditors.

If therefore the junior creditor has a fixed charge and the senior creditor only a floating charge, there is the question of whether the fixed chargee has also subordinated himself to preferential creditors.

One solution to this circularity problem is to treat the fixed chargee as having by the ranking agreement necessarily subordinated himself to the preferential creditors since, if he subordinates to a floating charge and if the floating charge ranks after preferentials, the fixed chargee also subordinates to preferentials. This is the solution adopted by the Australian cases of *Waters* v. *Widdows* [1984] V.R. 503; *Deputy Commissioner of Taxation* v. *Horsburgh* [1984] V.R. 773.

The other solution, conceded in *Re Woodroffes (Musical Instruments) Ltd.* [1985] 2 All E.R. 908, 912, is to subrogate the senior floating chargee to the junior fixed chargee's priority by law so that the senior floating chargee is paid first out of the proceeds of the fixed charge up to the amount secured by the fixed charge. If any balance is still due to the floating chargee, he must first pay the preferentials out of the proceeds of the floating charge, then pay his outstanding balance and then hand over any surplus to the fixed chargee.[9]

The second solution is plainly better for the senior creditor. Whether subrogation could be achieved by contract is a matter for conjecture.

In the ordinary case the senior creditor can obviate this problem by taking a first fixed charge on the same assets as are covered by the junior creditor's fixed charge. The situation might arise where this is not done for one reason or another or where the senior creditor's first fixed charge fails as a preference.

[9] See Professor R.M. Goode, *Legal Problems of Credit and Security* (2nd ed., 1988) (Sweet & Maxwell) pp. 97 *et seq.*

CHAPTER 9

PROTECTIVE CLAUSES: THE GUARANTEE ANALOGY

Turnover subordinations and guarantees   **9.1**

A turnover subordination is similar in substance to collateral security granted by the junior creditor over the junior debt to secure the senior debt. Because the junior creditor pays the debt owed by the debtor to the senior creditor, it is likely that the technicalities of guarantee law (as applied to collateral security) will be attracted to some turnover subordinations. This should be so even though a turnover subordination is not characterised as a security interest, but rather as an absolute transfer. The reason that the guarantee analogy seems broadly appropriate is that both guarantees and turnover subordinations involve a situation where one person (the guarantor or junior creditor) is obliged to pay a debtor's debt owed to another (the beneficiary of the guarantee or the senior creditor) and the law is protective of those in that position. This chapter will review the rules without detailed citation since the principles of suretyship are readily accessible in the standard works.

If there are several classes of subordinated debt stacked up in layers, it would be for consideration whether the most junior creditor is similar to a sub-guarantor or whether he is similar to a co-guarantor. This will affect such matters as rights of subrogation and contribution. The prime test should be whether the most senior creditor can claim turnover from the most junior creditor direct or whether the first junior creditor has the prior right subject in turn to turnover to the senior creditor.

Some of the principles set out in this chapter are most unlikely to apply to contractual subordinations to all debt but should apply only to turnover subordinations.

Subrogation by junior creditor   **9.2**

A junior creditor who has turned over dividends to a senior creditor probably has a right of subrogation to the senior debt and all securities for the senior debt.

This flows from the general rule that if one person at the request of a debtor pays the debtor's debt owed to a third-party creditor then the payer is entitled to be subrogated to the creditor who has been paid and for this purpose the creditor's claim is not deemed to be extinguished.[1]

---

[1] See generally Goff & Jones, *The Law of Restitution*, (3rd ed., 1986) Sweet & Maxwell, Chap. 14.

The classic examples are guarantees and liability insurance. Because in effect a turnover subordination amounts to the junior creditor using his asset to pay the senior creditor the same doctrine of subrogation should apply.

Subrogation by law is somewhat technical (especially when the debtor did not request that his debt be paid by a third party) and hence a subordination agreement should confirm the position by providing that the junior creditor is entitled to be subrogated to the senior creditor's claim and any guarantees or security for the claim if and when the senior debt has been paid in full.

The alternative of providing that the junior debt is deemed not discharged if the junior creditor has had to turn over a receipt to the senior creditor is odd and unlikely to be effective as against a liquidator who has paid dividends on the junior debt in discharge of the junior debt. It would be preferable to draft the debtor's liability as a liability to indemnify the junior creditor.

Some forms endeavour to cover the old chestnut that one cannot be subrogated to a debt which has been paid: these forms accordingly provide that recoveries by the senior creditor from the junior creditor are not deemed to reduce the senior debt so far as the debtor is concerned. This provision is not considered necessary so far as English law is concerned, since discharge of the senior debt is inconsistent with an express provision for subrogation.

The doctrine of subrogation in relation to both guarantee and insurance law generally requires that the guarantor or insurer must have paid the claim in full before he is entitled to be subrogated to the creditor paid. In order to avoid any question of whether the junior creditor can come alongside the senior creditor on the senior creditor's security after a partial payment only (or after a full turnover of the junior debt which is insufficient to pay the senior debt), the subordination agreement should expressly exclude the junior creditor's right to subrogation until the senior debt has been paid in full. A general non-competition clause is desirable, *i.e.* the junior creditor agrees that he will not claim subrogation, contribution or indemnity or otherwise claim against a debtor by virtue of a turnover if this could result in the junior creditor claiming in competition with the senior creditor.

If the junior creditor must turn over proceeds to pay senior claims which are invalid or non-provable or non-allowable on bankruptcy, such as post-insolvency interest, the junior creditor will have nothing to be subrogated to. Junior creditors sometimes use this as an argument against covering post-insolvency interest on the senior debt.

Subrogation should not normally apply in the case of a contractual subordination since the junior creditor pays nothing to the senior creditor.

9.3   Suspense account

If the turnover by the junior creditor is sufficient to pay the senior debt, the senior creditor should be entitled to place the turnover amounts on suspense account and not apply them towards the reduction of the senior debt. In this way the senior creditor maximises his proof against the debtor on an insolvency. The suspension should naturally terminate once the senior creditor has received proceeds from whatever source equal to the senior debt.

The validity of suspense accounts is well documented in English case law on guarantees, *e.g. Commercial Bank Australia v. Wilson* [1893] A.C. 181, P.C.

Waiver of defences clause   **9.4**

A "waiver of defences" clause adapted from guarantees should normally be included in turnover subordination agreements, except subordinations to all other debt.

Under such a clause, the junior creditor agrees that the subordination and his obligations under the subordination are not to be affected by:

— waivers granted to or compositions with the debtor or any other person;
— variations of the senior debt or of any security or guarantees for the senior debt;
— releases or non-perfection of any security or guarantees for the senior debt.

Under guarantee law, waivers in relation to or variations of the guaranteed claim release the guarantor unless he agrees to them. The same might apply to variations of the senior debt, such as extensions of the due date for payment for it might be said that the junior creditor's position is prejudiced or that he agreed to be subordinated only to the specified senior debt and not some varied senior debt.

Release of security or guarantees for the senior debt by the senior creditor may allow the junior creditor to treat his obligation to turn over proceeds under the subordination as diminished to the extent that the junior creditor's rights to the security on subrogation are thereby lost to him. Further the junior creditor's risk of loss by virtue of his obligation to turn over recoveries is increased if the senior creditor diminishes his own potential recoveries. These principles are well established in guarantee law.

A junior creditor would be better protected if he restrained the senior creditor from releasing guarantees or security (at least if the junior creditor does not have security over the same assets) since the loss of these reduce the junior creditor's rights on subrogation and potentially increase the required turnover to pay the senior debt. The junior creditor also has an interest in ensuring that the senior creditor properly perfects any senior security by registration and notice.

In the case of contractual subordinations, the question of whether variations of the senior debt release the junior creditor should primarily depend upon whether the junior creditor agreed to be subordinated only to some specific senior debt and not a varied senior debt. Since a contractual junior creditor probably does not have a right of subrogation, releases of security and the like by a senior creditor should not normally weaken the subordination.

The waivers should not be necessary in subordinations to all present and future debt of all other creditors since the consent to subordination to all creditors ought to carry with it a consent to variations and releases by a particular senior creditor.

9.5   Contribution between junior creditors

If there are two equal junior issues constituted by a turnover subordination and one of the junior creditors turns over dividends to the senior creditor but the other does not, then the paying junior creditor should as a matter of law have a right of contribution against the other junior creditor to the extent the paying junior creditor has paid more than his share.

The junior creditor should be prohibited from claiming contribution from another junior creditor in competition with any claim by the senior creditor against the contributing junior creditor.

Some junior issues state that a junior creditor is obliged to turn over only its own proportion of the senior debt so as to avoid one set of junior creditors being obliged to sue the other. This is because contribution actions against anonymous bondholders may be impractical. An analogy is to be found in rateable proportion clauses in insurance contracts.

In contractual non-turnover subordinations, no junior creditor should be liable to contribute to another because no junior creditor is obliged to pay a senior creditor.

9.6   Duration of subordination

In appropriate cases a subordination agreement should provide that the subordination is a continuing subordination and applies to the ultimate balance of the senior debt, notwithstanding any intermediate payment in whole or in part of the senior debt.

Where the senior debt is a term debt, then once it is paid the subordination will come to an end and there is no need for the clause.

Where however the senior debt is revolving, such as fluctuating debit balances on bank current account, then, by analogy with guarantee law and on the basis of the rule in *Clayton's* case, the subordination of junior debt may cease as soon as the senior debt is reduced to zero even though subsequently the senior debt springs up again by new advances.

Where the junior creditor subordinates all present and future debt owing to him to all present and future debt owing to a particular senior creditor, such as a bank, consideration should be given as to whether there should be some provision for termination of the subordination by the junior creditor lest the courts imply that the junior creditor has the right to cancel the subordination on reasonable notice. The subordination agreement may provide that the junior creditor can terminate the subordination on giving not less than the specified number of days' notice and that in such event the subordination will continue to apply in respect of senior debt which (a) is outstanding at the date of expiry of the notice, or (b) is subsequently incurred pursuant to a transaction or obligation entered into prior to the expiry of the notice, or (c) is subsequently incurred under an arrangement entered into prior to the expiry of notice which is not legally binding on the senior creditor, such as a line of credit. In this way the bank can ensure that existing lines will remain senior without being obliged to cancel them on termination of the subordination.

On the other hand, a termination of the subordination could effectively deter the senior creditor from making new advances and hence restrict the senior creditor's ability to finance a work-out.

In an appropriate case it should be an event of default in any senior debt instrument that a termination of the subordination is to entitle the senior creditor to accelerate the senior debt concerned.

It should not be necessary in bond issues which are subordinated to all other present and future debt to provide that the subordination is continuing or to include provisions for termination, since the subordination avails all senior debt so long as the junior bond is outstanding.

Exhaustion of recourse by senior creditor 9.7

A subordination agreement may provide that the senior creditor is not obliged to exhaust recourse against securities or guarantors or the debtor before claiming the benefit of the turnover of proceeds under the subordination. This is probably the law in any event.

A guaranteed creditor is not usually obliged to exhaust recourse against the principal debtor or security or other guarantors before claiming under the guarantee unless the guarantee otherwise provides. But a waiver of any rule that the principal creditor must exhaust recourse is commonly inserted in guarantees.

Senior debt non-provable 9.8

The subordination agreement may provide that the junior creditor is obliged to turn over recoveries on the junior debt even though the senior debt is invalid, unenforceable or non-provable and even though the senior creditor has agreed to a composition reducing or renouncing the senior debt, as if there were no such defect.

In principle there is no objection to such a term and indeed many guarantees validly provide that the guarantor must pay the principal creditor even if the principal creditor is unable to claim from the principal debtor, as where the guaranteed debt turns out to be *ultra vires*.

A serious disadvantage for a junior creditor is that, having turned over proceeds to pay the invalid or non-allowable senior claim, the junior creditor has nothing to be subrogated to: paragraph 9.2

A general protection obliging the junior creditor to turn over if the senior debt is invalid for any reason would be unusual, except for post-insolvency interest. Under the insolvency laws of many countries post-insolvency interest is not recoverable by a creditor. This is certainly so in the United States (see s.502(b) of the Bankruptcy Code of 1978) and in Britain (see r. 4.93 of the Insolvency Rules 1986).

In three United States cases the courts have held that a senior creditor could not claim a turnover of dividends by the junior debtor to cover post-insolvency interest on the senior debt unless the subordination agreement expressly so provided.[2]

If the claim is secured, then interest at the agreed rate accruing after the insolvency order or earlier resolution may be taken out of the proceeds of realisation of the security only if the security is sufficient to cover that interest after payment of the principal and pre-insolvency interest. In other words the secured creditor cannot apply proceeds first to the non-provable post-insolvency interest so as to leave him with the ability to prove for principal and provable pre-insolvency interest: *Re London, Windsor & Greenwich Hotels Co., Quartermaine's Case* [1892] 1 Ch. 639. Section 506(a) of the United States Bankruptcy Code of 1978 provides that post-petition interest is recoverable if the security is sufficient to cover the whole of the secured debt including interest.

Costs payable by the insolvent may also be excluded from proof, *e.g.* if the judgment awarding costs was pronounced after the insolvency order or earlier resolution for winding-up.[3]

Another example of a non-provable debt is reimbursement contingencies offending the rule against double-proof. Thus if the senior creditor has issued a guarantee or standby letter of credit on behalf of the debtor and the beneficiary of the guarantee or letter of credit submits a proof in the liquidation of the debtor for the guaranteed debt before the senior creditor has paid the guarantee or letter of credit in full, the senior creditor is excluded from proof by reason of the rule against double proof.[4]

But if the beneficiary has been paid, the beneficiary holds dividends on his proof in trust for the paying creditor: *Gray* v. *Seckham* (1872) L.R. 7 Ch.App. 680. A junior creditor paying the senior creditor ought to be entitled to the senior creditor's rights to these dividends by subrogation.

Tort claims, *e.g.* for misrepresentation inducing the senior debt, are now provable in England: Insolvency Rules 1986, r. 13.12.

---

[2] *In re Kingsboro Mortgage Corp.*, 541 F2d 400 (2d Cir. 1975); *In re Time Sales Finance Corp.*, 491 F2d 841 (3d Cir. 1974); *In re King Resources Co.*, 385 F.Supp. 1269 (D.Colo. 1974).

[3] See, for example, *ex p. Bluck* (1887) 56 L.J.Q.B. 607, 655; *Re British Goldfields of West Africa* (1889) 2 Ch. 7, C.A.; *Re Collinson* (1977) 33 F.L.R. 39 (Western Australia).

[4] See, for example, *Re Sass* [1896] 2 Q.B. 12, 15; *Re Fenton* [1931] 1 Ch. 85, 115, C.A.; generally, the author's *English and International Set-Off*, paras. 10–97 *et seq.* As to the U.S. position, see s.502(e) of the Bankruptcy Code of 1978.

Return of preferential payment of senior debt   9.9

It should be made clear that if the debtor makes a payment of the senior debt which the senior creditor must subsequently return as a preferential payment or for any other reason, the junior debt continues to be subordinated to the new senior debt when it springs up again.

A payment in the suspect period would normally be preferential if the debtor is influenced by a desire to improve the position of the senior creditor or a guarantor for the senior debt on the debtor's insolvency.

A similar situation might arise if the senior creditor is a trustee of another debt issue and must disgorge a payment on the private senior debt on the ground that the senior creditor acted in conflict of interest in recovering its own private debt ahead of the claims of the creditors for whom the senior creditor is a trustee: paragraphs 10.11 and 10.12. The junior debt should be expressed to remain junior to the senior debt which is reinstated after the disgorgement.

Appropriation of payments   9.10

A clause should provide that the senior creditor may appropriate receipts and apply the proceeds of security towards a debt owed to the senior creditor other than the senior debt. This is to negative the possibility, that, where a senior creditor receives a payment from the debtor which he could appropriate either to the senior debt or to some other debt, the law might imply that he must appropriate first to the senior debt so as to exonerate the junior creditor as "guarantor" of the senior debt.

A similar possibility might apply if the senior creditor has general security which he could apply either to the senior debt or some other debt. If the senior creditor can apply the security proceeds to his other debt, he maximises his recoveries.

Senior creditor's responsibility for junior debt   9.11

An assignee by way of security of a debt has limited responsibilities to the assignor to safeguard and preserve the debt in the same way that a pledgee of a chattel must look after the chattel. Thus the assignee is liable to the assignor if he releases or compromises the assigned claim.[5]

Where the senior creditor is a transferee only of proceeds of the junior debt, it is doubtful that the senior creditor has any duties in relation to the junior debt, *e.g.* to present negotiable instruments in good time. However there is no harm in excluding whatever duties there may be.

---

[5] *Glyn* v. *Hood* (1860) 1 G.T. & J. 334. See also *ex p. Mure* (1778) 2 Cox Eq.Cas.; *Williams* v. *Price* (1824) 1 Sim. & St. 581.

CHAPTER 10

TRUSTEES FOR JUNIOR DEBT

10.1   Advantages of trustees

If the junior debt is an issue of securities which will be broadly held or if both classes of debt are secured, it is usually preferable to appoint a trustee and, in some cases, a trustee is essential.

Turnover subordinations. In the case of issues of junior debt securities subordinated by a turnover subordination to specific senior creditors, it would be impracticable for the senior creditors to seek out and claim turnover proceeds from each junior creditor. If the junior securities are bearer bonds, the junior creditors will be anonymous.

On the other hand, if the subordination of the junior issue is achieved by a contractual subordination to all creditors without any turnover obligation, this pragmatic factor does not arise and a trustee need be appointed only if local law requires a trustee. Many international issues of junior eurobonds by banks subordinated contractually to all other unsubordinated creditors have been made without a trustee.

Secured debt. If the senior and junior debt are secured, then a trustee is useful to hold the benefit of the security for the benefit of both creditors. While separate security could be given to each creditor and the priority and remedies regulated by an intercreditor agreement, the advantages of a common trustee include:

— the assets covered by the security are the same for both creditors;
— the enforcement remedies are the same;
— if there are many creditors, it is not necessary to vest security in numerous mortgagees or to grant subsequent additional security to all the creditors: it is enough to grant the security to the trustee alone;
— proceeds of realisation can be applied by the trustee in the prescribed order without the necessity for any turnover from the junior creditor;
— the trustee is responsible for perfecting the security and holding title deeds and the like on deposit;
— the insurance is common;
— there is no conflict with mandatory "order of registration" priorities;
— a trustee is necessary if the creditors wish to transfer their claims by novation: see below.

In the case of security for senior and junior debt involving many creditors, it would generally be hopelessly cumbersome to grant the security to each creditor separately.

Transfers by novation. If the debts are secured and the senior and junior credit agreements allow substitution of creditors by novation (paragraph 7.22), then a trustee is necessary to preserve the security on a novation. This is because the old debt in favour of the outgoing creditor is cancelled and replaced by a new debt in favour of the incoming creditor. Without a trustee the security would have to be re-created in favour of the incoming creditor. With a trustee the security is created once and for all in favour of the trustee for the benefit of a class of creditors, including future creditors who become beneficiaries by novation. There is no objection to creating a trust for future beneficiaries unidentified when the trust is created provided that it is possible to determine whether a particular claimant is within the intended class of beneficiaries when the trust property vests.

Novations are commonly employed as a method of transferring a participation in a syndicated credit as a means of enabling the outgoing bank to transfer its commitment to make new loans: various fiscal and regulatory factors have also influenced this method of transfer.

Other advantages. Apart from these factors, from the point of view of bondholders, trustees have the additional advantages that:

— a trustee can take enforcement action on behalf of bondholders (where this is allowed by the terms of the subordination) and thereby avoid the disproportionate expense of individual legal proceedings;
— if the junior bonds are widely held, a trustee has the necessary expertise and resources to recommend courses of action on a default by the issuer and to call meetings of bondholders whose resolutions would bind dissenting and absent bondholders who might otherwise block some sensible compromise.
— if the junior bond contains complicated clauses typical of some junk bonds, a sophisticated institution is available to monitor compliance and to review financial information provided by the issuer.

From the point of view of issuers and the senior creditors:

— a trustee can be given powers itself to grant minor waivers where the interests of the junior bondholders are not materially prejudiced or to convene a meeting to sanction alterations to any covenants which turn out to be over-restrictive. The trustee can thus shield the borrower (and also the senior creditors) from unreasonable action by minority junior bondholders blocking a transaction involving a technical breach and introduce a flexibility not otherwise available;
— on a work-out, the issuer deals with one representative, not a

multitude. This could be particularly important from the point of view of the senior creditors in risky change of control finance;

— the trustee can be given power to approve a substitution of debtor (under the guarantee of the issuer) if this is desirable, *e.g.* to avoid a new withholding tax on interest or, alternatively, to approve a consolidation or merger, and in each case to approve the new subordination documentation; and the trustee can approve a change of stock exchange on which the bonds are listed, if the rules of the original stock exchange become unduly onerous.

10.2   Requirements for a trustee

In some cases the parties do not have a choice: a trustee is required by the relevant stock exchange or by statute.

Stock exchange requirements. The International Stock Exchange in London requires the appointment of a trustee for domestic debt issues, but there is no statutory requirement for a trustee. The International Stock Exchange can waive the requirement in the case of international eurocurrency issues. The Luxembourg Stock Exchange does not require a trustee.

United States Trust Indenture Act of 1939. In the United States the Trust Indenture Act of 1939 was enacted following an SEC Report of 1936 which identified a number of abuses involving trustees and which emphasised the need for the presence of a trustee to protect bondholders and for the conferring of the necessary rights and duties upon the trustee to implement that protection.

The Act states that it is unlawful for any person, directly or indirectly, to make use of any means or instruments of transportation or communication in interstate commerce or of the mails to offer or sell bonds unless they are covered by a trust indenture which is registered and qualified under the Act: section 306. Broadly, an international bond issue which avoids violation of the Securities Act of 1933, such as under various foreign offering exemptions, will escape this Act since the exemptions are generally coextensive with those under the 1933 Act. The 1939 Act does not apply (amongst other cases) to private placements nor to bonds guaranteed by a United States officially-supervised bank. The SEC may on application exempt bonds proposed to be issued by issuers organised under foreign law.

Trust indentures must be filed with the SEC for screening in a manner similar to registration statements for public issues of other securities.

The *Canadian* legislation is similar to the United States 1939 Act: see the Canada Business Corporations Act, Part VII.

In *Singapore* "every corporation which offers debentures to the public for subscription or purchase in Singapore" must provide for the appointment of a "trustee corporation" as trustee for the holders of the debentures: section 97(1) of the Singapore Companies Act. However, the issue can be exempted by ministerial consent (see section 97(6)) and often is in the case of international issues. Issues to professional dealers in securities are not caught: see section 3(6)). The rule applies only to offerings "in Singapore."

The position under the Companies Codes in *Australia* is similar: see section 152(1).

Fiscal agents   10.3

A fiscal agent for a debt issue is wholly different from a trustee. Most importantly, a fiscal agent is the agent of the issuer and not the bond-holders. A trustee on the other hand is the representative of the bondholders.

Generally speaking the fiscal agent has no fiduciary duties towards the bondholders. Only occasionally will the fiscal agent be under a duty to call a default upon the specific request of a bondholder or to hold redemption moneys in trust in an account at another bank. A trustee on the other hand has extensive fiduciary and monitoring duties imposed by the trust deed and by law.

Trustee as creditor   10.4

The mechanics of the payment obligation in debt issues is either for the debtor to grant a payment covenant to the trustee parallel with the covenant given to the junior bondholders in their bond or to grant a single payment covenant to the trustee without a parallel covenant in favour of the holders of the debt securities.

In eurobond issues the issuer covenants directly with the bondholders in the bond and gives the trustee a parallel payment covenant. The trust deed provides that permitted payments to bondholders through the pay-ing agencies discharge the parallel covenant in favour of the trustee *pro tanto*. The bondholders are therefore direct creditors of the issuer, not merely through the trust. But after a default or other springing event crystallising the subordination, the trust deed generally provides that the trustee must require the paying agents and the issuer itself to pay the trustee direct which then holds the proceeds in accordance with the terms of the subordination.

On the other hand, English practice for ordinary domestic issues of registered debentures (as opposed to bearer eurobonds) is for the cove-nant to pay to be given only to the trustee for the debentureholders who are issued with stock certificates recording the terms of the covenant in favour of the trustee. Only the trustee is a creditor of the issuer and not the debentureholders.

The reason for the difference is that the market expects a bearer instrument to contain a direct covenant (it is doubtful whether it must do so to preserve negotiability) whereas domestic issues are invariably regis-tered issues where the same expectation is not present.

The presence of a parallel or single payment covenant is relevant to the restrictions on the rights of the junior creditors to enforce their debts. If there is a single covenant in favour only of the trustee, then, quite apart from any no-action clause in the trust deed itself, a junior creditor cannot petition for a winding up of the issuer since he is not a creditor: *Re Dunderland Iron Ore Co.* [1909] 1 Ch. 447. But the junior creditor can do so if he holds a bearer bond containing a direct covenant in favour of the holder even though there is a parallel covenant in favour of the trustee: *Re Olathe Silver Mining Co.* (1884) 27 Ch.D. 278. Contrast *Re Uruguay Central Hygheritas Railway Co. of Monte Video* (1879) 11 Ch.D. 372. But if in this case the junior bonds provide that only the trustee can sue, obviously the junior creditor has no right of suit: *Atlantic Acceptance Corpn. Ltd.* v. *Burns & Ditton Construction (1962) Ltd.* (1971) 1 W.W.R. 84 (Alberta Supreme Court).

10.5   Foreign reception of the trust

If the junior securities are to be held internationally, the reception of the trust in civil code countries falls to be considered. Some civil code countries such as Switzerland, the Netherlands, Luxembourg and Germany have adopted rough equivalents to a debt trustee and it is believed that many states which do not themselves recognise trusteeship are prepared to recognise a foreign law trust which is valid under the foreign governing law. But the courts in civilian countries which have not received the trust or recognised equivalent representatives have tended to treat trusteeship in one of two ways:

(a) In some cases they have treated the trustee as the sole owner. Here, the beneficial ownership by the beneficiaries is simply not recognised and the beneficiaries are treated as having only a contractual right against the trustee, *i.e.* there is a debtor-creditor relationship between trustee and beneficiary. In the result the beneficiaries are theoretically exposed to the insolvency of the trustee in that private creditors of the trustee have access to the trust assets.

(b) More commonly, civilian courts have recharacterised the trust in terms of civil law concepts of agency or *mandatarius, e.g. Kerr* v. *Societe Pyrenees Minerals* (Court of Appeals of Toulouse July 18, 1905, Clunet 1906, 451 at page 453). This solution gives the beneficiaries the ownership of the trust property but the refusal to acknowledge that the trustee is the legal owner and therefore entitled to deal with the trust property can have major inconveniences, particularly in relation to secured issues.

Many civil code states have granted the Anglo-American trustee a right to sue on behalf of bondholders.[1] By contrast, in the *Four Seasons* case in 1971 a Luxembourg court refused to recognise a bondholder resolution made under a trust deed authorising the trustee to claim in the bankruptcy of the issuer on behalf of the bondholders. Subsequently a decree was enacted in 1972 allowing the use of a *fiduciaire representant* who can represent bondholders in legal actions and insolvency proceedings.

---

[1] Rabel, *The Conflict of Laws, A Comparative Study* (1958–1964), Chap. 75, p. 467.

If a common trustee is appointed to hold the security on a leveraged bid financed by senior and mezzanine debt and if it is contemplated that the target group will grant security for the finance, then, apart from obstacles in the way of subsidiaries giving financial assistance for the purchase of their own shares, the grant of the security to a trustee may not be possible in relation to subsidiaries in civil code states which require the security to be granted to the real creditor. Unless the senior and junior creditors are a small club of institutions, this will generally be impracticable.

A recent convention has sought to tidy up the unhappy situation described above. The Hague Convention on the Law Applicable to Trusts and on their Recognition (implemented in Britain by the Recognition of Trusts Act 1987) provides in Article 8 that in contracting states the validity of a voluntary written trust, its construction, effects and administration will be governed by the governing law of the trust. This may be expressly chosen by the settlor. A trust created in accordance with that law is to be recognised as a trust: Article 11. A watery provision in Article 12 provides that a trustee may register assets in his capacity as trustee "in so far as this is not prohibited by or inconsistent with the law of the State where registration is sought." There are various overriding rules including the usual public policy exception: Article 18. The Convention is complex and the reader is referred to the analysis in Underhill & Hayton, *Law of Trusts and Trustees* 14th ed. 1987 pp. 823 *et seq.*

Qualifications of trustee   **10.6**

The general practice in the international capital markets for both ordinary and junior issues is for the trustee to be a professional trust corporation except in Germany where the representative is generally the lead manager of the issue.

Where statute imposes an obligation to appoint a trustee it is also generally provided that the trustee must be a corporation of a specified minimum financial standing and must be locally incorporated so as to be subject to the jurisdiction of the courts and to the supervision of a domestic authority who can monitor the trustee's financial standing and fiduciary reputation.

In *Britain* there are no statutory requirements for debt issues except that the International Stock Exchange, if it requires a trustee, insists upon a trust corporation, *i.e.* a United Kingdom trust corporation satisfying certain (unburdensome) capital tests. But, because the International Stock Exchange can waive a trustee in eurobond issues, foreign trust corporations are often allowed.

Both *Canada* and the *United States* require a local trustee for *regulated* issues but in the United States only one of the trustees need be a local trustee corporation under official supervision.

In *Singapore*, the trustee (if required) must be a local public corporation or a foreign public corporation prescribed as such by the Minister of Law.

In the case of private credits, there is no objection in England to an agent bank acting as common trustee of the security for both layers of debt.

10.7   Conflicts of interest generally

It is universally true that a trustee must not put himself in a position where his duty to bondholders conflicts or might conflict with his private interest (ego conflict) or a duty to other beneficiaries (divided loyalty). The reason for the rule is that where a trustee has discretionary powers, there is a risk that the exercise of the discretions might be polluted by personal interest or muddled by a divided loyalty. The foundation is not actual injury to beneficiaries but the hallowed orison "lead us not into temptation."

In *Aberdeen Rly. Co.* v. *Blaikie Bros.* (1854) 1 Macq. 461, H.L., Lord Cranworth L.C. said at 471:

"It is a rule of universal application that no one having such duties to discharge shall be allowed to enter into an engagement in which he has, or can have, a personal interest conflicting or which may possibly conflict with the interests of those whom he is bound to protect."

There must be a real sensible possibility of conflict, not some conceivable possibility in events not contemplated as real sensible possibilities: *Industrial Development Consultants* v. *Cooley* [1972] 2 All E.R. 162, 172. The possibility of the conflict is increased where the trustee has large discretionary powers as opposed to clearly defined duties.

The question of conflict is a common problem in relation to subordinations. For example, there is the question of whether a trustee may act for a subordinated issue and also a separate senior issue. In leveraged bids with layers of mezzanine debt, there is the question of whether the agent bank for the senior debt can act if it (or one of its related companies) is also a junior or senior creditor or financial adviser to the bidder. Mezzanine debt is often convertible or has attached warrants entitling the junior creditor to convert into shares of the issuer or its holding company so that the question may arise whether a bank can act as trustee for the junior creditors if it or one of its related companies is also itself a junior creditor who may potentially become a shareholder.

Other examples of potential conflicts, which are not idiosyncratic to subordinations, include situations where there are cross-shareholdings or cross-directorships or where the trustee has an investment department which invests in securities of the issuer on behalf of customers. The latter situation should usually be controllable by a Chinese Wall.

10.8   Contracting out of conflicts rule

It is generally possible for a trustee to act in conflict if the beneficiary consents and if the beneficiary is fully-informed as to what he is consenting to: the prohibition is not absolute. A beneficiary can relax a duty provided he "fully understands not only what he is doing but also what his legal rights are, and that he is in part surrendering them": *Boulting* v. *Association of Cinematograph Television and Allied Technicians* [1963] 2 Q.B. 606, 636. This stringent rule supports specific disclosure and it is not enough for the fiduciary merely to disclose that he has an interest. However, even if the creditor has consented, a conflict may expose the trustee to the risk of closer scrutiny of the trustee's conduct and to allegations of bad faith destroying any exculpatory protection: paragraph 10.9.

But in the United States and Canada it is not possible to contract out of the rules prohibiting certain conflicts of interest set out in the United States Trust Indenture Act of 1939 and the Canada Business Corporations Act respectively.

Further in England there are various provisions limiting the ability of trustees to exclude liability and these may be more rigorously interpreted if the trustee acts in conflict of interest. The Trustee Act 1925, section 61, provides that the court can exclude a trustee from liability from breach of trust only if he satisfies the stringent test that he "has acted honestly and reasonably, and ought fairly to be excused." Section 192 of the codifying Companies Act 1985 (which is paralleled in other English-related jurisdictions such as Australia, India and Singapore) provides that any provision contained in a trust deed for securing an issue of the debentures is void in so far as it would have the effect of exempting a trustee from or indemnifying him against liability for breach of trust where he failed to show the degree of care and diligence required of him as a trustee. However, the trustee can be released by three-quarters in value of the debentureholders at a meeting summoned for the purpose of the release "with respect to specific acts or omissions" but not generally.

In England, Australia and Singapore this provision (or its local equivalent) applies to any debenture trust deed, irrespective of whether there has been a public offering. The territorial ambit is not stated, nor is it clear whether the section will override a foreign law trust deed conferring wider exculpations.

Whether consumerist statutes (such as the Unfair Contract Terms Act 1977) limiting exclusion clauses in contracts generally or consumer contracts would apply to any trust deed "contracts" is a question of construction of the statute.

Effect of conflict **10.9**

If there is a conflict (even if consented to by the beneficiaries), then the following results may ensue:

(a) The trustee is more vulnerable to negligence proceedings: *Mutual Life Citizens Co.* v. *Evatt* [1971] A.C. 793. Exculpation clauses are more likely to be outflanked on the ground that the trustee acted in bad faith: *Dabney* v. *Chase National Bank*, 346 U.S. 863 (1953);

(b) Circumstances could arise where conflicting duties are imposed so that, whatever the trustee does, he will be liable to one party or another. If the trustee inhibits proper performance of his duties by acting for both sides, he does so at his own risk.

(c) The trustee may be liable to account for profits or benefits derived from his conflicting role, *e.g.* disgorgement of a private loan paid out to a bank trustee ahead of the bondholders: paragraph 10.12.

(d) Criminal penalties in certain cases where a statute outlaws conflicts for public issues, *e.g.* Singapore Companies Act, section 93.

As Cardozo J. observed in *Meinhard* v. *Salmon*, 249 N.Y. 458 (1928) at 464:

> "A trustee is held to something stricter than the morals of the market-place. Not honesty alone, but the punctilio of an honour the most sensitive, is then the standard of behaviour."

Of course, if a conflict actually surfaces, the trustee could resign but this apparent escape is, in practice, limited. This is because the bondholders lose an informed trustee when they need him most and because experience has shown that it can be difficult to find a replacement trustee in time.

10.10   Trustee for both senior and junior debt

Where the trustee is a *trustee of two issues* of the same issuer, one senior, the other junior, the possibility of conflict is often lessened by virtue of the limited action which the junior holders can take to protect themselves against the senior holders. This at least is true of capital issues by banks, but less true of mezzanine finance.

Normally it would be difficult for a trustee to act for both of a secured and an unsecured issue of debentures. But there should be no objection to a common trustee holding the security for both the senior and the junior creditors in, say, a financing of a leveraged bid and indeed this is the recommended arrangement for the reasons given at paragraph 10.1. In order to resolve the potential exposure of the trustee to divided loyalties, the trust deed should specifically direct the trustee to exercise his discretions, (*e.g.* to accelerate and the timing or manner of enforcement) in accordance with the directions of the majority senior creditors by value. There can only be a conflict if the trustee has a discretion, not where he has a duty to act as directed. The trust deed should absolve the trustee from taking any action if the majority senior creditors fail to give instructions when requested.

10.11   Trustee is private lender

In bid financings the trustee for the security is often the agent bank for the senior creditor who may have made loans to the debtor. A bank trustee of an issue of securities may also be the banker to the issuer—a situation not peculiar to subordinations.

Banks acting as trustees drew scathing judicial criticism from the courts in *Re Dorman Long & Co.* [1934] 1 Ch.D. 635, 671. This is because it was found that in practice the bank might be tempted to secure the payment of its own loan first, to call for private security or to insist on building up set-offs. The bank might be privy to information which is protected by banker's confidentiality but which is highly pertinent to the bondholders. There might be a temptation not to notify defaults, or an inclination to advance more private money to avert a default or not to accelerate the bonds if the acceleration might prejudice the recoverability of the private loan. Experience has shown that a bank lender who is also a trustee severely restricts its freedom of action as lender in the event of default and is exposed to bondholder action if holders go unpaid.

A particular problem for the bank trustee is the risk of being compelled to disgorge private receipts. This could happen if the bank is trustee for the junior creditors or a common trustee for the security and is also a private lender. It could also happen if the bank is a senior lender and also a trustee of some separate junior issue: see also paragraph 10.12.

Some of the United States cases on banks acting as trustee are relevant:

In *Dabney* v. *Chase National Bank of the City of New York*, 98 F.Supp. 807 (S.D.N.Y. 1951), *rev'd* 201, F. 2d 635 (2d Cir. 1953) *modifying* 196 F. 2d 668 (2d Cir. 1952), *appeal dismissed*, 346 U.S. 863 (1953), an action was brought against the trustee in order to restore loan payments which the trustee had received eight years prior to the declaration of bankruptcy of the obligor on the basis that the loan was made when the trustee had knowledge of the borrower's insolvency. The loan had been made and repaid during the trusteeship. *Held*: a trustee must not compete with the interests of investors and must give the bondholders undivided loyalty free from any conflicting personal interest. The court compelled the trustee to pay over to the bondholders sums collected by the trustee on its loan to the borrower.

In *York* v. *Guaranty Trust Co. of New York*, 143 F. 2d 503 (2d Cir. 1944) *rev'd* on statute of limitations grounds 326 U.S. 99 (1945), the bondholders claimed that they had suffered loss by reason of the trustee's inaction. The trustee had enabled the borrower to meet payments of interest by making private loans to the borrower but nevertheless the trustee failed to exercise its powers to commence liquidation proceedings and thereby to prevent further erosion of the assets. Subsequently the trustee proposed a scheme of arrangement involving the exchange of bonds for shares which was not accepted by all the bondholders. *Held*: the trustee's motive for failing to liquidate was its desire to protect its position as a creditor and that mere disclosure of the conflict could not exculpate the trustee. It was wilful misconduct and bad faith to occupy conflicting roles.

In *Dudley* v. *Mealey*, 147 F. 2d 268 (2d Cir. 1945), *cert. denied* 325 U.S. 873 (1945), the defendant bank, which was a trustee under a bond issue, set off amounts owing to it privately against deposits held by it as a bank. *Held*: the trustee should disgorge these sums received by set-off on the basis that the set-off had robbed the bondholders of an asset of the issuer. By becoming trustee the bank assumed a duty of undivided loyalty and was not free to enter into relations with the borrower which created a conflict of interest.

In *Starr* v. *Chase National Bank*, N.Y.L.J. September 21, 1936, (Sup.Ct.) page 771, Col. 6 (Supreme Court) the trustee, even after it knew of default on the bonds, had received substantial sums from the borrower which it used to pay back its own private indebtedness. It had also failed to attach certain free assets to the borrower which were available to it. *Held*: a trustee had an active duty to attach property available for the purpose where it had actual knowledge of a default. The trustee's conduct constituted bad faith so that reliance could not be placed upon an exculpatory clause exempting it from responsibility. On the other hand in *Hazzard* v. *Chase National Bank*, 159 Misc. 57, 287 N.Y. Supp. 541 (Sup.Ct. 1936) the trustee escaped by reason of an exculpation clause. The trustee was permitted by the trust deed to substitute collateral securities on presentation of an earnings statement. The trustee, which was also a private lender to the obligor, allowed a substitution of securities known to an executive of the trustee to be worthless. For this purpose the knowledge of the executive, who had nothing to do with the trustee department but was on the board of the obligor, was imputed to the bank as a whole. The trust deed said that the trustee was not liable except for "gross negligence or bad faith." *Held*: although the trustee had been negligent, neither gross negligence nor bad faith had been made out. The court nevertheless launched into a stinging attack on the trustee and the trust deed: "how unutterly unjust to the investing public is the modern trust indenture.... The untrained investor unquestionably depends upon the great financial institution named as trustee to supply the skill and the watchfulness and the prudence and the experience which he himself lacks.... This indenture was particularly vicious ... the fee of $1,100 per year in this case was grotesquely exorbitant for the negligible services performed and responsibility undertaken by the defendant."

For the disgorge provision in the Trustee Indenture Act of 1939, see paragraph 10.12.

In England the law is likely to be similar to the United States cases cited above by way of extension of the stringent rule that a trustee must not make a profit out of the trusteeship without the informed consent of the beneficiary: see the summary by Lord Denning M.R. in *Phipps* v. *Boardman* [1965] Ch. 992, C.A., affd. *sub nom. Boardman* v. *Phipps* [1967] 2 A.C. 46, H.L.

10.12   Regulatory restrictions on conflicts of interest

In *Britain* there are no statutory rules prohibiting trustees from acting in conflict and the matter is left to the fairly ferocious general law relating to fiduciaries. The International Stock Exchange rules for London listings prescribe that the trustee "must have no interest in or relation to the company which might conflict with the position of trustee." The rule refrains from elaboration.

In the *United States* the Trustee Indenture Act of 1939 has intervened to prevent a trustee of a *regulated* indenture from acting if there is a material conflict of interest. The Act, in a busy section 310(b), sets out nine interests which are deemed to be conflicting, *e.g.* cross-control, being a trustee under more than one indenture for the same obligor (except under certain conditions), being an underwriter of the securities, or if 20 per cent. or more of the trustee's voting shares are owned by the obligor and its directors or officers combined (or more than 10 per cent. owned by one such person). Only very limited interlocking of boards of directors is allowed. It is clear however that the Act does not override the common law responsibilities of a trustee so that these survive parallel to the 1939 Act: *Morris* v. *Cantor*, 390 F.Supp. 817 (S.D.N.Y. 1975).

Pragmatically, the Act does not prohibit a trustee from also being a private lender to or other creditor of the obligor. However section 311(a) of the Act is important for agent banks acting as security trustee for junior or senior creditors. This provides that if the trustee receives payment on any debt owed by the obligor to the trustee within four months prior or subsequent to uncured defaults then the trustee must keep the payment in a separate account and must share it with the investors if there is a subsequent bankruptcy in which the investors are not fully paid.

However, the section is not all-powerful since it excludes some creditor claims of the trustee in its private capacity (such as payments on securities having a maturity of one year or more at the time the trustee acquired them) and furthermore the four-month rule is rather short in the context of many defaults. On the other hand, as has been seen, case law has intervened to cause a trustee to disgorge private moneys received even outside the four-month period: paragraph 10.11.

In *Canada* the Canada Business Corporations Act prescribes by section 78 that if there is material conflict of interest between the trustee's role as trustee and his role in any other capacity, then within 90 days after he becomes aware of the conflict the trustee must either eliminate the conflict or resign from office. This provision is based on a similar provision in the United States Trust Indenture Act of 1939: section 310.

The *Singapore* Companies Act (section 97) deems that the following offend the independence rule for regulated trusteeships of corporate public issues in Singapore: the trustee or a group company holds more than 5 per cent. of the voting power of the borrower's shares; the borrower owes money beneficially to the trustee or a group company, subject to a detailed threshold of 10 per cent. of the debentures (this effectively rules out bank trustees); the trustee has guaranteed the debentures.

The Companies Codes in *Australia* set out independence tests on similar lines: section 152. Singapore tends to adopt Australian corporate legislation.

The *Luxembourg* 1972 Decree on trustees requires that *fiduciaire representants* for debt issues must be independent of the issuer and its controllers and do not find themselves in a position liable to create a conflict of interest. A non-complying trustee must rectify the position in three months or resign. No examples of conflict are given.

Variation of the terms of junior debt generally   10.13

Unless there is some measure of democratic control, an unreasonable or quiescent minority could dictate to the majority and imperil a beneficial arrangement necessary in an emergency or desirable for the common weal. This could be particularly prejudicial to the senior creditors.

In the case of subordinations of syndicated bank debt, the matter can be dealt with by usual majority bank clauses. With junior debt issues, the position is more complex because of the intervention of stock exchange rules and statutory controls. Common law jurisdictions do not generally make statutory provision for bondholder meetings, but trust deeds invariably do. These confer very wide powers on meetings to grant waivers, extend maturities, allow mergers, permit conversions of the debt securities into shares, alter the currency of the bonds and (sometimes) even to desubordinate.

The rules of the International Stock Exchange require that the trust deed (if one is required) for an issue listed on the exchange must provide that a meeting of bondholders is to be called on a requisition in writing signed by holders of at least one-tenth of the nominal amount of the bonds. In civil code countries, by contrast, statute enables bondholders representing a proportion of the outstanding bonds to call meetings to vote on matters of common interest: 5 per cent. is prescribed in Brazil, France, Germany and Switzerland but others have a higher percentage, with Belgium requiring an improbable 20 per cent.

The subject of the powers of bondholders to bind dissentient minorities is a large one and one may restrict the following analysis to a few outline points.[2]

10.14   Issues on which majority can bind minority

English eurobond practice for subordinated issues is to confer very wide powers upon bondholders' meetings but, in order to protect minority bondholders against abuse of majority power, to require high quorums and majorities for fundamental matters, e.g a vote of three-quarters of bondholders present at the meeting at which a quorum is three-quarters of the outstanding bonds (an almost impossible quorum in the case of bearer bonds). Curiously, the subordination itself is not always entrenched.

The policy of the Trust Indenture Act of 1939 is to protect the rights of individual bondholders under regulated indentures rather than to permit flexibility: see section 316.

10.15   Minority protection

Many jurisdictions protect minority bondholders against the abuse of majority power. For example, Article 326 of the Japanese Commercial Code provides that resolutions must be approved by the court and the court will not approve a resolution where (among other things) the resolution has come to be adopted in an improper manner, is markedly unfair or is contrary to the interests of the bondholders generally.

In *England*, bondholder resolutions can validly bind dissentient minorities: see, for example, *Re Joseph Stocks & Co. Ltd.* [1909] 26 T.L.R. 41 (bonds made irredeemable). It has been held that bondholders voting at a general meeting are not bound to disregard their own selfish interests but are entitled to vote in whatever way they think best for themselves: *Goodfellow* v. *Nelson Line* [1912] 2 Ch. 324, 333. But in *Re Holders Investment Trust* [1971] 1 W.L.R. 583, the court held, in a situation where preference shareholders were also ordinary shareholders, that the preference shareholders must vote in the interests of the class as a whole and disregard their private interests as ordinary shareholders. This somewhat special decision should be borne in mind by senior creditors who are also junior creditors. In any event, a resolution can be attacked if there is unfairness or oppression or discrimination between bondholders[3] or

---

[2] For a more detailed study, see the author's *Law and Practice of International Finance*, Clark Boardman (New York) Chapter 9.

[3] *Goodfellow* v. *Nelson Line* [1912] 2 Ch. 324; *Re New York Taxi-Cab Co.* (1913) 1 Ch. 1.

secret advantages are given to one bondholder,[4] or the resolution is not strictly within the terms of the power.[5]

Under the *EEC Admissions Directive*[6] undertakings are under a legal obligation to treat holders of *pari passu* debt securities equally except for certain offers of early repayment.

Bondholders' communities   **10.16**

In many civil code countries statutes establish and regulate bondholder communities. These statutes may reduce the ability of junior bond-holders to vary the junior debt.

In *Switzerland* the provisions for bondholders' communities are set out in Articles 1157 to 1186 of the Swiss Code of Obligations.[7] If bonds are issued "directly or indirectly by a public subscription [presumably meaning the Swiss public] under uniform loan terms by an obligor domiciled or having a business establishment in Switzerland" (which would appear to exclude foreign government issues but not foreign companies having a Swiss establishment) the creditors by law form a community of creditors. There is a separate community for each issue of bonds. There are specific provisions as to the decisions which the assembly of bondholders can take which bind dissentient bondholders and as to minimum majorities.

The rights granted to the community of creditors and the representative cannot be excluded or restricted by contract. Whether this would lead a Swiss court to override conflicting provisions in an English euro-bond trust deed appears unclear. In *France* a 1935 law provides that bondholders of a class of bonds issued by an SA be grouped as a matter of law into an association having legal personality: the *masse des obligataires*. Again there are entrenched provisions requiring unanimity and minimum majorities. However, a 1967 law exempts debt issued by French enterprises outside France. Where the issue is exempt, some French issuers have constituted a *société civile*. This is a type of civil partnership set up by the bond issue documentation and to which all bondholders belong. Typically the document provides for representation of bondholders, the exclusion of individual bondholder action, and bondholder meetings. The *société civile* of bondholders has been recognised by the French courts since 1927.[8]

In *Belgium* and *Luxembourg* the law is similar: see the Belgian Co-

---

[4] *British American Nickel Corp.* v. *O'Brien Ltd.* [1927] A.C. 369.
[5] *Mercantile Investment and General Trust Co.* v. *The International Co. of Mexico* [1891] [1893] 1 Ch. 484 n. 489, C.A.; *Hay* v. *Swedish and Norwegian Railway Co. Limited* [1889] 5 T.L.R. 460, C.A.
[6] Council Directive of March 5, 1979 co-ordinating the conditions for the admission of securities to official stock exchange listing (79/279/EEC).
[7] See *Swiss Securities Law*, English translation by Swiss-American Chamber of Commerce (1982).
[8] See Delaume, "Choice of Law and Forum Clauses in Euro-bonds," 11 *Columbia Journal of Transitional Law* 240, (1972); Frederic C. Rich, "Are bondholders' rights protected?" *Euromoney*, September 1981, 95.

ordinated Laws on commercial companies, Articles 91–95 and the Luxembourg law concerning commercial companies of 1915 as amended (Articles 86–90). Bondholders' meetings have a restricted competence.

As to *West Germany* see the Law concerning the Rights of Bondholders (Schuldverschreibungsgesetz) of 1899 (as amended), applying to bondholders of an AG.

In *Japan* the provisions for meetings of debentureholders of a Japanese *Kabushiki-Kaisha* (joint-stock company) are contained in Articles 319 to 341 of the Japanese Commercial Code.

10.17   Conflict with bondholder statutes

Difficult conflict of law problems could arise where the terms of a trust deed are in collision with the local statutes regarding bondholder representatives and communities. Fortunately, many of the statutes apply only to issues by local companies: exceptions are the Swiss and United States statutes.

The Swiss and United States codes prohibit contracting-out. The Luxembourg list of matters on which bondholders can pass resolutions has been held to be exhaustive. If contracting-out is not permitted and the statute applies to the issue, the local courts might treat the statute as a mandatory rule of public policy which overrides the governing law. In *Chemins de Fer Portugais* v. *Ash* (Cass. March 1922, 1944, S. 1945. I. 77, Rev. 1940–46 107) the Cour de Cassation refused to enforce, on the ground of public policy, a Portuguese judicial order confirming a plan approved by 91 per cent of the holders of bonds of a Portuguese railway company which waived a gold clause and authorised the obligor to issue preferential bonds.

Chapter 11

MISCELLANEOUS

Regulation of capital adequacy and solvency ratios   **11.1**

Subordinated debt may be treated as capital for the purposes of minimum solvency or capital adequacy standards applied by regulatory authorities to banks, insurance companies, securities businesses and the like whose continued solvency is deemed crucial to the integrity of the financial system or who take other people's money or both.

Banks. The central statement of the principles governing the supervision of the capital adequacy of international banks is the Report of July 1988 of the Basle Committee on Banking Regulations and Supervisory Practices on International Convergence of Capital Measurement and Capital Standards. The expectation was that these principles would be adopted by supervisory authorities worldwide in respect of banks conducting significant international business, although strictly it is an agreement between the Group of Ten central banks (Belgium, Canada, France, Germany, Italy, Japan, the Netherlands, Sweden, Switzerland, the United Kingdom and the United States, plus Luxembourg).

In a nutshell the affected banks will be required by 1992 to maintain capital of 8 per cent. of their assets and exposures. For this purpose capital is divided into two tiers comprising core capital (such as equity and disclosed reserves) and supplementary capital which can include certain categories of subordinated debt. The various categories of assets and exposures are given a risk weighting as a broad-brush method of determining their relative riskiness. Thus claims on OECD central banks have a zero risk weight, residential mortgage loans have a 50 per cent. risk weight, and ordinary loans to the private sector have a 100 per cent. risk weight. On the capital side, perpetual subordinated debt issues having the characteristics of equity and subordinated term debt having a maturity of more than five years can be included subject to various detailed qualifications and limits.

The Basle Convergence Agreement was implemented in the United Kingdom by the Bank of England's Notice No. BSD/1988/3 of October 1988. Details of the qualifying attributes of primary perpetual subordinated debt and of term subordinated debt are set out in the Bank of England's Notice No. BSD/1986/2 of March 1986, as amended by Notice No. BSD/1988/3.

For example, the qualifying requirements for perpetual subordinated debt include requirements that (a) the debt be subordinated to all other debt, (b) events of default be excluded subject to limited exceptions, (c) the debt is not repayable without the consent of the Bank of England, (d) the issuer has the option to defer interest payments, and (e) the debt is able to absorb losses while leaving the issuing bank able to continue trading, *e.g.* by providing for its compulsory conversion into equity if reserves become negative.

Cross-holdings by a bank of another bank's subordinated debt are a deduction from capital in accordance with detailed provisions. This is in order to ensure that the same capital is not used by more than one institution to support its operations by a process of double-gearing. The rationale is that cross-holdings of capital would make the banking system more vulnerable to the rapid transmission of a default by one institution to other institutions and hence threaten the system.

Similar concepts are in the process of being developed by actual or proposed European Community Directives in connection with the breaking down of national regulatory barriers to local bank establishment. In order to maintain competitive equality—the level playing field—the proposal is that supervisory authorities must require the same minimum solvency ratios. See especially the Council Directive on April 17, 1989 on the own funds of credit institutions (89/299/EEC) which in Article 4.3 sets out the minimum criteria for subordinated loan capital to qualify as "own funds" (the Community's term for capital) and which provides for the deduction from capital of certain holdings of subordinated debt in other credit and financial institutions (Article 2.1(13)).

The proposal for a Council Directive on a solvency ratio for credit institutions is based on Basle ideas.

See also the main proposed Second Council Directive on the co-ordination of laws relating to credit institutions.

Building Societies. Building Societies are also subject to a capital adequacy regime. The Building Societies (Supplementary Capital) Order 1988 (S.I. 1988 No. 777) sets out the terms which subordinated debt has to meet for this purpose. A Prudential Note 1988/1 of April 1988 has been issued by the Building Societies Commission providing guidance on the requirements. The rules are similar in approach to the Bank of England criteria for banks. The BSC Prudential Note is generous to lawyers in stating: "The legal instruments required to achieve the necessary contractual arrangement are typically lengthy and complicated. Societies should engage specialist lawyers to advise them."

Investment businesses

The Financial Services (Financial Resources) Rules 1987 made by the Securities and Investments Board pursuant to section 49 of the Financial Services Act 1986 set out certain minimum financial resources which must be maintained by certain firms carrying on investment business. One of the criteria relates to the maintenance of gross capital which is the amount of net assets adjusted in accordance with a formula. In making the calculation, liabilities in respect of eligible long term and short term subordinated loans can be disregarded subject to certain limits. In order to qualify as an eligible subordinated loan the loan must be made to the firm under the terms of a duly executed agreement in the relevant form scheduled to the Rules.

Special features of the form of long term subordinated loan include:

— a stipulation that the lender's only remedy for the recovery of amounts owing under the loan agreement is to institute proceedings for the insolvency of the borrower (which is defined in such a way as to exclude administration and other rehabilitation proceedings),

— provision that payment of any amount, whether principal, interest or otherwise, of the subordinated liabilities is conditional upon the borrower being in compliance with a stipulated net worth requirement both before and after the payment and, in the case of insolvency proceedings conditional upon the borrower being solvent both before and after the payment,

— provision that even though the borrower is in compliance with its net worth requirement, a payment of principal cannot be made if the Securities and Investments Board does not consent,

— a term that payments received by the lender in breach of these conditions are to be returned to the borrower and in the meantime held on trust,

— a term that the subordinated liabilities may not be secured and that the lender will not without the prior written consent of the Securities and Investments Board assign all or any of the subordinated liabilities.

Withholding tax   11.2

There is very little distinction for United Kingdom tax purposes between ordinary debt and subordinated debt.

Where interest is paid by a company, section 349(2) of the Income and Corporation Taxes Act 1988 ("T.A. 1988") imposes an obligation on the person by or through whom the payment is made to withhold income tax at the basic rate (currently 25 per cent.). There are two relevant exemptions to this. First where the company is a bank and the bank pays interest in the ordinary course of carrying on a bona fide banking business in the United Kingdom it will be exempted from the obligation to withhold tax: section 349(3)(b) T.A. 1988. Interest paid on a subordinated loan made to a bank will not however be treated as being in the ordinary course of its business and so basic rate tax will have to be withheld.

The second exemption from withholding is under section 124 of the T.A. 1988 ("the quoted eurobond exemption"). The exemption is available for ordinary debt as well as subordinated debt instruments and applies if the instrument is issued by a company, is quoted on a recognised stock exchange, is in bearer form and bears interest. A holder may receive his interest gross if he is not a United Kingdom resident or if he receives his interest through a recognised clearing system (which currently includes Euro-clear and Cedel).

11.3   Stamp duty

No United Kingdom stamp duty would be payable on a "contingent debt" subordination, a contractual subordination or a debtor-creditor turnover subordination whereby the junior debtor agrees to pay the senior creditor amounts equal to receipts on the junior debt. As to subordination trusts whereby the junior creditor holds receipts on trust for the senior creditor, there should be no United Kingdom stamp duty under the head of duty of "Conveyance or transfers on sale of any property" in the Stamp Act 1891, Schedule 1 because there is no conveyance or transfer effected by the instrument but only an agreement to transfer.

No stamp duty should be payable under the alternative head of any contract or agreement for the sale of any equitable estate or interest in any property whatsoever within section 59 of the Stamp Act 1891 because there is no consideration payable by the senior creditor to the junior creditor on the amount or value of which the duty could be levied.

An alternative reason for exemption might be that neither a maximum nor minimum consideration can be calculated.

11.4   Perpetuity rule

Subordination trusts are subject to the perpetuity rule whereby trust property must vest in the beneficiary within the perpetuity period. The purpose of this rule was to prevent people from tying up their property for ever by, for example, giving successive generations of their descendants only a life interest in the property. This laudable objective has the result, little dreamed of by the ancient courts, that subordinations of perpetual debt must be contractual subordinations or debtor-creditor turnover subordinations and not set up a trust.

As to other cases, the Perpetuities and Accumulations Act 1964 introduced the "wait and see" principle whereby a disposition is not void until it becomes established that the vesting must occur, if at all, after the end of the perpetuity period. Since the perpetuity period which is most likely to apply under the Act is 21 years (see section 3(4) of the Act), the subordination agreement could specify an alternative duration of up to 80 years under section 1(1) of the Act. In most cases it will be clear that the subordination is unlikely to last for anything like 21 years in which event it would not be necessary to specify a perpetuity period.

In Australia it has been held that perpetuity is a matter for the governing law of the trust: *Augustus* v. *Permanent Trustee Co. (Canberra) Ltd.* (1971) 124 C.L.R. 245.

Convertible junior debt **11.5**

Convertible subordinated debt has the usual advantages of convertible debt, *e.g.* the ability to convert sweetens the issue by giving the bond-holder the security of a fixed rate of interest but with an opportunity to make profits if the issuer's shares go up in value by more than the conversion premium.

In the case of a turnover subordination, on conversion of the junior debt the senior creditors will lose the benefit of the turnover of dividends and in the meantime the junior creditor may effectively be able to defeat the subordination of income by receiving dividends on his shares. Insider subordinations commonly prohibit conversion of the junior debt. In other cases conversion is often permitted since in practice the junior creditor is likely to convert only if the debtor's business prospers. The conversion option may reduce the interest rate on the junior debt and hence the financial load on the debtor. Whether equity can be repaid (and hence defeat a tighter debt subordination) is a matter for local corporate law. In Britain, private companies can purchase their own shares out of capital subject to various conditions including projected solvency for the coming year: Companies Act 1985, ss.171 *et seq.*

In the case of contractual non-turnover subordinations which are drafted as debt contingent on the debtor's solvency, the conversion of debt into shares must not infringe any rule that shares must not be allotted at a discount: see section 100 of the Companies Act 1985. The nominal amount of the junior debt, after taking into account its conditionality, must not be less than the par value of the shares: *Mosely* v. *Koffyfontein Mines Ltd. (No. 1)* [1904] 2 Ch. 108, C.A. The test is the nominal amount of the debt, not its actual value.

If perpetual subordinated debt of authorised banks is to qualify for tier 2 capital under the Bank of England's capital adequacy rules, it must (amongst other things) be compulsorily convertible into shares if reserves become negative: paragraph 11.1.

Corporate powers **11.6**

Consider whether the junior creditor has corporate power to enter into the subordination and whether the directors of the junior creditor may properly lend money on the basis that it is irrecoverable or handed over to a senior creditor in certain events. There is much law on the subject in relation to guarantees. The *ultra vires* will be virtually abolished as regards third parties by the Companies Act 1989 when the relevant section comes into force.

Rescission of junior debt **11.7**

If a junior creditor is entitled to rescind the junior debt a question may arise as to whether the junior creditor's claim for damages or restitution is also subordinated. If not, the subordination would be defeated.

For example, a junior creditor may be entitled to rescind the subordinated claim if it is evidenced by a bond and the prospectus for the bond issue contained fraudulent or negligent misstatements. In the United States some cases have held that the damages claim is also subordinated or alternatively that the junior creditor is not entitled to rescind.[1]

The United States position is now covered by section 510(b) of the Bankruptcy Code of 1978 which provides as follows:

> "For the purpose of distribution under this title, a claim arising from rescission of a purchase or sale of a security of the debtor or of an affiliate of the debtor, for damages arising from the purchase or sale of such a security, or for reimbursement or contribution allowed under section 502 on account of such a claim, shall be subordinated to all claims or interests that are senior to or equal the claim or interest represented by such security, except that if such security is common stock, such claim has the same priority as common stock."

The term "security" as used in this section includes both debt securities and equity securities: see section 101(35)(A).

11.8   Compulsory subordinations on insolvency

The above deals with subordinations achieved by the voluntary act of the junior creditor. There are classes of subordination on insolvency which are compulsory by law, the main types of which are listed below.

(a) Preferential creditors. Ordinary creditors may be subordinated to preferred creditors, such as employees and banks subrogated to employee claims. The Insolvency Act 1986, section 178 provides that in a winding-up certain preferential debts are paid in priority to other debts. These are primarily: money owed to the Inland Revenue for money taxed at source, VAT, car tax, betting and gaming duties, social security and pension scheme contributions, and remuneration, etc., of employees: see Schedule 6 to the Act.

(b) Depositors. In some jurisdictions general creditors may be subordinated to bank depositors or insurance policyholders. In England bank depositors rank equally with other secured creditors but are protected by a compensation fund up to certain limits: see the Banking Act 1987.

(c) Equitable subordination. Under the *Deep Rock* equitable subordination rules in United States bankruptcy law, typically a shareholder who mismanages an under-capitalised company to the detriment of its creditors may be liable, on the insolvency of the company, to have his claim subordinated to those creditors on grounds of fairness. In effect the delinquent shareholder's loan is converted into equity. Equitable subordination is recognised by section 510(c) of the United States Bankruptcy Code of 1978 and has attracted much recent case law.

---

[1] See, *e.g. In re Holiday Mart, Inc.*, 715 F2d 430 (9th Cir. 1983); *In re Weis Securities, Inc.*, 605 F2d 590 (2d Cir. 1978).

This concept is partially reflected in section 215(4) of the British Insolvency Act 1986 which allows the court to direct that a person liable for fraudulent or wrongful trading in relation to a company who is also a creditor is to be subordinated to the payment of all other debts owed by the company plus interest. A person who controls the management of the company, *e.g.* an over-intrusive bank, could be a "shadow director" (see section 741 of the Companies Act 1985) and, if so, could be liable for wrongful trading and be postponed by this section.

If a senior creditor is relying on a turnover of dividends from a junior creditor whose claim is equitably subordinated, the senior creditor will get no turnover if the junior creditor's claim is effectively treated as equity. In such a case the senior creditor may wish to argue that the junior debt should not be treated as equity under the *Deep Rock* doctrine.

(d) Profit-sharing loans. Under section 3 of the English Partnership Act 1890 which applies to loans (whether to companies or partnerships or anybody else—see rule 12.3 (2A) of the Insolvency Rules 1986) if interest varies with the profits of the borrower or the lender is to receive a share of profits, the lender is not entitled to receive anything in respect of his loan until the other creditors have been satisfied. This rule is widely adopted in other common law jurisdictions based on English law, such as common law Canada.

(e) Credit between spouses. Under the Insolvency Act 1986, section 329, bankruptcy debts owed in respect of credit provided by a person who was the bankrupt's spouse at the commencement of the bankruptcy rank in priority after those debts. The policy of the postponement is that a spouse is deemed effectively to have an equity interest in the other spouse rather than an interest as creditor. The principle has been applied to loans by mistresses: *Re Beale* (1876) 4 Ch.D. 246; *Re Meade* [1951] Ch. 774.

(f) Sums due to company members. Under the Insolvency Act 1986, section 74(2)(f), a sum due to any member of a company (in his character of a member) by way of dividends, profits or otherwise is postponed to other ordinary creditors of the company. If unpaid dividends have in fact been converted into a loan, then the loan escapes subordination: *Re L.B. Holliday & Co.* [1986] B.C.L.C. 227.

(g) Contraventions of Financial Services Act 1986. By rule 12.3(2A) of the Insolvency Rules 1986, as amended, certain claims resulting from a court order for disgorgement of profits made by a person as a result of carrying on investment business in contravention of the Financial Services Act 1986 or from a contravention of certain other provisions of the Act are not provable in a winding-up or bankruptcy until the claims of all other creditors have been satisfied. The rule also applies to claims under section 49 of the Banking Act 1987 for the disgorgement of profits made in carrying on an unauthorised deposit-taking business.

CHAPTER 12

INTERNATIONAL SURVEY

12.1   This Chapter contains a survey of the approach of some of the main jurisdictions to subordinations of debt and security. United States law on subordinations has been outlined in summary in previous Chapters. Although the contributions, written by leading lawyers in the jurisdictions concerned, are intended to indicate no more than the motorways of the law in this area, not the maze of side streets, the effect of the pooling of legal concepts in a variety of jurisdictions does have the result of illuminating many dark corners of the law. A great advantage of comparative law is that it sharpens the relief of one's own attitudes and potentially enrichens one legal system by solutions reached in another.

As in the earlier Chapters of this book, it was not thought practicable to deal in any detail with fiscal and regulatory law since the rules are currently undergoing such rapid change that any attempt to encapsulate them now would be out-of-date within months.

One result of the survey is to reveal virtual unanimity on the efficacy on insolvency of a properly drafted subordination agreement if the subordination is to all creditors and an acceptance that such a subordination does not infringe the bankruptcy policy of the mandatory *pari passu* payment of debts. But this harmony is not present when it comes to subordinations where the junior creditor wishes to be subordinated to only one senior creditor but to rank *pari passu* with the other creditors. This leads to some sort of turnover agreement, whether of proceeds or otherwise, and it is the characterisation and legal consequences of this transfer which give rise to particularly acute problems.

BELGIUM

Contributed by: **Wilfred Goris**
De Bandt, van Hecke & Lagae
Brussels

12.2   Contractual subordination

Validity. A contract of subordination is valid upon the insolvency of the junior creditor and/or of the debtor of the subordinated debt.

The Law on Preferences and Mortgages of December 16, 1851 provides in article 8:

> "The assets of the debtor are the common security of his creditors and the

proceeds of their sale will be distributed among them proportionally to their claims unless there are lawful reasons of priority among his creditors."

Freedom of contract allows a creditor to waive this legal right to equal treatment ("*pari passu*"). The waiver may either be agreed in favour of one or more specific creditors or, by a unilateral undertaking or by a contract with the debtor, in favour of all other creditors of the debtor. One might consider as an example of subordination the statutory rule limiting the effect of a payment which should normally entail subrogation. According to article 1252 of the Civil Code and article 538 of the Law of April 18, 1851 on Bankruptcy, a secured creditor may, notwithstanding a (partial) payment made by a guarantor or a co-obligor of the debtor to the secured creditor, continue to collect dividends or distributions from the assets of the debtor on the basis of the total amount of his claim; it is only when the secured creditor has been fully paid (by the guarantor(s) or otherwise) that the payers (guarantors and/or co-obligors) will be entitled to benefit from the normal effects of subrogation.

Insolvency tests and fraudulent trading. The subordinated ("junior") debt counts as a liability in order to determine whether the debtor is bankrupt. The voting rights of junior debt holders in any procedure for a general settlement with creditors ("concordat") before or after bankruptcy was declared, are counted on the basis that the junior claim is debt, not distinguished from other (unsecured) creditors.

The directors of the debtor cannot ignore junior debt when continuing to incur liabilities; they might become personally liable under fraudulent or wrongful trading rules.

A practice has developed of preventing bankruptcy by the subordination of claims. A typical situation concerns privately-held corporations operating with a limited capital and with substantial loans or trading debts owing to their controlling shareholders or other members of their group. Notwithstanding that losses exceed their capital, such entities may, according to the particular circumstances of the case, not be declared bankrupt *ex officio* if an affiliated creditor agrees to subordinate his claims to those of the other creditors.

Variations without the consent of the senior creditor. If the junior creditor and the debtor agree that the junior creditor's claim will be subordinated to other creditors who are not a party to the agreement, normally the junior creditor and the debtor could agree between them to revoke the subordination without the agreement of the senior creditors. But if the junior creditor's subordination is expressed as a stipulation in favour of the senior creditors as third parties ("*stipulation pour autrui*"), it is probable that the junior creditor could not agree to vary the subordination without the consent of senior creditors who had (be it implicity) accepted the benefit of the stipulation. Such variations would be excluded if the *stipulation pour autrui* was agreed to be irrevocable.

Set off (compensation). In the absence of any statutory rules on subordination the question of whether the subordination could be defeated by a set-off while both the debtor and the junior creditor are solvent is to be settled by proper drafting of the subordination agreement. Under general rules of contract law, a party may validly waive the benefit of a set-off (compensation) which might otherwise arise.

As to set-off on insolvency, the Law of April 18, 1851 on Bankruptcy provides in article 444:

> "As from the judgment of bankruptcy the bankrupt is by operation of law removed from the management of all his assets, even those which he might acquire during his bankruptcy."
> "All payments, transactions and acts effected by, and all payments made to, the bankrupt after said judgment, are void."

Set-off is considered, for the purpose of application of this rule, as a technique of making reciprocal payments: compare articles 1234 and 1289 Civil Code.

Consequently, bankruptcy prevents any set-off between debts and claims of the bankrupt and a counterparty. Exceptionally set-off is authorised even after bankruptcy between closely-connected claims and liabilities, e.g. those resulting from the same contract.

12.3   Turnover subordination

Availability of turnover subordination. If a junior creditor is to be subordinated to a single senior creditor or group of senior creditors, it is uncertain whether under Belgian law this can be validly achieved by an agreement by the junior creditor to transfer bankruptcy dividends and other proceeds he may receive on the junior debt to the senior creditor otherwise than by an assignment of his claim or the granting of a security interest in the claim.

An assignment (full transfer) of the claim of the junior creditor to the senior creditor might of course confer on the senior creditor more than is intended since the junior creditor would lose any interest in the collection of the receivable.

The result aimed at may be achieved under Belgian law by the creation of a security interest by the junior creditor over one of his assets to secure due payment by the debtor to the senior creditor. The creation of a security interest over the claim of the junior creditor may be achieved by a "pledge."

The security (pledge) over the junior claim should be created in the same manner as is required for the transfer (assignment) of that claim: article 1 of the Law of May 5, 1872 on (commercial) pledges and article 2075 of the Civil Code.

In order to render the pledge or the assignment of the claim of the junior debtor effective as against all interested parties (mainly the creditors of the junior creditor), the pledge or assignment must be notified by a bailiff (*huissier*) to the debtor or acknowledged by the debtor in a notarial deed: articles 2075 and 1690 of the Civil Code. This notification will entail expenses, including a stamp tax on the document drawn up by the bailiff or on the notarial deed and a registration tax on both the documents.

Further possibilities to be considered here are (i) the designation of the senior creditor as agent of the junior creditor for the collection of the dividend, or (ii) the designation, by agreement between the debtor (or the receiver of its bankruptcy) and the junior creditor of the senior creditor as the only party to which the payment of the debt (or dividend) may be validly made (*i.e.* "*adjectus solutionis gratia*"). Such techniques might achieve the aim pursued but their enforceability upon the insolvency of the junior creditor is not certain.

Secured subordinated debt   **12.4**

Ranking of security over the same asset. Generally speaking the benefit of the ranking of creditors may be the subject of valid contract: the creditor holding a first rank mortgage may agree to grant the benefit of his first rank to another mortgagee, provided always that the agreement does not prejudice other creditors of the same debtor. The amount of the debt secured by the specific priority right concerned cannot be increased.

It is thus possible for several creditors having security over the same asset, whether or not the law provides for any priority among them, to agree between themselves to rank senior and junior and to modify the distribution of the proceeds of the enforcement of their claims. Third parties would not normally be affected by this internal agreement between secured creditors.

Enforcement. The junior creditor has an independent right to enforce its claim and thereby to impose on the senior creditor a realisation of the asset concerned.

The contract of subordination may restrict the exercise of this right.

Representative of secured creditors. Under Belgian law, with very few exceptions, a right of priority or a security must be granted either to a specific creditor or with respect to a specific claim. The security (be it a mortgage, pledge of a chattel or a claim, or an undertaking to guarantee) cannot be held by a representative, fiduciary or trustee on behalf of the creditors who are the actual beneficiaries of the security. The security has to be held by the creditor himself.

One exception concerns the issue of bonds secured by a mortgage. The coordinated laws on commercial companies (article 97, 98 and 99) provide that the mortgage can be registered for the benefit of the joint bondholders, and that a trustee may be designated in order to modify or enforce the mortgage on behalf of the bondholders.

The above should be distinguished from the technique of designating a custodian for pledged chattels, whereby the creditor and the pledgor agree to deliver the chattels to the custodian, who will act on behalf of the pledgor (who is entitled to restitution upon payment of the debt secured) and of the creditor, who is entitled to enforce and to receive the proceeds in priority to other creditors of the pledgor and the debtor.

12.5 Taxation and subordinated debt

Apart from the feature peculiar to subordinated debt mentioned below, the normal tax rules which are applicable to any debt or debt instruments in general likewise apply to subordinated debt.

Where the subordinated debt assumes the characteristics of equity, interest payments on the debt might be re-characterised as distributions of profit, which are not deductible from taxable income of the debtor.

The deductibility of interest will be limited if the rate of interest exceeds an amount corresponding to a rate established by Royal Decree with reference to the rate applied by the monetary issuing institution of the country the currency of which is expressed to be the currency of the debt or alternatively the rate applied in the market of that country, increased by a margin of 3 per cent.: Art. 50–1° Income Tax Code. The limitation will be applied to the extent of the excess.

This interest rate ceiling is however not applicable, *inter alia*, to (i) publicly issued bonds or other debt securities and (ii) interest payments made to, or by, Belgian banks or certain other categories of credit or financial institutions.

The issuance of subordinated debt is not subject to any Belgian tax other than those generally applicable upon the issue of debt.

The transfer of a subordinated debt instrument is not subject to Belgian documentary taxes other than those applicable upon the transfer of any other debt instrument.

12.6 Capital adequacy and subordinated debt

As to *banks*, at the time of writing the Basle Agreement had not yet been implemented by Belgian legislation. The Banking Commission drafted new regulations on own funds implementing the Basle Agreement but those were not yet in force pending further revision in order to fully align them to the EEC Directives on own funds and solvency ratios of credit institutions.

Pending these anticipated changes, under present rules and practices, the Banking Commission imposes specific requirements in order to allow subordinated debt to qualify as capital for the purpose of the capital adequacy ratios applicable to banks. The main requirements are:

—duration of the debt: 3 years maturity (or in the case of advances, reimbursement at the earlier after 3 years) and a mandatory notice period of a minimum of 2 years (subject to the Banking Commission's approval); this will become 5 years under the new regulations;
—proper evidence of (i) the effectiveness of the subordination in accordance with applicable law and (ii) compliance in all respects with the law applicable to the subordinated creditor;
—denomination in Belgian francs; in the case of denomination in a foreign currency, the assimilation to own funds will be limited according to the pro rata portion of the bank's own funds attributable to its risks in foreign currency on non-residents.

The new regulations will likewise apply to Belgian *savings banks* and other *deposit-taking institutions*.

With respect to *insurance companies*, even though assimilation of subordinated debt to own funds for capital adequacy purposes has a regulatory basis, in practice the supervisory body (*Office du Controle des Assurances*) appears to accept this possibility only very exceptionally.

Compulsory subordination on insolvency   12.7

Belgian legislation does not provide for any situation in which a claim, whether a loan or a claim having any other origin, is compulsorily subordinated in the event of the insolvency of the debtor. As mentioned, however, a practice whereby a creditor accepts a subordination has developed as a means of avoiding a bankruptcy declaration *ex officio*.

CANADA

Contributed by: **S. B. Scott, Q.C.**
Borden & Elliot
Toronto

Introduction   12.8

Canadian law is based on a federal model. Jurisdiction over bankruptcy and insolvency is reserved to the federal government while the provinces have jurisdiction over such matters as private contracts, the validity of most security and the law of trusts. There is a doctrine of paramountcy pursuant to which, in the event of conflict between valid federal laws and provincial laws, the federal laws will prevail. All of the provinces of Canada, with the exception of Quebec, are common law jurisdictions; Quebec is a civil law jurisdiction. The law regarding subordination of debt in the common law provinces is derived largely from the English model. The provinces of Ontario, Manitoba and Saskatchewan and the Yukon Territory have, and the provinces of British Columbia and Alberta will shortly have, modern personal property security legislation based on Article 9 of the United States Uniform Commercial Code. This survey of Canadian law focuses on the law applicable in Ontario.

Contractual subordination   12.9

Section 141 of the Bankruptcy Act (Canada), R.S.C. 1985, c.B–3, provides that—

"Subject to this Act, all claims proved in a bankruptcy shall be paid rateably."

This provision corresponds roughly to the *pari passu* requirements of Section 107 of the Insolvency Act, 1986 (U.K.) and Rule 4.181(1) of the Insolvency Rules, 1986 (U.K.), as amended.

In *Re Orzy* (1923), 53 O.L.R. 323; [1924] 1 D.L.R. 250; 3 C.B.R. 737 (Ont. C.A.) the First

Appellate Division of the Ontario Supreme Court in Bankruptcy held that "in bankruptcy the rule of equality is absolute except where the Act itself gives priority to some debts over others." In this case, one creditor (O) had knowingly allowed the debtor to represent to his other creditors that the debt owed to O had been repaid. O was nevertheless permitted to prove a claim and was held to be entitled to a dividend. The court was concerned that if it were to recognise the rights of the other creditors against O, "the administration of bankrupts' estates might be encumbered with inquiries of a most embarrassing character, which it can never have been intended by the Legislature should be undertaken."

Notwithstanding this case, there is no policy reason why a creditor should not be permitted to subordinate his debt to other creditors, and the Commonwealth cases referred to in para. 3.1 would be persuasive. Contractual subordinations of debt remain enforceable between the parties despite the bankruptcy of the debtor, although contractual subordinations whereby the junior creditor is subordinated to all other creditors of the debtor are not common in Canada. In such a case, the junior creditor would not be entitled to a dividend from the bankrupt's estate until the senior creditors had been paid in full, although the junior creditor could prove a claim in bankruptcy. A contractual subordination would be effective in the event of the junior debtor's bankruptcy.

There is no distinction between junior debt and any other debt in determining the solvency of the debtor for bankruptcy or corporate law purposes. A person is insolvent, as defined in the Bankruptcy Act (Canada), when, *inter alia*, the fair or realisable value of his property is insufficient to enable payment of all his obligations, due and accruing due. Similarly, under the Canada Business Corporations Act, the solvency tests are based on the realisable value of the corporation's assets as compared with its liabilities and stated capital. Canadian law does not impose personal liability on officers and directors as is provided under the "wrongful trading rules" under the Insolvency Act, 1986 (U.K.).

In general, where the senior creditor is not a party to the subordination arrangement, the debtor and the junior creditor can vary the subordination without the consent of the senior creditor, although this may not be possible where the senior creditor has advanced money in reliance on the subordination.

Set-off, both legal and equitable, applies in bankruptcy (Bankruptcy Act (Canada), Section 97(3)). In order for set-off to operate, a creditor must prove a claim against the bankrupt estate. Set-off will generally not operate in respect of junior debt as the claim of the junior creditor, although provable in bankruptcy, would not be due until the claims of the senior creditors had been paid.

12.10   Turnover subordinations

An agreement to pay over proceeds received from the debtor would constitute a "transfer of an account" which would be subject to the Personal Property Security Act, 1989 (Ontario) and similar legislation in certain other provinces. Such a transfer would not be effective against a trustee in bankruptcy or assignee for the benefit of creditors of the junior creditor unless it had been perfected pursuant to the Act. The Act applies both to absolute assignments and to assignments as security.

Canada does not have any stamp duties or other documentary taxes on transfers of proceeds.

Secured subordinated debt 12.11

Creditors may take security over the same collateral and may agree amongst themselves as to their respective priorities. This applies to security in real property and in personal property. In respect of personal property, the Personal Property Security Act, 1989 (Ontario) provides that a secured party may subordinate its security interest to any other security interest and that such subordination is effective according to its terms.

It is clear that a junior secured creditor would have an independent right as a matter of law to compel a sale on a default, although any such realisation would be subject to the rights of the senior creditors. It would be prudent for this issue to be addressed in the intercreditor agreement.

There is no restriction against junior and senior creditors agreeing to appoint a representative or trustee to hold the security for the benefit of both the junior and senior creditors.

Taxation and subordinated debt 12.12

There are no special taxation rules which apply to subordinated debt as opposed to ordinary debt. Some taxation rules may, however, be particularly applicable to junior debt. The "thin capitalisation rules" limit the attractiveness of subordinated debt as an alternative to equity for certain foreign-owned Canadian resident corporations, as these rules limit the deductibility of interest payments on certain debt for Canadian income tax purposes. Further, where debt is sold at a substantial discount, which is more likely for junior than for ordinary debt, a portion of the proceeds may be deemed to be income for tax purposes.

Canada does not have issue taxes on issues of junior debt nor documentary taxes on transfers of such debt.

Capital adequacy and junior debt 12.13

Junior debt is permitted to constitute capital in calculating the capital requirements of financial institutions. Canada has adopted the Basle Agreement of 1988 in respect of Canadian banks, with effect from fiscal 1989. The Securities Act (Ontario) permits certain subordinated debt to be included in the capital adequacy calculations for dealers in securities and underwriters.

Compulsory subordinations on insolvency 12.14

Certain ordinary loans may be compulsorily subordinated to other creditors on a bankruptcy. Various preferred claims, such as limited claims for wages by employees of the bankrupt, limited claims by landlords and claims of the Crown, rank prior to the general body of creditors.

Further, the claims of a lender who received a rate of interest which varied with the profits or received a share of the profits of the business may be deferred until the claims of all other creditors have been paid in full. The United States doctrine of equitable subordination has not yet been adopted in Canada.

DENMARK

Contributed by: **Jens Zilstorff**
                 Plesner & Lunoe
                 Copenhagen

12.15 Introduction

Danish law is to a large extent silent on the subject of subordination of debt.

The legal situation, therefore, to a great extent depends on the specific circumstances present in a situation leading to a result of subordination of debt (*i.e* contract or promise from a junior creditor).

The main uses of subordination and the reasons therefor in Denmark do not differ from the situation in other countries, *e.g.* where a parent company subordinates debt owed to it by a subsidiary for capital requirement purposes, and where the debtor is in financial difficulties and the subordination is accepted in favour of the debtor's trade suppliers etc.

12.16 Contractual subordinations

Subordination of debt is an instrument which on the face of it is in opposition to the provisions in the Bankruptcy Act dealing with the *pari passu* payment of ordinary creditors of a debtor, whether corporate or private. After Articles providing for the payment of various preferential claims, Article 97 of the Danish Bankruptcy Act provides as follows:

> "Thereafter all other claims—except those covered by Section 98—are paid equally."

Although this is expressed to be mandatory, the better view is that the provision merely requires that no ordinary creditor is paid in priority to other (ordinary) creditors unless he has some special preference, *i.e.* a valid pledge or other valid security. Article 97 of the Danish Bankruptcy Act does not prevent a creditor from agreeing to be deferred to other creditors—either before or after the common debtor's bankruptcy—since an agreement to defer does not offend the fundamental policy of equality.

Contractual subordination may appear in two forms; either a subordination for the benefit of any and all of the other creditors of the common debtor or a subordination for the benefit of one particular or a specific group of creditors chosen by the junior creditor.

12.17 Contractual subordination for the benefit of all senior creditors

If a junior creditor for instance agrees with the senior creditor(s) and the common debtor that the junior creditor's debt will be subordinated on the insolvency of the common debtor, the basic principle is that the contract will be upheld by the Danish courts on the insolvency of the debtor. The junior creditor thus will only be paid after all other creditors of the common debtor, including the senior creditor, have been paid. The promise of subordination from the junior creditor is deemed "clean" and thus is given in favour of all other creditors, including the senior creditor, on equal terms.

If no senior creditor is party to the subordination contract and the junior creditor agrees solely with the debtor that the junior debt shall be subordinated to all other creditors, the junior creditor and the debtor could subsequently agree to cancel the subordination without the consent of the other (senior) creditors. This situation is often seen for instance in cases where a parent company subordinates a subsidiary's debt to other creditors for capital requirement purposes.

Although the general rule is that a non-published agreement between the junior creditor and the debtor may be cancelled without any consequences for the junior creditor, it may very often turn out that the junior creditor is bound by his promise of subordination. This for instance would be the case where the senior creditor by some means or another was made aware of the junior creditor's obligation of subordination and on the basis of the subordination—and to the knowledge of the junior creditor— enlarged his engagement and credit with the debtor in reliance on the subordination. Subordination by a parent company for capital requirement reasons will sometimes appear in the accounts of the subsidiary.

A subordination constituted solely by an agreement between the debtor and the junior creditor touches the principle in Danish law described as third party promises, and the solution of disputes will to a very large extent depend on the concrete situation from case to case.

> In the case of *Ingenir T. Dahl's Shipservice A/S in bankruptcy* v. *Eksport-kreditradet*, (*cf.* Ugeskrift for Retsvaesen 1964, p. 253), the Ministry of Commerce was to issue a guarantee for a loan advanced to the company by its bank. As a condition to the issue of the guarantee to the company's bank, the Ministry required that the company's subsidiaries in Sweden and Norway, having claims against the Danish company, subordinate their debts in favour of the Ministry's eventual claim arising out of the guarantee. The subsidiaries subordinated in favour of the Ministry, and the court held that the Ministry was entitled to claim dividends on the subsidiaries' claims against the Danish company, even though the subsidiaries at a later stage had subordinated their debts in favour of all other creditors of the Danish company. The contractual subordination in favour of the other creditors of the Danish company was regarded as null and void.

Contractual subordination for the benefit of specific senior creditors   **12.18**

Danish law also allows a contractual subordination under which a junior creditor is to be subordinated only to one particular creditor or a specific group of creditors instead of all other creditors of the debtor. Thus, it is possible under Danish law for an agreement to be entered into whereby a creditor prior to the debtor's bankruptcy "steps aside" with his claim in favour, for instance, of one senior creditor. According to Danish law, a subordination in favour of one creditor or a specific group of creditors is regarded as a transaction whereby the junior creditor assigns only his right to dividend until the senior creditor has been paid in full, and not as an assignment of his full claim. The validity of the agreement is not affected according to whether the debtor is a party or not. Subordination of this nature is often required by banks from a parent company before the bank, for instance, continues to lend money to the subsidiary. The particulars of an agreement of subordination in favour of a bank will often contain provisions by which the bank shall be entitled to register the junior creditor's debt in the bankruptcy estate and also by which the bank is authorised to exercise any and all of the junior creditor's rights, such as, for example, the right to vote for a trustee and to receive and acknowledge receipt of dividends until the bank has received full cover for its claims.

A leading case dealing with subordination is *Aktieselskabet Københavns Handelsbank* v. *Schou-Danlon A/S in liquidation* (Ugeskrift for Retsvaesen 1983, pp. 1141–1147). The dispute concerned the problem of whether a bank was entitled to receive a dividend from a company in liquidation (S) not only on the bank's own claim but also, by virtue of a declaration of subordination of June 30, 1960, on a recognised and approved claim belonging to another company (R). The companies R and S were both members of a group of companies which at the end of 1974 entered into liquidation. The document of subordination which undoubtedly existed in 1974 was originally issued for the purpose of securing a credit facility from the bank to S. The document, however, had no provisions with regard to the amount and reason for the debt. Although it was established that neither the bank nor the management of the group of companies in February, 1974—in connection with the granting of a further credit from the bank—were aware of the existence of the document of subordination from 1960, the court found that the document covered the whole of the credit which the bank had granted to S. Consequently, the bank enjoyed payment of the dividend payable on the claim belonging to R.

In the case of *Phoenix Materials Corporation* v. *The bankruptcy estate of Topsil af 1981 A/S* (Ugeskrift for Retsvaesen 1983, p. 1116), it was held that a declaration of subordination, although it was silent on the subject of voting rights, gave the senior creditor the right to vote on behalf of the junior debt for the election of a trustee.

The establishment of a subordination coming into effect subsequent to the debtor's bankruptcy may be achieved in two ways: either by the junior creditor granting the senior creditor security over the junior debt and its fruits, or by way of an agreement whereby the junior creditor transfers either his claim in full or only the expected proceeds, *i.e.* the dividend, to the senior creditor.

The first situation constitutes a pledge and the second situation a transfer of title to the junior creditor's claim either wholly or in part. Regardless of which of the two possible ways is chosen, the senior creditor will only be secured against the junior creditor's creditors if he has notified the common debtor, or rather the common debtor's bankruptcy estate, of the transfer of title or pledge. It should be noted that a junior creditor who transfers his full claim or only his right to the proceeds of the claim (either by way of transfer of title or by way of pledge) subsequent to the debtor's bankruptcy may experience difficulties in explaining the reason therefor. Even though formal notice has been given by the senior creditor to the debtor's bankruptcy estate as to his right to receive dividend etc., if the junior creditor becomes bankrupt, the senior creditor may find that the junior creditor's transfer is declared null and void by his bankruptcy estate.

It should also be noted that subordinated debt under Danish legislation will count in determining whether the debtor is insolvent, for instance for the purposes of a bankruptcy petition.

It is possible, however, under Danish law for a contractual subordination to prescribe that the payment of the junior debt is contingent or conditional upon the senior debt being paid in full. There are no specific provisions in the Danish Bankruptcy Act on this subject, but certainly it is for the junior creditor to agree whatever conditions he wishes to attach to his claim. If the junior debt is contingent upon the senior debt being paid in full, the effect will be that, if the common debtor is insolvent, the junior creditor would have no claim at all.

An agreement of subordination entered into prior to the debtor's bankruptcy does not attract Danish stamp duty. The opposite is the case if the subordination is established after the debtor's bankruptcy, for instance, by way of a transfer by the junior creditor of his right to dividend to the senior creditor or of the junior creditor's full claim. At this time it is an established fact that the claim (the proceeds of the junior debt) is transferred by way of subordination. Such a transfer will be liable to a stamp duty calculated as one per mille of the nominal amount transferred.

Set-off   **12.19**

Under Article 42 of the Danish Bankruptcy Act, a set-off of mutual debts is permitted under certain circumstances in the event of bankruptcy. In general, it is therefore possible for a creditor to set off his debt against the debtor's debt to the creditor if the claims are genuine and originate at a time prior to the debtor's bankruptcy or suspension of payments. It is, however, not mandatory for a creditor to claim that his own debt be set off, and thus a junior creditor may waive his right to set off. In the case of a contractual subordination, it is arguable that a junior creditor, although nothing has been promised in this respect at the time of subordination, by his acceptance of the subordination has waived his right to claim set-off in that the subordination would be defeated if the junior creditor were allowed to set off.

A subordination in favour of one or more but not all creditors of a debtor, whether in the form of an assignment or mortgage/pledge of the junior debt, transfer of proceeds etc. will normally lead to the result that the senior creditor(s) will only enjoy the same rights as the junior creditor would have had if he had not subordinated. This means that the senior creditor in this situation may be subject to objections by the bankruptcy estate, for example, as to the validity of the junior creditor's claim.

12.20   Secured senior and junior debt

Under Danish law it is possible for two creditors to have security over the same asset(s) and for the creditors amongst themselves to agree which of them should rank senior or junior. This goes for both tangible assets and for real property, aircraft, ships and negotiable instruments.

In general, any security by way of pledge should be registered with the relevant public authority. The registration for instance of mortgages over land should be notified to the local land registry, whereas mortgages over aircraft and ships should be registered with the relevant central registration bureau in Copenhagen. Security by way of pledge of public listed bonds and shares should be registered with Vaerdispapircentralen, an institution set up by law dealing with the registration of rights etc. to public listed bonds and shares. But for some negotiable instruments, such as private negotiable IOUs, the security is established by the physical handing over of the IOU to the creditor.

The registration systems for rights registrable with public authorities as described above prescribe an order of registration which is generally the date order in which the secured creditor has his right registered at the relevant registry.

The various registration systems, however, do not prevent the creditors from agreeing between themselves to rank their debts in whatever priority they wish. Their agreement to this effect, however, should be duly registered and if not, they would rank in the order of priority prescribed by the relevant registration law. This would be of particular interest to any third party, especially the creditors of one of the secured creditors involved.

Subject to observance of the relevant provisions concerning enforcement and realisation of the assets securing the creditor, a junior secured creditor has a right to compel a public sale of the assets concerned if there is default on the junior debt, even though the senior creditor objects. The settlement, however, of the proceeds from the realisation should be made with due respect to the ranking and, therefore, the senior creditor must be paid first. A junior creditor may, by way of an agreement with a senior creditor, agree to waive his right to exercise an enforced sale or only to claim enforced sale if the senior creditor is in agreement. However, if the junior creditor has become bankrupt, one cannot disregard the fact that Danish courts ultimately will permit an enforced sale even though the senior creditor does not give his consent since the junior creditor's bankruptcy estate has an independent interest in having the estate finally wound up.

It is possible under Danish law for creditors whose security is physically handed over to them by the debtor to appoint a representative to administer the secured assets during the duration of the security period.

The proceeds of an enforced sale will normally be distributed by the public authority, in general the bailiff taking care of the enforced sale, in accordance with the registered rank of each creditor's right.

Taxation   12.21

Under Danish taxation rules it is generally assumed that, from the debtor's point of view, subordinated debt should be treated in the same way as any other debt and thus the debtor has the ability to deduct interest on the debt in computing taxable profits. There are at present no withholding taxes on interest payments on loans.

Stamp duty on a loan contract, for instance with a bank, is payable at the rate of three per mille of the loan amount. A transfer of a loan, *i.e.* shift of creditor, is subject to a stamp duty of one per thousand whereas in general there is no stamp duty payable in cases of shift of debtor.

Capital adequacy   12.22

In respect of banks, special provisions are found in the Danish Legislation Regulating Banks and Savings Banks. In accordance with this piece of legislation, banks may receive subordinated capital if this is permitted by the banks' bylaws and if the bank has the right to give notice of termination, *i.e.* repay the received funds. In the event of liquidation such contributed capital must be used first to settle normal creditors and thereafter the depositors. Subordinated debt complying with these rules is treated as capital for the purpose of the minimum solvency or capital adequacy standards flowing from the requirements in the Danish Law on Banking which require that the equity of a bank must amount to at least 8 per cent. of the bank's overall debt and commitments.

Special and very detailed rules are in force concerning insurance companies.

On January 17, 1990 the Minister of Industry proposed a bill in the Danish Parliament as an amendment of the Law on Banking whereby, amongst other things, it was proposed to incorporate into Danish law the EEC Directive of April 17, 1989 on the equity of credit institutions (89/299). At the time of writing it is expected that this Act will be adopted by the Danish Parliament during 1990 and come into force as of January 1, 1991.

Compulsory subordinations on insolvency   12.23

The question of compulsory subordination in Danish law has to a great extent surfaced in situations where a loan agreement is established for the purpose of injecting money into the debtor's enterprise on terms whereby the creditor may participate in the enterprise's profits in various ways but in a manner whereby no publication as to the injection of money is made. In legal theory, the question is referred to as the problem concerning "quiet companies."

Based upon Danish legal theory and case law, the main rule is that a person injecting money into an enterprise without publication thereof and enjoying a right to profits in various forms or perhaps even a kind of ownership will be regarded as a creditor on equal terms with other creditors of the debtor. In earlier case law, Danish courts established that, even although profits were to be paid instead of or on top of interest payments on the borrowed amount, this did not have any influence on the fact that a loan agreement was established. The fact that the lender has control or influence on the management of the company has also not prevented the same result. However, in a relatively recent judgment of the High Court, referred to in Ugeskrift for Retsvaesen 1978, p. 205, the court decided that the lender should not be treated as creditor and thus was in fact subordinated on the debtor's bankruptcy. Typically a compulsory subordination will lead to the result that the claim should be settled after settlement of the ordinary creditors but before share capital.

FINLAND

Contributed by: **Lauri Peltola,**
Procope & Hornborg
Helsinki and London

12.24   Introduction

Subordination is a concept which is not known in the Finnish Companies Act. However, the Finnish Commercial Banking Act does include a section on requirements under which subordinated debentures may be issued by a commercial bank in order to qualify as the bank's equity.

In spite of the legal "non-existence" of subordination the concept is relatively commonly used in Finland. However, one is not aware of any judgments on subordination and therefore the validity and construction of the subordinations created in Finland have not been tested in the courts. For the above reasons any comments made below on subordination are made under certain reservations.

12.25   Contractual subordination

It seems that subordination in Finland has been used almost exclusively for the purpose of avoiding a limited company being wound-up owing to the mandatory rules of limited companies being obliged to maintain the shareholders' equity at a minimum level, in principle, one-third of the paid-up share capital. Accordingly, subordination has been used mainly between group companies and in the relationship between shareholder/ creditor and the debtor company.

It has been accepted by the Finnish audit profession that a subordinated debt of a junior creditor may be taken into account as part of shareholders' equity in assessing whether or not the mandatory winding-up ratio has been exceeded. However, for accounting purposes a subordinated debt nevertheless remains a debt.

As regards personal liability and questions as to fraudulent trading, it is believed that a properly subordinated debt arrangement should be sufficient to avoid adverse consequences. However, one is unable to refer to any court cases to support this opinion.

Finnish law contains detailed provisions regarding the priority between various creditors of a bankrupt limited company, such as liquidation costs, claims based on employment, taxes, secured creditors, trade receivables, etc.

Obviously, any agreement to obtain better priority to the detriment of other similarly (or better) ranked creditors would be void unless the preferred status has been created prior to the bankruptcy strictly in accordance with the requirements of the law such as the creation of a floating charge. However, it seems that an agreement to the contrary effect, *i.e.* an agreement whereby the priority will become inferior should not be considered void. Problems may perhaps arise in the event that the junior creditor whose receivable has been subordinated itself goes into liquidation. It has not been tested in the courts whether the liquidators of the junior creditor would be able to challenge the validity of the subordination agreement, or perhaps, nevertheless to use the subordinated debt for set-off which in normal cases is allowed under Finnish law on liquidation. In particular, if a subordination is made within the six month "critical period" before the bankruptcy of the junior creditor, the arrangement may well be declared void in certain circumstances.

On the one hand the right of set-off is relatively wide under Finnish law, but on the other hand a right to set off against a subordinated debt would in the event of liquidation of the debtor be very much in contradiction to the underlying idea of subordination. Therefore, it seems that the right to set-off should not apply, in particular, if an express prohibition to this effect has been incorporated in the subordination agreement.

Turnover subordinations   **12.26**

An arrangement whereby a junior creditor assigns the dividends to be paid by the trustees of a bankrupt company in respect of the junior debt to the senior creditor until the senior debt is paid seems to be unknown in Finland. But this is not to say that it would be void under Finnish law.

A turnover subordination agreement would normally be binding on the junior creditor and the senior creditor. If the debtor, *i.e.* the trustees of the liquidated company, are not notified of the turnover subordination agreement, any dividend will be paid to the junior creditor and will in the event of the liquidation of the junior creditor be part of the assets of the junior creditor. To eliminate this risk, the trustees should be properly notified of the agreement between junior creditor and senior creditor.

On the other hand such an agreement which has been notified to the trustees is probably very close to an assignment of the underlying junior debt since any dividend paid by the trustees essentially is (partial) payment of the junior debt. It is also questionable whether the trustees would in practice accept instructions from the junior creditor and senior creditor to pay dividends "to the senior creditor until the senior debt is paid." Such instructions might easily lead to claims against the trustees for paying a dividend to the wrong creditor. Therefore it is probable that in practice the trustees would insist that the instructions should apply either to the entire junior debt or to a fixed part thereof. Thus, the difference between a turnover subordination and an assignment of the junior debt may be very nominal indeed.

A turnover subordination is purely a contractual arrangement which cannot be registered to obtain any preferred status of security.

12.27   Secured subordinated debt

In accordance with the leading principle of "freedom of contract," it is possible for secured creditors to agree between themselves to rank senior and junior. Under the Finnish system, negotiable registered bonds issued by the debtor company are used for secured loans. An intercreditor agreement regarding the internal ranking of the secured creditors is valid only between the contractual parties. Accordingly, if a registered bond subject to such an agreement is transferred to a bona fide third party creditor the intercreditor agreement would not be binding on the transferee creditor. For the above reason it is recommended that any agreement regarding changes in ranking of security should be properly recorded in the registry of charges maintained by the authorities.

Despite any agreement to the contrary, a junior creditor will always have an independent right to compel a sale on a default and thus to force the senior creditor into a realisation. Should the junior creditor in doing so be in breach of the agreement between the junior creditor and the senior creditor, the senior creditor may be entitled to damages for the breach of the agreement.

If a junior or senior creditor compels a sale of the debtor's assets, the realisation of the assets must be carried out by public authorities, or, in the event of the liquidation of the debtor, by the trustees. In both cases the assets concerned must be held for the benefit of both senior and junior creditor (and other creditors) and the proceeds distributed in the priority order as set out by law.

12.28   Taxation

From a tax point of view a subordinated debt should not attract a tax treatment different from ordinary borrowings.

No Finnish stamp duties apply to subordination arrangements.

12.29   Compulsory subordination

Under Finnish law subordination cannot be compulsory but must always be based on an agreement between the junior and senior creditor.

FRANCE

Contributed by: **Jacques Terray/**
Sophie Boyer Chammard
Gide Loyrette Nouel,
26 Cours Albert 1er
75008 Paris

French law on subordination of debts is reasonably developed. Specific **12.30**
laws legitimizing subordination have been enacted. At the same time a
corpus of literature has grown up forming an important body of doctrine.
In France, doctrine traditionally enjoys persuasive authority.

Statutory subordinations

France is one of the few countries which has expressly regulated the
rules applicable to subordinated debt by statute. Three laws have recognised subordination and given it validity.

Prêts participatifs. The Act no. 78–741 of July 13, 1978 on the *prêts* **12.31**
participatifs was the first statute to give legal status to subordination.

Although the term of "*participatifs*" seems to imply a right to a share of
profits, the "*prêts participatifs*" need not carry such a right and are first
and foremost a subordinated loan.

The object of the Act was to improve the level of equity of companies.
However, the loan is not counted as equity for legal purposes, such as
insolvency tests, etc, but rather as debt (see below) and accordingly the
prêts participatifs may truly be regarded as subordinated debt.

Articles 26 and 27 of the 1978 Act deal with the order in which debts
should be paid on insolvency.

Article 26 sets out the definition of a *prêt participatif* as a claim which
will only be paid on liquidation of the company after payment in full of all
other creditors.

Article 27 provides that the payments in respect of the *prêts participatifs* follow the general rules in the event of bankruptcy proceedings.

In fact the Bankruptcy Act 1985 provides for a compulsory period
during which the company is encouraged to recover; in particular all
payments of interest in respect of any debt contracted by the company are
frozen. This period starts when the company is declared insolvent and
lasts until the continuation or liquidation of the company is decided.

Prêts participatifs constitute a general subordination insofar as junior
creditors rank after all other creditors. Moreover, they are loans, and as
such, they cannot be assigned as easily as securities would be.

In addition, this method of raising capital has been criticised on the
ground that the *prêts participatifs* can be redeemed and are therefore not
as good as equity capital. They merely cheapen the cost of capital without
achieving the benefit to creditors of equity which is fully locked-in. As a
result, the use of *prêts participatifs* has declined.

Titres participatifs. Another method of creating subordinated debt was **12.32**

introduced by the Act no 83–1 of January 3, 1983, included in the Companies Act of 1966. Again the policy of the Government was to permit a strengthening of the capital base of companies. The Act creates participating securities, (*titres participatifs*), the issue of which is reserved to government-owned companies or cooperative companies. The *titres participatifs* were a way to introduce in government-owned companies, securities having the same money rights as shares for their holders, without diluting the capital.

Article 283–6 of the 1966 Companies Act provides that these securities can be paid only at the expiration of the life of the company or at least not before seven years. The securities rank after the *prêts participatifs* and their holders are remunerated according to the results of the company.

12.33   **Subordinated bonds.** The last and most important Act which sanctions subordinated debt is the Act no. 85–1321 of December 14, 1985 adding a new article 339–7 to the Companies Act of 1966 and allowing various composite bonds to be issued.

Article 339–7 states:

> "In the issue of securities representing debts of the issuer company [. . .], it can be provided that these securities will be redeemed only after payment of all other creditors, although before creditors of *prêts* or *titres participatifs*".

Subordinated bonds present an advantage when compared with *prêts participatifs*: as securities, they can easily be transferred.

Accordingly creditors will rank as follows on the liquidation of the company:

— secured creditors
— all ordinary creditors
— subordinated bond-holders (article 339–7, 1.66)
— lenders under *prêts participatifs* (article 26, 1.78)
— lenders under *titres participatifs* (article 283–6, 1.66).

The Acts therefore established a ladder of three classes of junior creditors ranking after all other creditors.

However as we have seen, the Acts have a limited scope and do not provide for all possible applications in the field of subordination.

For instance, by providing a set order of ranking between the different forms of subordination, the Acts may – or may not – exclude a different order set up by the parties.

Therefore doctrine came to consider non-statutory subordination in order to widen the scope of statutory subordination.

12.34   **Alternatives to statutory subordination**

There is a long standing debate on whether subordination, other than statutory subordination, is valid under French law.

The problem is of importance since, as we have seen, statutory subordination does not allow a wide range of applications. The debate arose however because the Civil Code sets up a public policy rule: Article 2092 and 2093 of the French Civil Code provide that all ordinary creditors have a right against all present or future assets of the debtor and that they must be paid *pari passu* out of the debtor's assets.

Moreover the Bankruptcy Act of January 25, 1985 affirms this principle of equality in article 166–1:

"The amount of the assets [which is left after payment of costs and privileged creditors] is divided up *pari passu* between all ordinary creditors".

If this principle is applied literally, a non-statutory subordination is not valid in the absence of an express statutory provision. However most authors seem to agree on its validity (H. Le Roy "Les clauses de préférence et de subordination en droit français des emprunts", RDAI no. 7, 1986, p. 725; Vasseur: Cours de Droit).

In fact the equality principle is set up in order to protect ordinary creditors. One unsecured creditor is impeded from seeking to place himself in an advantageous position to the detriment of other ordinary creditors and from being paid in priority to other creditors. But it does not prevent a creditor from agreeing to be deferred to other creditors without causing any damage or loss to them and from giving up the benefit of the public policy rule of protection.

Moreover, as the law does not expressly prevent parties to a contract from altering their order of payment, the principle of freedom of contract should allow subordination.

In the end, the right to be paid *pari passu* with all unsecured creditors is akin to an ownership right. The creditor may use it and abuse it, or assign it. Nothing prevents an owner from giving up or postponing his right to be paid (I. Urbain-Parléani, thèse, "les comptes courants d'associés", LGDJ 1986); (Vasseur).

This conclusion is confirmed by case law on the renunciation of the right to equal treatment. For example, in a 1931 case (June 25, 1931, Rec. Douai, 1931, 276) a guarantor gave up his right to claim against the debtor, for the benefit of a bank. The clause was held to be valid.

To conclude, case law and doctrine tend to admit non-statutory subordination although they contemplate different civil law principles to justify it. We will now describe the various grounds that have been found by legal writers to support the lawfulness of subordination in the absence of a statutory provision.

Security. One possible method of achieving subordination to one creditor but equality with the others would be to grant security over the junior debt in favour of the senior creditor to secure the senior debt. But this security might conflict with any negative pledges binding on the junior creditor. Also, it would fail on the insolvency of the junior creditor, unless the formalities of article 2075 of the Civil Code are complied with: the security must be duly notified to be the debtor by a *huissier* (bailiff), or accepted by the debtor in formal manner.

Cession d'antériorité. Subordination has sometimes been treated as a   **12.35**
contract of assignment of priority or anteriority (*cession de priorité*, or *cession d'antériorité*).

This is a contract between the junior creditor and the senior creditor by which the former assigns his right of priority to the latter.

It is primarily a method of altering priorities between secured creditors. In fact, doctrine developed this method by refering to article 2134 of the Civil Code on mortgages, (L. Cioni, Petites Affiches, March 16, 1981, no. 32 p. 6). It is questionable whether this procedure can apply to unsecured debts as opposed to secured debts.

Stipulation pour autrui. This is a contract between a settlor (the debtor) and a promisor (the junior creditor) whereby the settlor requires the promisor, as part of his consideration, to act for the benefit of a third party (beneficiary). In the case of junior debt, the promisor would agree to be paid after the senior creditors are fully paid and to transfer recoveries to the senior creditor.

This technique is much used in France as it is simple and capable of adaptation to different situations. It is precisely this civil law principle which is used for assigning the benefit of insurance. It is often suitable in cases where a trust under English law would be used. A stipulation seems therefore the appropriate equivalent to the common law trust of proceeds.

Generally, no formalities are required to perfect the transfer of proceeds, other than in special cases arising under the ordinary law. For example, the contract of stipulation may be subject to the agreement of the board of directors where the junior creditor is a partner or a director of the company (pursuant to article 101 of the Companies Act 1966).

Cession d'antériorité and stipulation have been largely discussed by the doctrine. However, they both present disadvantages and the recent researches of the doctrine have turned to the contingent debt release.

12.36   **Contingent debt release.** This is a contract between the junior creditor and the debtor providing that the junior creditor gives up his claim if, but only if, the senior creditors cannot be paid. Therefore the junior creditor's payment is contingent on the senior debt being paid in full.

The contingent debt release is a simple combination of two principles of the Civil Code. Article 1282 allows a creditor to give up his right of payment; and pursuant to article 1168 an obligation can be conditional on an event occurring. In our case, the event is the payment of the senior creditors.

As soon as senior creditors are paid, the condition occurs and the junior creditor recovers his claim.

The junior debt is undetermined until the senior creditors are paid. But the junior creditor can still declare his debt to the receiver (in England, prove his debt) pursuant to the Bankruptcy Act of January 25, 1985. The junior debt will be taken into account in the same way as any other debt.

This seems to be the most suitable justification to subordination. In fact, it can be applied on insolvency as well as during the life of the company. Moreover it is binding on and enforceable against everybody. In addition, it does not infringe the principle of equality since a creditor can use or not use his ownership right as he wishes.

Contractual or turnover subordination. It must here be emphasized that the problem of contractual or turnover subordination does not arise under French law in the same terms as under English law.

Under French law, a junior creditor can enter a contract with one senior creditor only, whereby the junior debt is subordinated to the senior debt; this is valid and binding under French law, as long as it does not affect the equality between other unsecured creditors.

For instance, if an insolvent debtor whose assets are 100 has a junior debt of 50, a senior debt of 50 and a trade debt of 50 (total 150), the three creditors should receive, according to the *pari passu* rule and without the subordination, 33 each.

Under French law, the contract of subordination between the junior creditor and the senior creditor does not affect the situation of the trade creditor, who will receive 33. But the junior creditor will pay 17 to the senior creditor so that the senior creditor receives his 50 in full. The result therefore is that the senior creditor is paid before the junior creditor (who retains 16); the trade creditor does not benefit from and is not affected by the subordination. And subordination to one creditor only does not automatically create subordination to all other creditors as is the case under English contractual subordination.

Moreover, the practical consequences are the same in all cases; whether the justification is a *stipulation pour autrui* or a contingent debt release, there are no particular formalities to comply with. For instance, the formalities of article 1690 applicable to the transfer of debts do not apply to subordination since there is no transfer of the debt itself under French Law, but simply a change in the order of payment.

Therefore, subordination under French law does not create any technical difficulty and the legal techniques allowing subordination are the same whether a debt is subordinated to one creditor only or to all other creditors.

One distinction may be made however between statutory and non-statutory subordination; in fact, Parliament only considered subordination to all other creditors. But non-statutory justifications to subordination allow either general subordination to all other creditors or subordination to one senior creditor only.

Set-off 12.37

A problem could arise when a junior creditor owes a debt to the debtor: can he set off this debt against the subordinated debt?

If this were possible, set-off would have the same result as if the junior creditor was being paid first, before all other creditors, and therefore set-off would defeat subordination.

The French Bankruptcy Act excludes set-off on insolvency, and thus it should not create a problem when subordinated debts are concerned.

This is however subject to exceptions permitted by case law in relation to bank current accounts and cross claims arising out of the same transactions or connected transactions. These exceptions have become numerous and case law now interprets very widely the criterion of "connected transactions".

Set-off however is not mandatory and could be waived by the junior creditor. If it is not waived the difficulty could be avoided by providing that on insolvency of the common debtor the junior debt is contingent upon the senior debt being paid in full (see earlier). Until then, the junior creditor will have no certain claim and hence nothing to set off.

12.38   Insolvency tests

An important question is the status of the junior debt in determining whether the debtor is insolvent for the purpose of bankruptcy proceedings. Because of its hybrid status the junior debt – when it is subordinated to all other debts – could be considered either as part of the equity of the company or as a normal debt.

The 1978 law on *prêts participatifs* is unclear as it states that "to appreciate the financial situation of companies [they] are considered as equity".

It is generally accepted however that this is a financial and economic criterion, so as to improve the credit of companies. The legal approach is different: the *prêts participatifs* are subordinated debt and must be treated as debt, not as equity.

This is subject to the principles of the Basle Agreement applicable to banks; see below.

In fact, when checking the criteria which should alert the directors of a company as to its insolvency, for instance when determining whether the assets of a company have become less than half of its equity, subordinated debt is considered as debt.

This was held in an *obiter dictum* in a recent case of the Court of Appeal, Paris, July 8, 1987, which interpreted article 26 and 27 of the Act of 1978 (*op. cit.*). A company issued a *prêt participatif* and then became bankrupt. The court, discussing a point of procedure, held that "although article 26 of the Act considers the *prêt participatif* as equity during the life of the company when solvent, article 27 states however that junior lenders must be paid on liquidation after all other creditors". The result is that junior lenders are creditors for procedural purposes (and not shareholders).

However as far as banks are concerned, France has adopted the principles set out in the Basle Agreement on Convergence of Capital of July, 1988. This provides for subordinated debt of banks to be treated as supplementary capital for capital adequacy purposes, subject to various limits. Details of the Basle Agreement are given elsewhere in this work.

12.39   Procedure

Since subordinated debt is debt, subject to the exceptions mentioned above, the junior creditors are considered as normal creditors and hence they must follow the normal procedure necessary to enforce their right.

Accordingly, as soon as the bankruptcy proceedings have started, the junior creditor must declare his debt and his rank. This is the equivalent of the English proof of insolvency.

This was held in the case quoted above, Court of Appeal, Paris July 8, 1987:

On liquidation, junior lenders are to be paid "after all other creditors [but are not shareholders]. The result is that the junior lender is a genuine creditor as regards the bankruptcy proceedings and that his debt being borne before the declaration of insolvency, the junior creditor must [comply with the procedure]".

In other words, the creditor must prove his debt, and the receiver must consider the junior debt as a normal debt and verify it. The only difference with other debts is that the junior debt will be paid after other debts.

Subordination of secured creditors   12.40

The junior and senior creditors may be secured creditors. As far as real property is concerned, there is no objection under French law to two creditors being secured on the same property and for one of the secured creditors to accept to be paid after the other.

Practically, nothing prohibits the parties from agreeing between themselves a particular order of priority.

As between the two creditors, it does not matter that the registration systems, as far as mortgages over land are concerned, prescribe an order of registration and of priority depending on the date of registration. The parties themselves can agree to be bound by a different order of priority, although they will rank in the prescribed order as regards third parties.

The rights of enforcement of the junior secured creditor will not be modified although the debt is subordinated. A junior secured creditor has the right to compel the public sale of the assets concerned if there is a default on the junior debt, even though the senior creditor objects. However, the senior creditor must be paid first out of the proceeds of sale.

It is considered that an agreement between the senior and the junior creditor whereby the junior creditor agrees not to exercise his right of sale without the consent of the senior creditor, would be valid.

Taxation   12.41

The principle that subordinated debt is debt is to be applied to taxation. There are no special rules on taxation in that field.

However the same line must be drawn as in other fields: as soon as the remuneration of the debt is not merely interest but is a dividend or a share of profits, the company would lose the tax advantages allowing it to deduct payment of interest.

GERMANY (FDR)

Contributed by: **Dr. Wolf-Dietrich Krause-Ablass**
Bruckhaus Kreifels Winkhaus & Lieberknecht
Dusseldorf-Brussels

12.42 Contractual subordinations

In the Federal Republic of Germany contractual subordination is primarily used as a vehicle to avoid the bankruptcy of a corporation if the corporation's liabilities are in excess of its assets: see below. Apart from this, other forms of contractual subordination are possible, although they seem to be of less practical importance, such as subordination agreements among two or more creditors and the subordination of preferred bankruptcy claims, both of which are discussed below.

Subordinations to avoid bankruptcy. Pursuant to section 64 of the German GmbH Law the management of a company with limited liability (GmbH) is obliged to apply for bankruptcy if the company is insolvent or if its liabilities are in excess of its assets ("overindebtedness"). In order to avoid an application for bankruptcy caused through overindebtedness, a creditor (usually the debtor corporation's parent company or a bank acting with the support of the parent company) and the debtor corporation may agree upon a subordination of debt on the following lines:

> "The subordinated creditor's claim shall be subordinated behind the claims of all other creditors, and payments upon the subordinated creditor's claims shall be made only out of profits shown in the company's balance sheets or out of a liquidation surplus."

An alternative form of clause is as follows:

> "The subordinated creditor undertakes not to enforce his claim to the extent and as long as this is necessary in order to avoid any overindebtedness of the corporation."

Subordination clauses of the above type have been recognised by court decisions and in the legal literature as being legally valid under civil law and bankruptcy law: BGH, judgment of February 9, 1987, Betriebsberater 1987, 728; Scholz, *GmbH-Gesetz*, 7th ed. note 52 ad s.84.

If, in spite of subordination, the debtor corporation becomes bankrupt, the subordinated creditor has no claim against the bankrupt estate, as he has waived his claim by virtue of the subordination: Scholz/Lwowski, *Das Recht der Kreditsicherung*, 6th ed. 591.

In this connection, the question of the effect on the subordination of a declaration of a set-off may arise. Pursuant to section 53 of the German Bankruptcy Code (*Konkursordnung/ KO*) a claim which can be satisfied by way of set-off against a debt owing to the bankrupt estate is not affected by bankruptcy proceedings. The right of set-off may be exercised even with respect to future and conditional claims: section 54 KO.

However, if the subordinated creditor by virtue of the subordination agreement has waived his claims in the event of bankruptcy, the subordinated creditor would not be allowed to exercise a right of set-off under sections 53 *et seq.* KO. Accordingly, the subordination is not invalidated by the set-off provisions in sections 53 *et seq.* KO.

Subordination agreements between creditors. A subordination can be agreed among two or more creditors whereby a creditor (junior creditor) subordinates his claim to the claim of another creditor (senior creditor). For this purpose the junior creditor may commit not to collect his claim until the senior creditor's claim is fully satisfied: Scholz/Lwowski, *op. cit.* 591. However, this would lead to the result that not only the senior creditor but also other creditors who are not a party to the subordination agreement enjoy the benefits arising from the non-collectability of the junior creditor's claim.

This subordination to all creditors can be avoided if the junior and senior creditors agree that the junior creditor will act like any other creditor in relation to the debtor by collecting his claim against the debtor without any restriction but on terms that any payment received must be transferred by the junior creditor to the senior creditor until the senior creditor's claim has been fully paid: Scholz/Lwowski, *op. cit.*

In the event of the bankruptcy of the debtor company, the junior creditor under a turnover subordination would have the same status as the senior creditor *vis-à-vis* the bankrupt estate. Accordingly, he is entitled to receive payments from the bankrupt estate which subsequently must be transferred by him to the senior creditor, until the senior creditor's claim is satisfied. If the junior creditor has a right of set-off pursuant to sections 53 *et seq.* KO, this would not be affected by the internal subordination agreement. Accordingly, the junior creditor could recover his debt by declaring a set-off, but any amount recovered by the set-off would have to be transferred to the senior creditor.

Subordination of preferred bankruptcy claims. The German Bankruptcy Code (KO) contains a list of preferred claims against the estate (sections 57–60 KO) and a catalogue for the ranking of creditors in bankruptcy (section 61 KO). It is recognised that the ranking may be changed by way of agreement with the receiver (Konkursverwalter): Kilger, Konkursordnung, 15th ed, note 1 at para. 60. For example, a creditor having a preferred claim against the estate may waive his rank in order to permit bankruptcy proceedings to be instituted: this would not be allowed by the court, unless the funds of the estate are sufficient to allow the relevant claims to be satisfied. An agreement of this type by which employees of the bankrupt company accepted a lower ranking of their salary claims was confirmed by the Bremen Labour Court in a judgment of September 6, 1983. ZIP 1983. 1360–ZIP 1984. 623.

Subordination of security 12.43

Priorities. Often, two or more creditors may be secured on one and the same asset, by way of mortgages on real property, aircraft or ships, pledge of goods etc. Usually, the ranking of security is determined by the order in time in which the security has been registered or granted. For example, section 879 of the Civil Code (BGB) with respect to mortgages or other rights concerning real estate provides:

> "The ranking among several rights with which real estate has been encumbered is to be determined, if such rights are registered in the same section of the land register, by the sequence of the entries. If the rights are registered in different sections, the right registered at an earlier date shall have prior ranking; rights registered on the same day shall have equal rank."

In general, such ranking can be changed by agreement. For instance, with respect to mortgages or other rights on real estate, the ranking may be changed pursuant to section 880 BGB as follows:

> "The modification of ranking requires the agreement of the subordinated and the promoted right-holder and the registration of such modification in the land register.... If a mortgage, land charge or annuity charge is to be ranked down, the consent of the landowner is also required...."

Similar rules apply with respect to mortgages on ships (section 26 of the Law concerning Rights on Ships) and mortgages on aircraft (section 26 of the Law concerning Rights on Aircraft).

In the case of a pledge of moveable goods, the situation is somewhat different. According to the prevailing opinion of legal commentators, a change of rank of a pledge cannot be agreed with effect *in rem* but only with internal effect among the holders of the pledge agreeing to the change: Staudinger, BGB, 12th ed, note 9 at para. 1209.

Under German law there are other securities which usually are owned by one creditor only. This applies to security ownership of moveable assets ("Sicherungseigentum"). Once a security ownership has been granted to a creditor, it is not possible for another creditor to obtain a security ownership interest in the asset, except with the approval of the senior holder of the security. If, however, the senior holder of the security agrees and if the consent of the person providing the security to the senior holder is obtained, it is possible to create joint security ownership in favour of the senior and junior creditor. Both of them could establish, by way of internal agreement, their priority with respect to the distribution of proceeds from the sale or any other enforcement of the security over the asset concerned.

Enforcement rights. In general, each (senior or junior) creditor holding a security right in one and the same asset may enforce his right by way of public sale or otherwise in accordance with the applicable legal provision governing the security, if the secured claim of the relevant creditor has become overdue and/or if the other legal conditions required for the enforcement are fulfilled by the relevant creditor. However, the proceeds of the enforcement must be distributed among the various creditors according to their rank so that the senior creditor must be paid out of the proceeds first. It is, however, possible for the senior and junior creditors to conclude an agreement that both parties (or the junior creditor) will not start enforcement without the consent of the other party. Other conditions and regulations concerning enforcement of the security may be agreed as well. Of course, the effects of the agreement would be limited to the creditors who are a party to the agreement. An example of this type of agreement are pool agreements among banks or other security-holders pooling their security rights against a certain debtor.

Subordination of participation rights ("Genussrechte")   **12.44**

Profit-sharing rights may be given to a creditor of a company in the form of so-called "Genussrechte" (participation rights). As there is no uniform definition of these participation rights, the company and the relevant creditor are free to agree on various terms of profit-sharing or other participation rights. Accordingly, "Genussrechte" are rather flexible instruments enabling the company to raise funds without granting membership rights, voting rights etc. "Genussrechte" may be issued as subordinated debt having a similar function to equity capital. If the issuing company is a bank, the "Genussrechte" will be treated as liable capital under the German Banking Act (Kreditwesengesetz/KWG), if it meets the conditions provided by section 10 subsection (5) KWG as follows:

> "1. if it participates fully in any loss;
> 2. if it can be reclaimed only after the bank's creditors have been satisfied;
> 3. if it has been placed at the bank's disposal for a term of at least five years;
> 4. as long as the claim to repayment does not, or according to the contract cannot, become due in less than two years;
> 5. if, on conclusion of the contract, the bank pointed out expressly and in writing the legal consequences stated in sentences 2 and 3; and
> 6. in so far as the profit-sharing capital does not exceed twenty-five per cent of the liable capital as defined in sub-section (2) and (3) without an additional amount pursuant to sub-section (2) sentence 1 No. 3; the Federal Supervisory Office may allow exceptions if the participation right capital is paid to cover losses of liable capital.
> Participation in a loss may not be subsequently changed, nor may the subordinated ranking be restricted or the term or period of notice shortened. A premature repayment shall be returned to the bank without regard to any agreements to the contrary. If securities are issued with respect to participation rights, the legal consequences specified in sentences 2 and 3 shall be pointed out in the conditions of subscription and issue. A bank may acquire its own participation rights documented in security form only, if it acquires them in connection with a purchase commission."

Furthermore, pursuant to section 8(3) of the German Income Tax Law distributions of any kind on participation rights are tax deductible expenses, if the participation right does not grant a share in liquidation proceeds. The German Tax Administration has, however, tried to limit the tax deductibility by a restrictive interpretation of this provision: Pougin, *Genussrechte*, 1987, p. 12.

Compulsory subordinations   **12.45**

If a shareholder of a company with limited liability (GmbH) grants a loan to the GmbH, then, in the event of the bankruptcy of the GmbH or court composition settlement proceedings, the claim for repayment of the loan is excluded pursuant to section 32a of the German GmbH Law:

> "(1) If at a time when shareholders acting as prudent businessmen would have granted equity capital to the company, a shareholder instead gives a loan to the company, he cannot claim repayment of the loan in bankruptcy proceedings or in court composition settlement proceedings. . .
> (2) If at a time when shareholders acting as prudent businessmen would have granted equity capital to the company, a third party instead grants a loan to the company and if a shareholder has provided security for or guaranteed repayment of the loan, the third party in bankruptcy or court composition settlement proceedings can only claim a *pro rata* satisfaction of his loan to the extent that he has not been satisfied after enforcement of the security or guarantee.
> (3) These provisions apply correspondingly to other legal acts of the shareholder or a third party which economically correspond to the granting of a loan pursuant to sub-section (1) and (2)."

Furthermore, section 32b of the GmbH law provides:

> "If the company in the case provided for in Section 32a sub-sections (2) and (3) repaid the loan during the year prior to commencement of bankruptcy, the shareholder providing the security or acting as guarantor must refund to the company the amount so repaid. This liability exists only up to the amount of the shareholder's guarantee or to the value of the security furnished when the loan was repaid. The shareholder is free from such obligation if the assets used as security of the creditor are placed at the company's disposal for satisfaction. These provisions apply correspondingly to other legal acts which economically correspond to the granting of a loan."

Section 32a and 32b of the GmbH Law also apply to a commercial law partnership if none of the general partners is a natural person, namely in the case of a GmbH & Co. KG (sections 129a and 172a of the Commercial Code/HGB). Securities granted for debts covered by sections 32a and 32b of the GmbH Law can be rescinded by the receiver in bankruptcy. The same applies in the event of satisfaction of the debt during a period of one year prior to commencement of bankruptcy proceedings: section 32a KO.

The German courts have decided that, even without bankruptcy or court composition settlement proceedings, a shareholder's loan substituting equity (as defined by the above statutory provisions) must not be repaid by the GmbH if and to the extent that by repayment of the loan the company's net assets would be reduced below the amount of its registered share capital: BGH, Judgment of March 26, 1984, BGHZ 90, 370. The same principles are to be applied with respect to loans substituting equity capital of the stockholder of a stock corporation (Aktiengesellschaft) holding an "entrepreneurial" participation, which generally is the case if he owns more than 25 per cent. of the corporation's stock capital: BGH, judgment of March 26, 1984. BGHZ 90, 381.

12.46   Tax issues

Apart from the tax issue mentioned above with respect to participation rights, another tax issue has been discussed recently, but not finally answered by the Federal Supreme Tax Court (Bundesfinanzhof) with respect to a contractual subordination in order to avoid bankruptcy. The question is whether taxwise such subordination must be treated as a profit caused by cancellation of debt. In its decision of October 18, 1989 (IV B 149/88, Betriebsberater 1989, 2444), involving preliminary proceedings, the court did not finally decide the issue. However, the Supreme Tax Court raised serious doubts as to whether a subordination agreement under which payments upon the subordinated claim were to be made only out of profits shown in the balance sheet or out of a liquidation surplus would create a profit caused through cancellation of the debt.

Basle Agreement on Convergence of Capital of July 1988   **12.47**

In the Federal Republic of Germany the Basle Agreement on Convergence of Capital has been implemented on a voluntary basis by way of gentleman's agreements between the Federal Banking Supervisory Office and banks operating internationally. Under the gentleman's agreement the bank concerned undertakes to maintain a capital ratio of not less than 6.5 per cent. from the date of signing the agreement until the end of 1990, of 7.25 per cent. from January 1, 1991, until the end of 1992, and of 8 per cent. as from January 1, 1993. Compliance with these requirements must be reported by the bank to the Federal Banking Supervisory Office on a regular basis, and the correctness of the report is to be checked and confirmed by the bank's auditors in connection with their audit of the bank's annual statements: see the Letter of the Federal Banking Supervisory Office of January 5, 1989—I 3—363—15/88.

Brief details of the Basle Agreement are given elsewhere in this work.

GREECE

Contributed by: **Theodoros B. Karatzas**
Law Offices
Karatzas & Perakis
Athens

Introduction   **12.48**

Debt subordination is not an unknown concept in Greek legal practice but its use is very limited.

In a few cases the financing of a company with limited capital resources is accompanied by the subordination of certain debts, usually those of a person having a strong interest in the company obtaining the financing.

The main use of subordinated debt is to improve the capital resources of a borrowing company and is taken in lieu of an increase of its share capital, which in the opinion of the lender would otherwise be necessary.

This limited practice has not yet given rise to opportunities for the courts to try a dispute based on a debt subordination agreement. Equally the authors have not dealt with the matter although there are already some hints: see L. N. Georgakopoulos, *Manual of Commercial Law*, Vol. 1, Part 2—Companies, 1985, s.28, II, 7 and E. E. Perakis, *Introduction to the Law of Restructuring of Undertakings*, 1987 s.73.

In connection with a debt subordination transaction it should be noted that the principle prevailing in Greek law in case of a debtor's insolvency or forced execution against him is that ordinary prudent unsecured creditors must be paid *pari passu*. This principle is clearly stated in the following provisions of law:

(a) Article 977 s.3 of the Code of Civil Procedure, dealing with the distribution of the proceeds of forced sale of a debtor's assets;

(b) Article 660 of the Commercial Code governing the distribution of the proceeds of liquidation in bankruptcy among unsecured creditors;

(c) Article 1920 of the Civil Code providing for the payment of debts of a deceased person's estate. Some court decisions and authorities have accepted the view that the above provision is also applicable to other forms of liquidation, including the voluntary winding-up of companies.

In this connection it should be noted that a seizure or attachment of a debtor's assets does not create a lien in favour of the creditor initiating the seizure or attachment.

12.49 Contractual subordinations

An agreement whereby payment of a debt is subordinated to the prior payment of another debt of the same debtor should be a valid transaction and binding upon the parties concerned under Article 361 of the Civil Code, which confirms the principle of private autonomy (freedom of contract). Further, although there is no case law, it is considered that the agreement should not offend the principle of *pari passu* payment on the insolvency of the common debtor since the subordinated creditor agrees to rank after other creditors and therefore the other creditors are not prejudiced but on the contrary are benefited. Since the matter is not covered by authority, it may be advisable to state that the junior debt is, on the insolvency of the common debtor, conditional upon the senior debt first being paid in full.

The subordination agreement may take the form of a tripartite agreement between the senior creditor, the junior creditor and the debtor. It may also be in the form of a bilateral agreement between the debtor and the junior creditor in favour of the senior creditor (*pactum in favorem tertii*).

In some instances, the subordination is limited to a mere covenant and a corresponding event of default in a loan agreement between the intended senior creditor and the debtor.

By way of analogy, in many guarantees the guarantor effectively subordinates his claim by virtue of an agreement not to exercise his rights of subrogation if, after the payment the guaranteed amount, a surplus remains owing to the creditor. Under the above arrangement the guarantor must refrain from exercising his rights of subrogation against the debtor until and unless the non-guaranteed part of the creditor's claims is fully discharged, thus avoiding the situation where the non-guaranteed part of the claim ranks *pari passu* with the guaranteed part upon the new beneficiary (the guarantor) exercising his subrogation rights.

Subordination in all the forms specified above is binding only upon the contracting parties and those in whose favour it was agreed and cannot be opposed to third parties; it does not create rights *in rem*, but merely contractual obligations. Therefore a contractual subordination does not fully protect the senior creditor in case of forced execution, liquidation or bankruptcy.

The possibility of unilaterally varying the junior debt to the detriment of the senior creditor depends upon the language of the subordination. But generally speaking, unilateral variations of the junior debt cannot be raised against the senior creditor if the subordination is expressed to be in his favour and he has declared his acceptance of the agreement.

Turnover subordinations   **12.50**

In an effort to improve the efficiency of the contractual subordination the senior and junior creditors may, validly under Greek law, agree that any amount the junior creditor receives from any *pari passu* distribution of the proceeds of realisation of any of the assets of the common debtor, is assigned to the senior creditor. Instead of an assignment of proceeds, the junior creditor may assign to the senior creditor the entire subordinated debt as a security for the payment of the senior debt (fiduciary assignment).

Under Greek law any form of assignment is perfected only when it is notified to the debtor. As from the date of the notification of the assignment, it is binding upon the debtor who thereafter cannot discharge his obligations except by paying the assignee. This also applies to the case of set-off. Insolvency set-off is not possible under Greek law (although some court decisions have held to the contrary) so generally the subordination would not be destroyed by a set-off between the junior creditor and the common debtor if the debtor has become bankrupt.

Generally, trustees for creditors are not possible under Greek law, although it appears that the representative of bondholders under a bond loan issued by a "*societe anonyme*" and secured by a mortgage may be considered under certain circumstances to be the equivalent of a trustee. As regards fiscal implications, it should be noted that an assignment of proceeds or an assignment of the whole of the junior debt are not subject to stamp duty if they are construed as creating a security in favour of the senior debt (as they should be). If the assignment is construed as an independent transaction then it is subject to Greek stamp duty amounting to 2.4 per cent. of the amount involved for commercial transactions and 3.6 per cent. in all other cases.

12.51 Secured subordinated debt

Security *in rem* is available in Greece in the form of mortgages of immovables, ships and aircraft and in the form of pledges of chattels. The rule is that securities rank according to their order of registration, with the exception of mortgages registered on the same day, which have equal ranking, and pledges, which rank in their chronological order since pledges are not registrable.

Usually the security for the senior debt is registered first and the security for the junior debt is registered at least one day after the registration of the first security. However, if a debt secured by a first mortgage is to be subordinated to a debt which is to be secured by a mortgage on the same asset, the two creditors may between themselves agree to exchange their priority ranking. Under the strict letter of the law this agreement is permissible only between successive mortgagees, although there is no reason to prohibit the variation of ranks between non-successive mortgagees provided that this is not detrimental to the interest of other mortgagees who register their mortgages at some point in time between the successive mortgages.

A second-ranking mortgagee has a right to insist on a public sale when his debt becomes due without any limitation.

A secured creditor has the right to be satisfied in priority from the proceeds of liquidation of the creditor's assets over which he has a security interest (pledge or mortgage), subject to the rights of creditors possessing a lien.

In the case of a bond issue the bondholders may appoint a representative to hold the security for them. This is restricted to bond issues. There is no objection to the same representative acting for several classes of bondholders (senior and junior) and distributing the proceeds accordingly.

12.52 Capital adequacy and subordinated debt

Under Greek law the test for a debtor's solvency is not the ratio between assets and liabilities but the ability to pay his obligations as they fall due. Hence, a person or a company may be declared bankrupt if he ceases payments even if the above ratio is excellent. In banking practice subordinated debt is, under certain conditions (such as loans by major shareholders), considered as quasi equity.

12.53 Compulsory subordinations

A creditor may be compulsorily subordinated in the following cases:

(a) Article 32 of L. 3190/1955 on "limited liability companies" provides that debts owing to the companies' partners can be repaid only after third parties have been fully satisfied.

(b) Article 3 of L. 2190/1920 on "*societés anonymes*" provides that preferred shares shall be repaid prior to the repayment of common shares.

Of course, claims enjoying a lien or secured by a pledge or mortgage rank in priority to the claims of unsecured creditors.

ITALY

Contributed by: **Dr. Disiano Preite**
Chiomenti e Associati
Milan

Contractual subordination 12.54

There is very little law on subordinated debt in Italy.

If a junior creditor agrees with a senior creditor and the common debtor that the junior creditor's debt will be subordinated to that of the senior creditor on the insolvency of the common debtor, it is probable that this contract will be upheld on the insolvency of the debtor if under the subordination agreement the junior creditor fully waives his right to file for admission to the bankruptcy proceeding and also if the junior creditor simply binds himself not to accept repayment before the full satisfaction of the senior debt.

The provision in the Bankruptcy Act (article 52) dealing with the *pari passu* payment of ordinary creditors of a corporate debtor provides as follows:

"The bankruptcy opens the concurrence of the creditors over the bankrupt's assets. Every credit, even if secured, must be ascertained following the norms established in chapter V, except as otherwise provided for by the law."

Although this is expressed to be mandatory, the better view is that the provision merely requires that no ordinary creditor is paid in *priority* to other creditors unless he has some special preference. It probably does not prevent a creditor from agreeing to be *deferred* to other creditors, since an agreement to defer does not offend the fundamental policy of equality.

To understand contractual subordination we must first briefly recall what the law is when the debtor is *not* insolvent.

If the senior creditor is not a party to the subordination agreement, for the senior creditor to have a right to enforce against the debtor a contractual subordination agreement entered into by the debtor with a junior creditor, the agreement must be framed as a "contract in favour of the third party" (article 1411 civil code). This entails that the junior creditor enters into an obligation with the debtor, in favour of the senior creditor, not to accept the repayment of his credit before the senior creditor's reimbursement. The contract binds the debtor toward the third party (senior creditor) only after the latter gives his agreement.

Credits may be subordinated in favour of other future credits, since a subordination agreement may benefit third parties to be subsequently identified, so long as the identification criteria are established at the time of the agreement itself.

Note that in case of a subordination to a series of future creditors, the debtor (not the subordinated creditor) is always free to withdraw his promise in favour of new creditors mentioned in the agreement, until these creditors have agreed to the subordination contract. The debtor is therefore free, on the basis of a single contractual subordination agreement, to vary the number of his future senior creditors.

In case of bankruptcy the junior creditor will either have no claim, if he previously waived his right to enter the bankruptcy proceedings, or a claim accompanied by an obligation not to accept payment until the senior creditor is fully satisfied.

In the latter case the bankrupt's assets which should be assigned to the junior creditor under the *pari passu* rule will not be frozen until the end of the bankruptcy procedure. They will instead be distributed *pari passu* to all the remaining creditors until the senior creditor has been fully satisfied. If there were any remaining assets, then the junior creditor would have a right to receive the residue.

It must be recalled that under Italian law, insolvency proceedings may start even if the insolvent's assets have a value greater than his total assets, as long as he is unable to regularly perform his obligations.

Example: Assume a junior creditor J with a L50 credit, a senior creditor S with L10, and creditors C and C1 each with L10. The assets of debtor D are L60. Assume that each creditor may be satisfied for 75 per cent. of his credit. C and C1 will first be entitled to L7.5 each. Then the L37.5 to which J would be entitled will be divided between S, C and C1 until S has L10 (*i.e.* each take L2.5). Ultimately J takes the residue, *i.e.* L32.

It is therefore possible to subordinate a creditor to some and not only to all other creditors.

12.55   Contingent junior debt

Another method of conferring efficacy on a contractual subordination would be to provide that, on the insolvency of the common debtor, the payment of the junior debt is contingent or conditional upon the senior debt being paid in full. It is well established in Italian insolvency law that contingent claims against a bankrupt debtor are provable only in their valued amount. Section 95, co. 2 of the Bankruptcy Act deals with the proof of contingent debts of a bankrupt as follows:

> "The credits mentioned in the last paragraph of art. 55 [*i.e.* contingent credits] are included with reserve among the admitted credits [in the bankruptcy proceeding]."

Hence, if the junior debt is contingent upon the senior debt being paid in full, the effect would be that, if the common debtor were insolvent, the junior creditor would have a claim, subordinated, however, to the full payment of the senior creditors.

Further, by creating contingent debts, as in the example given above, a junior creditor may be subordinated both to one or more senior creditors or to all other creditors of the common debtor.

Variations of subordination 12.56

If the senior creditor is not a party to the subordination contract, as where, for example, the junior creditor agrees solely with the debtor that the junior debt will be subordinated to all other creditors, the junior creditor and the debtor could subsequently agree to cancel the subordination without the consent of the senior creditor.

This holds even if it could be shown that the senior creditors knew of the subordination and incurred their credits in reliance on the subordination except if the contract was constituted as described above in favour of the third party and expressly accepted by the senior creditors.

Insolvency test and fraudulent trading 12.57

Junior debt counts in determining whether the debtor is insolvent for the purposes of a bankruptcy petition.

The directors of the debtor corporation may not ignore junior debt for the purpose of ascertaining whether new liabilities may lead to personal liability for fraudulent or wrongful trading.

Set-off 12.58

Under section 56 of the Bankruptcy Act, set-off of mutual debts is permitted on bankruptcy, though the set-off is not mandatory and can be waived by the junior creditor.

In any case the set-off can be avoided by providing that on the insolvency of the common debtor, the junior debt is contingent upon the senior debt being paid in full: contingent credits may not be subject to a set-off.

Turnover subordinations 12.59

The subordination of a junior creditor to a single senior creditor could also be achieved by some arrangement whereby the junior creditor turns over dividends on the junior debt to the senior creditor until the senior debt is paid.

One method would be for the junior creditor to grant security over the junior debt in favour of the senior creditor to secure the senior debt. This could be effected by a pledge of the junior credit. No registration would be required of this charge, but the transfer would not be effective on the insolvency of the junior creditor unless it were notified in the form prescribed by Article 2800 of the Civil Code or the debtor formally consented to the transfer. A transfer by way of security may conflict with negative pledges (contracts against the grant of security) binding on the junior creditor.

The transfer might attract a documentary tax of up to 0.5 per cent. but this would depend upon the circumstances.

An alternative method would be an agreement by the junior creditor to transfer absolutely to the senior creditor all insolvency dividends and other recoveries received by the junior creditor on the insolvency of the common debtor. This is a transfer of proceeds. The formalities applying to assignments apply to transfers of proceeds in order and must be complied with to render the transfer effective against creditors of the junior creditor.

Another possible alternative is for the subordination agreement to state that the debtor is directed to pay all dividends on the junior debt direct to the senior creditor until the senior debt is paid in full. However, it is likely, though somewhat debated, that the debtor's obligation to pay the dividends to the senior creditor, will be considered to be terminated by the bankruptcy declaration. The senior creditor would in that case be unable to compel the insolvency representative to comply.

12.60 Bond trustee

It is possible for a fiduciary or other representative to be appointed to hold the benefit of the junior debt for a class of junior bondholders and to turn over proceeds to the senior creditors.

12.61 Secured debt

There is no objection in principle to two creditors being secured on the same asset and for one of the secured creditors to rank after the other.

12.62 Variation of priorities

The registration systems for mortgages over land, aircraft and ships prescribe an order of registration which is generally the date order in which the secured creditors register their mortgages at the relevant registry. However, even in this case it is considered that the creditors may agree between themselves to rank their debts in whatever priority they wish. But, as regards third parties, they will rank in the order of priority prescribed by the registration law.

12.63 Rights of enforcement

A junior secured creditor has a right to compel a public sale of the assets concerned if there is a default on the junior debt, even though the senior creditor objects. However, the senior creditor must be paid first out of the proceeds of sale. It is considered that an agreement between the senior and junior creditor that the junior creditor will not exercise this right of sale without the consent of the senior creditor would be valid.

12.64 Trustee of security

It is possible for a fiduciary or representative to be appointed to hold the security for the benefit of both creditors on terms that the proceeds of sale are applied in the order of priority agreed by the creditors.

Taxation 12.65

Taxation law on subordinated debt is highly uncertain and lacks any official decision by the tax authorities.

Generally, however, it may be said that subordinated debt should be treated in the same way as any other debt for most taxation purposes, in particular deductibility of interest by the debtor, withholding taxes, issue taxes and transfer taxes. However, it is possible that, if the junior debt is substantially equity, then payment of interest may be treated as payment of a dividend and hence lose the tax advantages of interest on debt, *e.g.* deductibility of interest and the different rules regarding withholding tax.

Capital adequacy 12.66

Italy is likely in due course to adopt the principles set out in the Basle Agreement on Convergence of Capital of July, 1988. This provides for subordinated debt of banks to be treated as supplementary capital for capital adequacy purposes, subject to various limits. Details of the Basle Agreement are given elsewhere in this work.

Compulsory subordination 12.67

A creditor may be compulsorily subordinated on the insolvency of a debtor in the following cases (amongst others):

1. Where the creditors are also shareholders and the credit has been qualified as instrumental to a possible future increase of the issued or authorised capital.
2. Where the creditor absolutely dominated the management of the debtor corporation, *de facto* dissolving any effective distinction between its assets and the debtor corporation's assets.

However, in the case of insurance companies, banks and others, the claims of policyholders, depositors and the like do not rank ahead of the claims of long term creditors. But this area of law is detailed.

JAPAN

Contributed by: **Takaki Takuoka**
Blakemore & Mitsuki
Tokyo

Legal authorities for subordinated debt 12.68

There are no code provisions or case law specifically with respect to subordinated debt in Japan.

Subordinated bonds recently have become a matter of special interest to Japanese banks in view of the release issued by the Director General of the Banking Bureau of the Ministry of Finance (*Kura-Gin* No. 2424 dated December 22, 1988) with respect to the capital adequacy of banks. This implements the principles set out in the Basle Agreement on the International Convergence of Capital Measurement and Capital Standards of July 1988. Japanese city banks devised a proposed model for subordinated bond issues in September 1988 (published in *Kinyu-Zaisei Jijo*, in the issue of October 17, 1988) with a view to the smooth obtaining of official recognition by the Government of a form of subordination for bonds. At the time of writing, the Government's position on this proposal had not yet been disclosed.

The Government has been reluctant to permit subordinated bond issues by a Japanese or non-Japanese corporation under the governing law of Japan, presumably on account of the lack of specific legal provisions in an area related to the protection of investors. However, the authorities may under certain conditions permit subordinated issues by a foreign corporation under an appropriate governing law of a foreign country where the subordination is valid. Recently, the authorities exceptionally permitted a subordinated issue under the governing law of Japan made by an international organisation (African Development Bank Japanese Yen Bond—first offering in November, 1989), presumably on the ground that the bankruptcy of an international organisation of this status was unlikely since it is owned by Member States who are liable to make additional contributions.

On the other hand, in the case of a subordinated loan involving only a few senior creditors, investor protection is not usually a major obstacle because the number of relevant parties is limited and the regulations concerning the protection of investors are generally not invoked.

12.69   Possible legal framework for subordinated debts

Under the Japanese legal system, the following two structures could be considered:

(1) A structure under which the senior creditors have a right, *vis-à-vis* the common debtor or the junior creditor, to the prior payment of the senior debt; and

(2) A structure under which, although the senior creditors do not have this right, the junior creditor's debt is subordinated by virtue of a condition imposed on the junior debt, so that the senior creditors effectively receive the prior payment of their debts.

Senior creditors have a right to prior payment. Under this structure, the following two arrangements could be considered.

(a) Contractual subordinations

It could be provided that the senior creditors have a direct right as against the common debtor to prior payment.

The objection to this formulation is that it would conflict with provisions in the Bankruptcy Law which prescribe the equal treatment of ordinary creditors (or at least would not be consistent with the procedures laid down by those provisions).

Article 40 of the Bankruptcy Law provides:

> "Obligations which are to be performed in the same rank of priority shall each be paid in proportion to the amount of the respective claims."

Article 258, paragraph 2, provides:

> "Claims for which dividends are to be distributed shall be distinguished, depending upon whether or not a right of priority exists: those having priority rights shall be entered in accordance with the rank of priority, and as for those which are devoid of priority rights, entries shall be made distinguishing between those subordinated by virtue of the provisions of Article 46 and others."

Evidently subordinated debts as referred to therein are only those provided as such by the Law.

On the other hand, the Corporate Reorganisation Law allows the reorganisation plan to treat one ordinary creditor differently from other ordinary creditors to a certain extent. Article 229 of the Corporate Reorganisation Law provides:

> "The terms and conditions of the reorganization plan shall be equal as among the persons who possess a right of the same nature; provided, however, that with regard to reorganization creditors and reorganization secured creditors, this shall not apply in the case where equity is not impaired even if special stipulations are made in respect of those claims of which the amount is small, or if discriminatory stipulations are otherwise made among such persons."

However, there is some uncertainty as to whether the court would allow the subordination in a reorganisation plan.

(b) Turnover subordinations

It could be provided that the junior creditor is obliged to turn over to the senior creditors any payments made to the junior creditor by the common debtor.

Two arrangements are possible, one where the senior creditors are a party to the subordination agreement and the other where they are not.

Where the senior creditors are parties, an agreement by the junior creditor with a group of specific senior creditors to the effect that the junior creditor will turn over to the senior creditors any payments made to the junior creditor by the common debtor should be valid. This would be the best method of subordination where the junior creditor wishes to be subordinated only to a limited number of creditors and not to all other ordinary creditors. The junior creditor would be required to prove the substance of the turnover transaction in order to avoid the tax authorities treating the transfer as a "gift" and not being deductible from income.

The junior creditors should secure the rights of the senior creditors by way of assignment for security (*joto-tampo*) of the future claims against the common debtor under notarial act (*kakutei hizuke*). Article 467 of the Civil Code provides:

> "1. The assignment of a nominative claim cannot be set up against the obligor or any other third person, unless the assignor has given notice thereof to the obligor or the obligor has consented thereto.

2. The notice or consent mentioned in the preceding paragraph cannot be set up against a third person other than the obligor, unless it is made in writing under a notarial act (*kakutei hizuke*)".

A clause in the agreement between the junior creditor and the senior creditors to the effect that the junior creditor authorises the trustee in bankruptcy to pay directly to the senior creditor the debt to be paid to the junior creditor would be invalid under the Bankruptcy Law: see Article 40 and Article 258, paragraph 2 of the Bankruptcy Law as referred to above.

Alternatively, the junior creditor could agree with the common debtor to the same effect, but without the senior creditor being a party. Under Japanese law, the junior creditor would be liable to the senior creditors to perform its obligation under the agreement upon a declaration by the senior creditors that they accept the third party beneficiary privilege under this agreement. Until that time, the junior creditor and the common debtor may agree to delete the subordination clause without the consent of the senior creditors.

Article 537 of the Civil Code provides:

"1. Where a party to a contract has agreed therein to effect an act or performance in favour of a third person, the third person is entitled to demand such act of performance directly to the obligor.
2. In the case mentioned in the preceding paragraph, the right of the third person shall come into existence as from the time when he declares to the obligor his intention to accept the benefit of the contract."

One weakness of this arrangement is that, if there are a great number of senior creditors, it would be impractical to expect that all of them would make the declaration. If the agreement provides that the senior creditors are entitled to the privilege without a declaration, the provision would be held invalid according to a Supreme Court decision of July 5, 1916, *Min-roku* Vol. 22, pp. 1336 *et seq.* Although the majority of scholars disagree with this ruling, the Supreme Court decision is still an authoritative judicial precedent, and it would be unsafe to follow the opinion of these scholars.

Junior debt is conditional. Under this arrangement the junior creditor's debt is subordinated by virtue of a condition imposed on the debt to the effect that payment of the junior debt is conditional on the payment of the senior debt.

The senior creditors do not have a right to prior payment but effectively obtain the benefit of prior payment of their debt from the common debtor as a result of the condition imposed on the junior creditor's debt. The structure would not conflict with the Bankruptcy Law or the Corporate Reorganisation Law.

As to the validity of the condition, for the purposes of the common debtor's corporate reorganisation, the subordination of the junior creditor should be effective if the agreement provides that payment is conditional "upon the senior debt being paid in full." However, in the event of the common debtor's bankruptcy, the condition should state that payment of the junior debt is conditional "upon the senior debt being scheduled to be paid in full at or prior to the time of the submission to the court of the final dividend list by the trustee in bankruptcy."

Article 271 of the Bankruptcy Law provides:

> "The trustee in bankruptcy shall deposit the amount of dividends to be distributed for any of the following claims:. . .(4) Claims subject to a condition precedent and future claims;. . . ."

Article 275 provides:

> "In cases where a claim subject to a condition precedent or a future claim has not become capable of being exercised within the period of exclusion for the last distribution, the creditor concerned shall be excluded from the distribution of dividends."

The period of exclusion for the last distribution expires when the final dividend list is fixed. Consequently, in order for the junior creditor to avoid being excluded from the remaining dividend payment under the bankruptcy procedures, the condition must be met prior to the time when the final dividend amount is fixed.

A condition limiting the subordination only to some senior creditors would in practice be impossible under these insolvency procedures.

A disadvantage of this structure is that the junior creditor and the common debtor could at any time agree to amend the agreement and to delete the subordination clause even though they had agreed between themselves not to do so.

As to insolvency set-off, although a set-off of mutual debts is permitted under the Bankruptcy Law upon exercise of one party, the senior creditor's benefit of prior payment is not, in the case of a "conditional debt" subordination, impaired by the junior creditor's exercise of set-off because the junior creditor may not set off a debt against the common debtor until the condition is met, namely that the senior debt has been paid in full.

Secured debts   12.70

Ordinary mortgages. The registration systems for mortgages over land, buildings, residential houses, aircraft, ships and certain other properties prescribe an order of registration which is generally the date order in which the secured creditors register their mortgages at the government registration office.

However, the order may be changed by agreement between the relevant parties: registration of the change and notice thereof to the debtor are required to secure the new order. Assume that the debt amounts of the first mortgagee, the second mortgagee, and the third mortgagee are Y10m, Y20m and Y8m respectively.

If the first mortgagee *agrees to transfer* its priority order of mortgage to the third mortgagee, the order of priority changes between them, and the right and priority of the second mortgagee remains unchanged. The result is that the order could be Y8m to the third mortgagee, Y2m to the first mortgagee, Y20m to the second mortgagee, and Y8m to the first mortgagee.

If the first mortgagee *agrees to waive* its priority order of mortgage in favour of the third mortgagee, they will have an equal priority. The result is that the order will be Y10m to the first and the third mortgagee in equal shares, Y20m to the second mortgagee, and Y8m to the first and third mortgagee in equal shares.

If the first mortgagee, the second mortgagee and the third mortgagee *agree to change* their order, the order will change accordingly.

Revolving mortgages. In case of an ordinary mortgage, once payment is made, in whole or in part, to the senior mortgagee, the registration of the senior mortgage does not cover a subsequent advance of new money by the senior mortgagee. However, there is another system called a "revolving mortgage (*ne-teitou*)" under which registration of the senior mortgage covers a subsequent advance by the senior mortgagee up to the registered amount. It is possible for two or more revolving mortgagees to share the same priority order as regards their security with the consent of the mortgagor. Mortgagees with the same priority order may agree between themselves to rank their mortgages in whatever priority they wish and register the priority.

Enforcement. Each mortgagee has the right to compel a public sale of the assets concerned without the consent of the other mortgagee or mortgagees if there is a default on its debt. However, the senior mortgagee must be paid first out of the proceeds of sale.

Trustee of security. Since a mortgage is generally not allowed to be registered under a name other than that of the creditor, it is not possible for a fiduciary or a representative to be appointed to register the mortgage for the benefit of both creditors on terms that the proceeds of the public sale are applied in the order of priority agreed upon by the creditors, unless the credits to the common debtor are granted in the name of the fiduciary or representative. An exception to this is that a commissioned company for secured bonds can be registered as the mortgagee for the benefit of the bondholders, but it may not act as such for two classes of bonds.

Taxation. Subordinated debts would generally be treated in the same way as any other debt for the purposes of Japanese taxation, such as deductibility of interest by the debtor and withholding tax.

LUXEMBOURG

Contributed by: **Janine Biver**,
Loesch & Wolter
Luxembourg

12.71 Contractual subordinations

Except for regulations issued by the Banking Supervisory Authority IML (*Institut Monétaire Luxembourgeois*) for the inclusion of subordi-

nated debt of credit institutions in equity for the purposes of the calculation of various ratios, there is no legal provision in Luxembourg
concerning contractual subordination of debts, nor is there any case law.

There is however no material reason why a contractual provision
whereby a junior creditor agrees with a senior creditor and the common
debtor that the junior creditor's debt will be subordinated to that of the
senior creditor, either before or after an insolvency of the common
debtor, should not be upheld in the insolvency proceedings of the debtor.

Article 561 of the Luxembourg Commercial Code dealing with distributions in bankruptcy proceedings provides for the *pari passu* payment
of all ordinary creditors and reads as follows (in free translation):

> "The amount of the movable assets of the bankrupt, after deduction of costs and
> expenses incurred in the management of the bankruptcy, aids which might have
> been granted to the bankrupt or to his family and the amounts paid to privileged
> creditors, will be distributed to all creditors, pro rata to their announced and
> verified claims."

Luxembourg courts have held that the principle of equal treatment of all
the creditors of the estate of a bankrupt is mandatory and of public order
(*d'ordre public*): Lux. January 22, 1909, Superior Court of Justice June
18, 1909, PAS 8, 22.

Notwithstanding this principle however, a subordination agreement
does not seem to offend the fundamental policy of equality between all
the creditors, since it is not intended to grant a privilege to one creditor.
On the contrary, as the subordinated creditor has agreed to be deferred to
other creditors, the situation of the other creditors is improved by the
subordination. Belgian commentators have no doubt as to the validity of
such clauses in bankruptcy proceedings and, since Luxembourg courts
tend to look to Belgian case law and legal commentaries, it can be
expected that the Luxembourg courts would uphold the validity of such a
contractual subordination.

Contingent junior debt   12.72

If a subordination is effected by a clause whereby on the insolvency of
the common debtor, the payment of the junior debt is contingent or
conditional upon the senior debt being paid in full, the clause might be
interpreted as being a suspensory condition. In such case the claim is
declared with the bankruptcy receiver only on a conservatory basis: if the
condition is not met, that is to say, if the senior creditor is not repaid in
full, the bankruptcy receiver would have the right to disregard the junior
creditor's declaration of claim.

If the debtor is insolvent and the junior creditor had agreed that his
claim would be junior to a claim of one or more or even all the other
creditors, then, if it appeared that these creditors would not be repaid,
the junior creditor would have no claim at all.

Variations of subordination   12.73

There are various possibilities for establishing the subordination of a
debt:

(1) Agreement between the junior creditor and the senior creditors;
(2) Agreement between the junior creditor and the debtor;
(3) Unilateral undertaking of the junior creditor.

In the case of (2) and (3) it is conceivable that the junior creditor would be able, in case (2) by agreement with the debtor and in case (3) by a unilateral declaration, to cancel the subordination without the consent of the senior creditor(s).

It is possible, however, that such an undertaking from the junior creditor constitutes a so-called "stipulation pour autrui" (stipulation in favour of a third party). According to Article 1121 of the Civil Code, if the creditor benefited by the stipulation has declared his willingness to take advantage thereof, the stipulation may not be revoked. The same result could arise if the senior creditor knew of the subordination and granted his credit in reliance on the subordination.

12.74 Set-off

A problem with legal set-off might arise, at least before insolvency proceedings, since Article 1289 of the Civil Code rules as follows (in free translation):

> "If two persons are debtors one of the other, a set-off operates between them and extinguishes both debts. . ."

It is generally held that the so-called "legal set-off" instituted by Article 1289 operates legally and automatically. However, according to court rulings, this automatic set-off may be waived.

In the judgment of the Superior Court of Justice of October 1, 1963 (published in Pasicrisie 19, 209), the court held:

> "Legal set-off is the one which occurs by law, even without the knowledge of the debtor, if the conditions for the set-off are fulfilled, *i.e.* reciprocity of debts between the same parties, identity of the object, liquidity and exigibility of the two debts, *unless* it derives from the circumstances that the parties intended to exclude the legal set-off in their relationship or that one of the parties has waived its right to the legal set-off."

It would therefore be desirable to include a waiver of any set-off in the subordination agreement. If the subordination agreement contains a clause whereby the payment of the junior debt is contingent upon the previous payments of one, more or all of the creditors of the debtor, the conditions for the legal set-off would probably not be fulfilled.

Set-off does not create a problem upon the insolvency of the debtor. According to Article 445 and decisions of Luxembourg courts, any set-off, whether legal, judicial or contractual is, in principle, forbidden after the bankruptcy judgment, except for very narrow exceptions permitted by case law, such as cross-claims arising out of the same transaction or connected transactions, and bank current accounts.

12.75 Turnover subordinations

If a junior creditor is to be subordinated only to one senior creditor (or to a group of senior creditors) and not to all other creditors of the common debtor, the junior creditor may agree to pay amounts received from the debtor and bankruptcy dividends in the debtor's bankruptcy in respect of the junior debt to the senior creditor until the senior debt is paid. In order to ensure that the junior creditor fulfils his obligations under such an agreement, the senior creditor might consider requiring that the claim against the debtor is assigned to him on terms that the assignment ceases at the moment when the senior debt is totally paid. It might in addition be provided that the junior debtor pledges, in favour of the senior creditor, his claim against the debtor as security for the senior creditor's claim against the debtor.

In order to render these agreements opposable as against third parties, including the debtor and the bankruptcy receiver of the debtor, the following formalities must be complied with:

(a) In the case of a *pledge* of the claim against the debtor in favour of the senior creditor, then, if the debtor is domiciled in Luxembourg, the pledge would have to be notified to the debtor by bailiff's deed (Article 2075 of the Civil Code) or accepted by him in an authentic deed. In both cases, the pledge would have to be registered, but only a small fixed amount would be payable as registration fee.

(b) In the case of an *assignment* of the junior claim to the senior creditor, the formalities to be accomplished in order to render the assignment opposable as against third parties would be those provided for by the law governing the assigned (junior) claim. If this claim was governed by Luxembourg law, a notification or an acceptation by the debtor in an authentic deed would be necessary. The registration fee would be 0.24 per cent. calculated on the total amount involved.

(c) A so-called "*delegation*" could be considered. In this case the junior creditor would give an order to the debtor to assume obligations against the senior creditor. Such a delegation may be "perfect" or "imperfect." In the case of a perfect delegation, the junior creditor would no longer be under any obligation to the senior creditor if the senior creditor and the debtor agreed with the junior creditor that a new obligation would exist between the senior creditor and the debtor. In the case of an imperfect delegation, the senior creditor would have, besides the common debtor, the junior creditor as his debtor. In both cases, no formalities would under Luxembourg law be necessary, but it should be noted that, if a delegation is submitted to any official authority (*autorité constituée*) in Luxembourg, a registration fee of 0.24 per cent. would become payable.

An assignment of the junior claim, despite the fact that a registration fee will become payable, might be preferable, since if a pledge is agreed upon, the pledge may only be realised once the senior debt has become due and payable and the debtor does not pay his debt.

Moreover in the case of a pledge, there is a further possible difficulty. If the junior debt is not yet in existence, it might be argued that the pledge has been given over a future claim. Despite the fact that it is now generally held in Belgium and France—and Luxembourg courts tend to have regard to these precedents—that a pledge can be given over future claims and despite the fact that in addition the Luxembourg Civil Code, like the French and Belgian Codes, states that future assets can be the object of transactions, there is still no Luxembourg legal provision which precisely confirms the validity of a pledge of future claims. There is no case law on the point.

It should be noted that the legal provisions on the pledge of securities expressly provide that securities coming into the possession of the creditor or an agreed third party in the future can be the object of a pledge.

A further difficulty might arise from the fact that the amount of the transferred or pledged proceeds cannot be indicated.

It may be assumed that under Luxembourg law any of these methods of turnover would in substance be treated as security and hence potentially conflict with negative pledge clauses.

12.76   Bond trustee

If the debtor is a company incorporated in and has its registered office in Luxembourg, it is conceivable that a fiduciary or other representative could be appointed to hold the benefit of the junior debt for a class of junior bondholders and to turn over proceeds to the senior creditors. However such a representative could not be designated by the debtor, but the junior bondholders themselves would have to meet and give the representative instructions to hold the benefit of the junior debt in the above manner and to turn over the proceeds to the senior creditor or creditors.

12.77   Secured debt

There is, under Luxembourg law, no objection in principle to two creditors being secured on the same asset and whereby one of the secured creditors ranks after the other. This is normally achieved automatically by the ranking of the charges as follows:

—for immovable property, aircraft and ships, the order of ranking is determined by the date on which the secured creditors register their mortgages at the relevant registry;

—for pledges on claims, where a notification is necessary, the order of date of registration of the document and the notification deed confer the priority ranking;

—for pledges on other assets, the order of date of registration, where necessary, confers the priority ranking;

—for pledges on shares, no registration is provided for and the order of date of the signatures of the deed would normally prevail. If disputes arise, the exact date of signature can be proved by any means, including witnesses.

In all these cases it is generally held that it is possible for the creditors to agree between themselves to rank their claims in whatever priority they wish.

In the case of mortgages, a priority agreement may be published if, for example, a first ranking creditor abandons his priority, either totally or only in part, for the benefit of another creditor.

Except where such a transfer or priority is published, the creditors will, as regards third parties, rank in the order of priority prescribed by law.

Assuming that the junior creditor's claim is not conditional upon the fulfilment of the debtor's obligations towards the senior creditor, and that the junior secured creditor's claim has become payable, the junior creditor would be able to compel a public sale of the assets concerned, at least in the case of mortgages, although the senior creditor must be paid first out of the proceeds of sale.

It might be possible to constitute a Luxembourg bank or financial institution as a fiduciary appointed by the junior and senior creditors, holding the security for the benefit of both creditors on terms that the proceeds of sale are applied in the order of priority agreed by the creditors.

Taxation   **12.78**

Generally, subordinated debt should be treated in the same way as any other debt for most taxation purposes, in particular deductibility of interest by the debtor, and taxes on transfers of claims.

Capital adequacy   **12.79**

At the time of writing, Luxembourg is on the point of adopting the principles set out in the Basle Agreement on Convergence of Capital. Even though all the rules and regulations have not yet been published, the supervisory authority already in practice applies the principles of such Agreement.

THE NETHERLANDS

Contributed by: **M. A. Blom**
                         Nauta Dutilh
                         Amsterdam

Advice on tax aspects: **M. P. M. van de Ven**
                         Moret, Ernst & Young

Contractual subordinations   **12.80**

There is very little law on subordinated debt in the Netherlands. A very useful source of information on this subject is the thesis of Van Hees, entitled *De achtergestelde vordering, in het bijzonder de achtergestelde geldlening* ("The subordinated claim, in particular the subordinated loan of money," Kluwer, 1989) which contains an extensive and very current investigation of this topic. It should be noted, however, that some of his conclusions are disputed by other authors.

12.81 Subordinations permitted by law

If a junior creditor agrees with a senior creditor or senior creditors and the common debtor or with only the common debtor that the junior creditor's debt will be subordinated to that of certain or all of the senior creditors on the insolvency of the debtor, there can be little doubt that this contract will be upheld on the insolvency of the debtor.

The provisions in the laws of the Netherlands dealing with the *pari passu* payment of ordinary creditors of a debtor provide (in rough translation) as follows:

> *Article 1177, Netherlands Civil Code*
> "All moveable and immovable assets of the debtor, both present and future, may be subject to claims for the satisfaction of his personal obligations."
> *Article 1178, Netherlands Civil Code*
> "Those goods serve as common security for his creditors; the proceeds thereof are divided among them, *pari passu*, in proportion to the claim of each of them, unless there would be among the creditors legal reasons for priority."

These articles are considered to require merely that no ordinary creditor is paid in *priority* to other creditors unless he has some special preference. They do not prevent a creditor from agreeing to be *deferred* to other creditors. In the legal literature the validity of subordination is accepted. Furthermore in the draft of a new Civil Code, which is expected to be enacted in the near future, subordination is specifically permitted.

There is no case law specifically dealing with the question of whether subordination is possible as a matter of law. However, what little case law there is concerning subordination gives no reason to doubt that the subordination of a debt is acceptable under present law as well.

12.82 Junior debt contingent

Under Netherlands law there is uncertainty as to the legal basis for a subordination. The view taken in the Netherlands is that a subordination clause must normally be read (in the Netherlands context) as meaning that on the insolvency of the common debtor, the payment of the junior debt is made conditional upon the senior debt being paid in full. This would mean that if the agreement states only that the junior debt is subordinated to the senior debt (and does not for example contain provisions granting security over the junior debt in favour of the senior creditor), the junior creditor would be paid only after all other creditors of the common debtor (holding unsubordinated claims), including the senior creditor, had been paid. Van Hees (*De achtergestelde vordering, in het bijzonder de achtergestelde geldlening*, p. 129 and pp. 113–115) takes the view that a subordinated debt is governed by a legal structure *sui generis* (of its own kind), though it is closely related to a conditional debt.

He believes that a subordination clause would lead to one of two results, namely (i) the senior creditor is paid as if the junior creditor did not exist on the basis that the share of each of the other creditors is determined as if no subordination had taken place, the subordinated claim being paid in so far as the senior claim did not receive any "extra" payment under the system, or (ii) the senior creditor receives not only his own share, but also that of the junior creditor.

Bankruptcy of the debtor   12.83

It is well established in the Bankruptcy Code of the Netherlands that contingent claims against a bankrupt debtor are provable only in their valued amount. Sections 130 and 131 of the Bankruptcy Code deal with the proof of contingent debts of a bankrupt as follows (again, in rough translation):

> *Article 130, paragraph 1 Netherlands Bankruptcy Code*
> "A claim subject to a condition precedent can be admitted for its value at the moment at which the bankruptcy was declared."
> *Article 131, paragraph 1 Netherlands Bankruptcy Code*
> "A claim whose maturity date is uncertain, or which entitles the claimant to periodical payments, will be admitted for its value on the day on which the bankruptcy was declared."

Hence if the junior debt is contingent upon the senior debt being paid in full, the effect would be that, if the common debtor were insolvent, the junior creditor would have no claim at all.

This would obviously lead to strange results in a situation where the debt is valued at nil and subsequently additional assets are discovered in the bankruptcy estate, which, if discovered at an earlier stage, would have led to a positive valuation of the junior debt. Several solutions could be adopted here, one being that articles 130 and 131 of the Bankruptcy Code are deemed not to apply in respect of subordinated debt. Another is the application of article 130, paragraph 2 of the Bankruptcy Code. This paragraph reads as follows (in rough translation):

> "If the trustee in bankruptcy and the creditors cannot agree on this manner of verification, such a claim will be admitted conditionally for its full amount."

On the basis of this paragraph, the subordinated debt could possibly be valued after all other claims have been paid if there is a fair chance that the valuation will turn out to be correct.

Here again it should be pointed out that Van Hees (*De achtergestelde vordering, in het bijzonder de achtergestelde geldlening*, pp. 129 and 113–115) reaches different conclusions on the basis of his premise that a subordinated debt is governed by a legal structure *sui generis*. In his system the questions discussed above in connection with articles 130 and 131 of the Bankruptcy Code do not play a role.

Variations of subordination   12.84

If the senior creditor is not a party to the subordination contract, as where, for example the junior creditor agrees solely with the debtor that the junior debt will be subordinated to all other creditors, the junior creditor and the debtor could subsequently agree to cancel the subordination without the consent of the senior creditor. Their ability to do so would be limited if the subordination clause is phrased in such a way that it can be read as creating a third party right ("derdenbeding") in favour of the senior creditors—a right which is based on article 1353 of the Netherlands Civil Code. This right can be enforced by each senior creditor who has declared his acceptance thereof. A change could not be made to the detriment of a senior creditor who has accepted the third party right.

The right of unilateral variation might also be limited by the so-called Actio Pauliana, set forth in article 1377 of the Netherlands Civil Code, pursuant to which each creditor can invoke the nullity of every act of its debtor that harmed creditors and that was performed without an obligation on the debtor's part to perform the same, provided that both the debtor and the person with whom or on whose behalf he acted were, at the time he so acted, aware of the fact that harm to other creditors' interests would result therefrom. A de-subordination of a subordinated debt could under certain circumstances certainly qualify as such an act.

Further, one could imagine that a variation could (again, under certain circumstances) be a tortious act *vis-à-vis* senior creditors, if it could be shown that the senior creditors knew of the subordination and extended their credits in reliance thereon.

12.85   Set-off

Under section 53 of the Netherlands Bankruptcy Code, set-off of mutual debts is permitted on bankruptcy. The set-off is not mandatory and can be waived by the junior creditor. It is possible that set-off will be deemed to have been waived by the mere fact that the debt is subordinated. If the set-off has not in fact been waived, set-off would be possible for the value of the subordinated claim, determined on the basis of articles 130 and 131 of the Netherlands Bankruptcy Code set forth above. If the junior debt is contingent upon the senior debt being paid in full and the debtor is insolvent, the subordinated claim should be valued at nil, so no set-off would effectively take place.

If a subordinated debt is not considered to be a conditional debt, or is considered to be a conditional debt to which articles 130 and 131 of the Bankruptcy Code do not apply, set-off in bankruptcy would in principle be possible. As mentioned above it is possible that set-off will be deemed to have been waived. Preferably set-off should be waived explicitly.

12.86   Turnover subordinations

If a junior creditor is to be subordinated only to the senior creditor and not to all other creditors of the common debtor, then, as mentioned above, a contractual subordination will not achieve this object (note that, as explained above, Van Hees takes a different position). This could only be achieved by some arrangement whereby the junior creditor turns over dividends on the junior debt to the senior creditor until the senior debt is paid.

One method would be for the junior creditor to grant security over the junior debt in favour of the senior creditor to secure the senior debt. This could be effected by a fiduciary transfer. No registration would be required of this transfer. A transfer by way of security might conflict with any negative pledges binding on the junior creditor.

An alternative method would be an agreement by the junior creditor to transfer to the senior creditor all insolvency dividends and other recoveries received by the junior creditor on the insolvency of the common debtor. Under Netherlands law this would be treated as an obligation of the junior creditor to pay to the senior creditor amounts equal to the amounts received. Should the junior creditor in turn go bankrupt, then the proceeds of the junior claim will fall into the bankruptcy estate of the junior creditor and the senior creditor would be treated as a common creditor of the junior creditor for the amount due to him.

Once again it should be noted that if the position Van Hees takes is correct, the subordination would of itself already result in all or part of the proceeds of the junior debt being paid out to the senior creditor, without passing through the junior creditor's estate.

Bond trustee   12.87

Netherlands law does not specifically provide for the possibility of a fiduciary or other representative being appointed to hold the benefit of the junior debt for a class of junior bondholders and to turn over proceeds to the senior creditor. This would in principle have the result that, under a turnover subordination, the senior creditor would have to claim recoveries from each junior creditor: this might be impracticable if there are many junior creditors. In view of case law, however, it might be possible to find a solution to this problem, leading to a result similar to the result that can be reached by appointment of a trustee under English law. Whether this is achievable depends on the actual circumstances.

Secured debt   12.88

There is no objection in principle to two creditors being secured on the same asset and for one of the secured creditors to rank after the other. However, the legal structure would depend on the type of asset and also the type of asset will determine whether or not the ranking will hold if the junior creditor goes bankrupt or if he does not act as agreed.

Variation of priorities   12.89

The registration systems for mortgages over land, aircraft and ships prescribe an order of registration which is the date order in which the secured creditors register their mortgages at the relevant registry. No variation of this order is possible under present law. The draft of the new Civil Code envisages the possibility of the order being changed. Obviously, arrangements could be made also in this case for the junior creditor to turn over to the senior creditor amounts received as a result of a higher ranking in respect of the asset.

12.90   Rights of enforcement

A junior secured creditor will often have the right to compel the public sale of the assets concerned if there is a default on the junior debt, even though the senior creditor objects. However, the senior creditor must be paid first out of the proceeds of sale if he has a higher ranking. If he does not have a higher ranking, again a turnover obligation should solve the problem. An agreement between the senior and junior creditor that the junior creditor will not exercise a right of sale without the consent of the senior creditor would be valid.

12.91   Trustee of security

The position is similar to that with respect to a bond trustee. Although Netherlands law does not specifically provide for the possibility of a fiduciary or representative being appointed to hold the security for the benefit of both creditors on terms that the proceeds of sale are applied in the order of priority agreed by the creditors, it is not unthinkable that an acceptable solution can be found, depending on the circumstances.

12.92   Taxation

The tax aspects of junior debt of a Netherlands debtor may be summarised as follows: Netherlands tax law does not provide for debt to equity ratios on the basis of which debt may be regarded as equity, or for a specific set of rules regarding subordinated debt. Subordinated debt is in principle treated in the same way as any other debt, in particular as regards the deductibility of interest by the debtor. Payment of interest is not subject to withholding tax as opposed to the payment of a dividend. However, under certain circumstances, especially where the creditor is also a shareholder, it is possible that junior debt will be treated as equity. Debt may be regarded as equity if special conditions are attached to the debt or if there are special circumstances at the moment the debt was created. The payment of interest may then be treated as payment of a dividend. Dividends may not be charged against profits taxable in the Netherlands. Consequently the tax advantage of the deductibility of interest on debt is lost. For the sake of completeness it should be noted that on the basis of Netherlands statutory tax law interest payable by the debtor on profit sharing (subordinated) bonds is treated as dividend. Under a tax treaty concluded by the Netherlands, the income may however be recharacterised as interest.

12.93   Capital adequacy

The Netherlands is likely in due course to adopt the principles set out in the EEC Council Directive 89/299/EEC of April 17, 1989, on the own funds of credit institutions (O.J. No. L124, May 5, 1989, p. 16) and in the Basle Agreement on Convergence of Capital of July, 1988. These provide for subordinated debt of banks to be treated as supplementary capital for capital adequacy purposes, subject to various limits. Details of the Basle Agreement are given elsewhere in this work.

SWEDEN

Contributed by: **Olof Waern**
G. Sandströms Advokatbyrå
Stockholm

Contractual subordinations   12.94

There are no judicial decisions or statutes relating to subordinated debt in Sweden and accordingly the validity of subordinations on insolvency is untested.

Nevertheless subordinations have been used in Sweden. A suitable clause in a debenture is as follows:

> "This subordinated debenture will in the event of the company's bankruptcy or liquidation only carry a right to payment from the company's assets after the payment of the company's other debts in full."

Although section 18 of the Swedish Priority Act provides that ordinary creditors of a bankrupt company must be paid *pari passu* and although this is expressed to be mandatory, it is considered that the section is intended to prevent priority being given to one creditor. The preferred view is that the section does not prevent a creditor from agreeing to be deferred to other creditors. The other creditors are benefited by the subordination and the bankruptcy policy of equality is not disturbed. But there is no authority on the point.

Turnover subordinations   12.95

If a junior creditor is to be subordinated only to one senior creditor and not to all other creditors of the common debtor, then a contractual subordination will not achieve this object. This is because the postponement of the payment of the junior creditor to one senior creditor on insolvency is inevitably a postponement to all other creditors. A subordination to only one creditor could only be achieved by some arrangement whereby the junior creditor turns over bankruptcy dividends received in respect of the junior debt to the senior creditor until the senior debt is paid.

One method would be for the junior creditor to grant security over the whole of the junior debt in favour of the senior creditor to secure the senior debt. This could be effected by a pledge. Details of this security would not require to be registered or filed with any public registry in Sweden, nor would the security document attract any Swedish documentary taxes. A transfer by way of security in this way might conflict with any negative pledges binding on the junior creditor.

An alternative method would be an agreement by the junior creditor to transfer absolutely to the senior creditor all insolvency dividends and other recoveries when received by the junior creditor on the insolvency of the common debtor. This is a transfer of the proceeds of a debt as opposed to an immediate security assignment of the whole of the junior debt.

12.96   Secured debt

Under Swedish law, there is no objection in principle to two creditors being secured on the same asset and for one of the secured creditors to rank after the other.

12.97   Variation of priorities

The registration systems for mortgages over land, aircraft and ships prescribe an order of registration which is generally the date order in which the secured creditors register their mortgages at the relevant registry. However, even in this case it is considered that the creditors may agree between themselves to rank their debts in whatever different priority they wish. But, as regards third parties, they will rank in the order of priority prescribed by the registration law.

12.98   Rights of enforcement

In very general terms a junior secured creditor normally has the right to compel the public sale of the assets concerned if there is a default on the junior debt, even though the senior creditor objects. However, the senior creditor must be paid first out of the proceeds of sale. It is considered that an agreement between the senior and junior creditor that the junior creditor will not exercise this right of sale without the consent of the senior creditor would normally be valid—at least if the junior creditor is not in bankruptcy.

12.99   Trustee of security

Under Swedish law it is possible for a fiduciary trustee or other representative to be appointed to hold the security for the benefit of both creditors.

12.100   Taxation

Generally, subordinated debt should be treated in the same way as any other debt for most Swedish taxation purposes, in particular deductibility of interest by the debtor and withholding taxes. However, it is possible that, if the junior debt is substantially equity, then payment of interest may be treated as payment of a dividend and hence lose the tax advantages of interest on debt, *e.g.* deductibility of interest and the different rules regarding withholding tax. The position is detailed.

SELECT BIBLIOGRAPHY

American Bar Foundation, *Commentaries on Model Debenture Indenture Provisions* (1971).

Calligar, "Subordination Agreements," 70 *Yale Law Journal* 376 (1961).

Calligar "An Analysis of Bank Loan Subordination Agreements," 147 *Banker's Magazine* 5 (1964).

Carlson, "A theory of Contractual Debt Subordination and Lien Priority", 38 *Vandervell Law Review* 975 (1985).

Dobbs, "Debt Subordination," Chapter 13 in Ruda (ed.) *Asset Based Financing: A Transactional Guide*, Matthew Bender (1988).

Everett, "Subordinated Debt—Nature and Enforcement," 20 *Business Lawyer* 953 (1965).

Fitzgerald, "The pitfalls and alternatives to subordinated loans," *International Financial Law Review* 17 (November 1983).

Golin, "Debt Subordination as a Working Tool," 7 *New York Law Forum* 370 (1961).

Goode, *Commercial Law* (1982), pp. 724–727, Penguin Books.

Goode, *Legal Problems of Credit and Security* (2nd ed., 1988) pp. 23–24, 95–98.

Henson, "Subordinations and Bankruptcy: Some Current Problems," 21 *Business Lawyer* 763 (1966).

Lingard, *Bank Security Documents*, (2nd ed., 1988), Chap. 19.

Lopes, "Contractual Subordinations and Bankruptcy," *Banking Law Journal* 204 (1980).

McCormick & Creamer, *Hybrid Corporate Securities: International Legal Aspects* (1987) Sweet & Maxwell.

Milnes Holden, *The Law & Practice of Banking, Vol. 2, Securities for*

Bankers' Advances. (7th ed., 1986) Chap. 8 (Second Mortgages), Pitman.

Nicolaides, "Priorities for subordinated debt" 4 *Butterworths Journal of International Banking and Financial Law* 247 (June 1989).

Tyler, *Fisher & Lightwood's Law of Mortgages* (10th ed., 1988), Butterworths.

Wood, *English & International Set-off* (1989) Sweet & Maxwell.

The forms set out below illustrate basic types of subordination agreement, notably turnover subordination trusts between both unsecured and secured creditors, intercreditor agreements between senior lenders and mezzanine lenders financing a leveraged bid, a contractual or "contingent debt" subordination and usual subordination clauses for a capital note issue by a bank.

A full form trust deed constituting subordinated debt is not included on account of the length of these documents but some suggestions are made as to the key terms which should be included in a normal trust deed in order to convert it into a junior trust deed.

If a debtor-creditor turnover subordination not involving a trust of proceeds is required, one or other of the forms for a turnover subordination trust could be suitably modified.

All lawyers know that, however many standard forms one drafts and however omnibus they are, the forms stubbornly refuse to suit the particular case when one comes to actually use them. These forms are no exception to this general rule and hence should be regarded as little more than an assembly of clauses which might save the user the trouble of having to completely reinvent subordination on each occasion.

Although the forms are expressed to be subject to English law, it is hoped that they will be helpful in other jurisdictions, subject of course to appropriate adaptions. For example, a lawyer in a civil code jurisdiction may wish to replace the obligations of the junior creditor to hold proceeds on "trust" for the senior creditor by obligations to hold proceeds as "the property of" the senior creditor and to transfer the proceeds to the senior creditor.

Form 1

1. ALL MONEYS TURNOVER SUBORDINATION AGREEMENT FOR UNSECURED CREDITORS: FULL FORM

Note on the form

The senior and junior creditors are unsecured.

All moneys, *i.e.* the junior creditor subordinates all present and future liabilities owed to him by the borrower to all present and future liabilities owed by the borrower to the senior creditor.

The senior creditor is a party.

THIS SUBORDINATION AGREEMENT is dated [   ] and made BETWEEN:

(1) [BORROWER] (the "Borrower");
(2) [SENIOR CREDITOR] (the "Senior Creditor");
(3) [JUNIOR CREDITOR] (the "Junior Creditor");

1. DEFINITIONS

(a) *Terms defined* In this Agreement:

"Event of Default"	means any event of default or other event entitling the creditor concerned to accelerate the due date of any liability.
"Junior Debt"	means all present and future liabilities of the Borrower to the Junior Creditor, absolute, contingent or otherwise, whether or not matured, whether or not liquidated, and whether or not owed solely or jointly by the Borrower or to the Junior Creditor solely or jointly, including without limitation (a) liabilities which the Junior Creditor acquires by purchase, security assignment or otherwise, (b) interest, (c) damages, (d) claims for restitution and (e) costs.
"Junior Finance Documents"	means all present and future documents and agreements relating to the Junior Debt.
"Pending Event of Default"	means any event which with giving of notice, lapse of time, determination of materiality or fulfilment of

	any other condition (or any combination of the foregoing) would be an Event of Default.
"Permitted Payments"	means the payments and receipts permitted by Clause 4 so long as they are so permitted.
"Senior Debt"	means all present and future liabilities of the Borrower to the Senior Creditor, absolute, contingent or otherwise, whether or not matured, whether or not liquidated, and whether or not owed solely or jointly by the Borrower or to the Senior Creditor solely or jointly, including without limitation (a) liabilities which the Senior Creditor acquires by purchase, security assignment or otherwise, (b) interest, (c) damages, (d) claims for restitution and (e) costs.
"Subsidiary"	means an entity from time to time:

(a) of which another entity has direct or indirect control or another entity owns directly or indirectly more than 50 per cent. of the share capital; or

(b) which is a subsidiary of another under the laws of the jurisdiction of its incorporation.

(b) *Assigns* Without prejudice to any restrictions on assignments or other dispositions, references to the Borrower, the Senior Creditor and the Junior Creditor include their respective successors and assigns.

(c) *Headings* Headings are to be ignored in construing this Agreement.

2. BORROWER'S UNDERTAKINGS

So long as any Senior Debt is or may become outstanding, the Borrower will not (except as the Senior Creditor has previously consented in writing)

(a) (subject to Clause 6) pay or repay, or make any distribution in respect of, or purchase or acquire, any of the Junior Debt in cash or kind except for Permitted Payments;

(b) permit any of its Subsidiaries to purchase or acquire any of the Junior Debt;

(c) set off against the Junior Debt except for Permitted Payments;

(d) create or permit or subsist security over any of its assets for any of the Junior Debt;

(e) merge or consolidate into or with any other company;

(f) take or omit any action whereby the subordination achieved by this Agreement may be impaired.

3. JUNIOR CREDITOR'S UNDERTAKINGS

So long as any Senior Debt is or may become outstanding, except as the Senior Creditor has previously consented in writing, the Junior Creditor will not:

(a) (subject to Clause 6) demand or receive payment of, or any distribution in respect or on account of, any of the Junior Debt in cash or kind from the Borrower or any other source, or apply any money or assets in discharge of any Junior Debt, except in each case for Permitted Payments;

(b) set off any of the Junior Debt except for Permitted Payments;

(c) permit to subsist or receive any security for any of the Junior Debt;

(d) permit to subsist or receive any guarantee or other assurance against loss in respect of any of the Junior Debt;

[(e) permit the Junior Debt to be evidenced by a negotiable instrument unless the instrument is legended with this subordination or is deposited with the Senior Creditor;]

[(f) convert any of the Junior Debt into shares of the Borrower]

4. PERMITTED PAYMENTS

(a) So long as no Senior Debt is overdue and unpaid and no Event of Default or Pending Event of Default has occurred under any document relating to any Senior Debt, (subject to Clause 6) the Borrower may pay and the Junior Creditor may receive and retain payment of, the following:

(i) scheduled payments of interest on the Junior Debt not earlier than the date the same are scheduled to be due in accordance with the original terms of the Junior Finance Documents and not exceeding interest at a commercial rate of return;

(ii) [SPECIFY OTHER PERMITTED PAYMENTS]

(b) In this Clause, a payment or receipt includes a payment or receipt by set-off.

5. TURNOVER OF NON-PERMITTED RECOVERIES

(a) *Non-permitted payment* If

(i) the Junior Creditor receives a payment or distribution, in cash or kind, in respect of or on account of any of the Junior Debt from the Borrower or any other source other than a Permitted Payment,

(ii) the Junior Creditor receives the proceeds of any enforcement of any security, or payment under any guarantee, for any Junior Debt, or

(iii) the Borrower or any of its Subsidiaries makes any payment or distribution, in cash or kind, on account of the purchase or other acquisition of any of the Junior Debt,

the Junior Creditor will hold the same in trust for and pay and distribute it to the Senior Creditor for application towards the Senior Debt until the Senior Debt is irrevocably paid in full.

(b) *Non-permitted set-offs* If any of the Junior Debt is discharged by set-off (except for a Permitted Payment), the Junior Creditor will immediately pay an amount equal to the discharge to the Senior Creditor for application towards the Senior Debt until the Senior Debt is irrevocably paid in full.

(c) *Non-permitted security proceeds* If the Junior Creditor receives proceeds of realisation in cash or in kind in respect of any security for the Junior Debt, it will hold the same in trust for, and pay and distribute them to, the Senior Creditor for application towards the Senior Debt until the Senior Debt is irrevocably paid in full.

6. SUBORDINATION ON INSOLVENCY

If

(i) any resolution is passed or order made for the winding-up, liquidation, dissolution, administration or reorganisation of the Borrower, or

(ii) the Borrower becomes subject to any insolvency, bankruptcy, reorganisation, receivership, liquidation, dissolution or other similar proceeding, voluntary or involuntary and whether or not involving insolvency, or

(iii) the Borrower assigns its assets for the benefit of its creditors or enters into any arrangement with its creditors generally, or

(iv) the Borrower becomes subject to any distribution of its assets, or

(v) any analogous event occurs anywhere

THEN:

(a) the Junior Debt will be subordinate in right of payment to the Senior Debt

(b) the Senior Creditor may, and is irrevocably authorised on behalf of the Junior Creditor to, (i) claim, enforce and prove for the Junior Debt, (ii) file claims and proofs, give receipts and take all such proceedings and do all such things as the Senior Creditor sees fit to recover the Junior Debt and (iii) receive all distributions on the Junior Debt for application towards the Senior Debt

(c) if and to the extent that the Senior Creditor is not entitled to do any of the things mentioned in (b), the Junior Creditor will do so in good time as directed by the Senior Creditor

(d) the Junior Creditor will hold all payments and distributions in cash or in kind received or receivable by the Junior Creditor in respect of the Junior Debt from the Borrower or its estate or from any other source in trust for the Senior Creditor and will pay and transfer them to the Senior Creditor for application towards the Senior Debt until the Senior Debt is irrevocably paid in full

(e) the trustee in bankruptcy, liquidator, assignee or other person distributing the assets of the Borrower or their proceeds is directed to pay all payments and distributions on the Junior Debt direct to the Senior Creditor until the Senior Debt is irrevocably paid in full. The Junior Creditor will give all such notices and do all such things as the Senior Creditor may direct to give effect to this provision.

7. TREATMENT OF DISTRIBUTIONS

(a) *Realisation* If the Senior Creditor receives any distribution otherwise than in cash in respect of the Junior Debt from the Borrower or any other source, the Senior Creditor may realise the distribution as it sees fit and the Senior Debt shall not be deemed reduced by the distribution until and except to the extent that the realisation proceeds are applied towards the Senior Debt.

(b) *Transfer of distributions* The Junior Creditor will at its own expense do all such things as the Senior Creditor may require as being necessary or desirable to transfer to the Senior Creditor all payments and distributions which must be turned over or held in trust for the Senior Creditor, including endorsements and execution of formal transfers, and will pay all costs and stamp duties in connection therewith.

(c) *Currencies* If the Senior Creditor receives any payment required to be paid by the Junior Creditor under this Agreement or paid in respect of the Junior Debt in a currency other than the currency of the Senior Debt, the Senior Creditor may convert the currency received into the currency of the Senior Debt at a prevailing market rate of exchange and the Senior Debt shall not be deemed reduced by the payment until and except to the extent that the proceeds of conversion are applied towards the Senior Debt.

(d) *Failure of trust* If for any reason, a trust in favour of, or a holding of property for, the Senior Creditor under this Agreement is invalid or unenforceable, the Junior Creditor will pay and deliver to the Senior Creditor an amount equal to the payment, receipt or recovery in cash or in kind (or its value, if in kind) which the Junior Creditor would otherwise have been bound to hold on trust for or as property of the Senior Creditor.

8. ENFORCEMENT BY JUNIOR CREDITOR

So long as any of the Senior Debt is or may become outstanding, unless Clause 6 applies or unless the Senior Creditor has previously consented in writing, the Junior Creditor will not:

(a) accelerate any of the Junior Debt or otherwise declare any of the Junior Debt prematurely payable on an Event of Default or otherwise;

(b) enforce the Junior Debt by execution or otherwise;

(c) initiate or support or take any steps with a view to any insolvency, liquidation, reorganisation, administration or dissolution proceedings or any voluntary arrangement or assignment for the benefit of creditors or any similar proceedings involving the Borrower, whether by petition, convening a meeting, voting for a resolution or otherwise.

9. VOTING

So long as the Senior Debt is or may become outstanding,

(a) the Senior Creditor may (and is hereby irrevocably authorised to) exercise all powers of convening meetings, voting and representation in respect of the Junior Debt and the Junior Creditor will provide all forms of proxy and of representation needful to that end,

(b) if and to the extent that the Senior Creditor is not entitled to exercise a power conferred by the above the Junior Creditor (i) will exercise the power as the Senior Creditor directs, and (ii) will not exercise it so as to impair this subordination.

10. CONSENTS

(a) *New transactions* The Junior Creditor will have no remedy against the Borrower or the Senior Creditor by reason of any transaction entered into between the Senior Creditor and the Borrower which violates or is an Event of Default or Pending Event of Default under any Junior Finance Document and the Junior Creditor may not object to any such transaction by reason of any provisions of any Junior Finance Document.

(b) *Waivers* Any waiver or consent granted by the Senior Creditor will also be deemed to have been given by the Junior Creditor if any transaction or circumstances would, in the absence of such waiver or consent by the Junior Creditor, violate any Junior Finance Document or constitute an Event of Default or Pending Event of Default under any Junior Finance Document.

11. REPRESENTATIONS AND WARRANTIES OF THE BORROWER

The Borrower represents and warrants to the Senior Creditor

(a) *Status* The Borrower is a limited liability company, duly incorporated and validly existing under the laws of [   ].

(b) *Powers and authority* The Borrower has the power to enter into and perform, and has taken all necessary action to authorise the entry into, performance and delivery of, the existing Junior Finance Documents and this Agreement and the transactions contemplated by those Junior Finance Documents and this Agreement.

(c) *Legal validity* The existing Junior Finance Documents and this Agreement constitute its legal, valid and binding obligations enforceable in accordance with their terms.

(d) *Non-conflict* The entry into and performance by the Borrower of, and the transactions contemplated by, the Junior Finance Documents and this Agreement do not and will not:

(i) conflict with any law or regulation; or
(ii) conflict with the constitutional documents of the Borrower or of any of its Subsidiaries; or
(iii) conflict with any document which is binding on the Borrower or on any of its Subsidiaries or any asset of the Borrower or of any of its Subsidiaries.

(e) *Authorisations* All authorisations, consents, registrations, filings, notarisations and the like required or desirable in connection with the entry into and performance by it, the validity and enforceability of, and of the transactions contemplated by, the Junior Finance Documents and this Agreement have been obtained or effected (as appropriate) and are in full force and effect.

12. REPRESENTATIONS AND WARRANTIES OF JUNIOR CREDITOR

The Junior Creditor represents and warrants to the Senior Creditor

(a) *Legal validity* This Agreement is within its powers, has been duly authorised by it, constitutes its legal, valid and binding obligations enforceable in accordance with their terms and does not conflict with any law or regulation or its constitution documents or any document binding on it and that it has obtained all necessary consents for the performance by it of this Agreement.

(b) *Disclosure* There has been provided to the Senior Creditor true and complete copies of the existing Junior Finance Documents containing all terms relating to the Junior Debt.

(c) *Ownership* The Junior Creditor is the sole beneficial owner of the Junior Debt and of the benefit of the Junior Finance Documents free of encumbrances, options and subordinations in favour of any person other than the Senior Creditor.

[(d) *Set-off* The Junior Debt is not subject to any set-off, counterclaim or other defence.]

13. REPETITION OF REPRESENTATIONS AND WARRANTIES

The representations and warranties in Clauses 11 and 12 are deemed to be repeated by each of the Borrower and the Junior Creditor respectively on each date so long as any Senior Debt is outstanding with reference to the facts and circumstances then existing.

14. INFORMATION BY JUNIOR CREDITOR

(a) *Defaults* The Junior Creditor will promptly notify the Senior Creditor of the occurrence of any Event of Default or Pending Event of Default under any Junior Finance Document.

(b) *Amount of Junior Debt* The Junior Creditor will on written request by the Senior Creditor from time to time notify the Senior Creditor in writing of details of the amount of the Junior Debt and give the Senior Creditor copies of all Junior Finance Documents as soon as entered into.

15. SUBROGATION BY JUNIOR CREDITOR

If any of the Senior Debt is wholly or partially paid out of any proceeds received in respect of or on account of the Junior Debt, the Junior Creditor will to that extent be subrogated to the Senior Debt so paid (and all securities and guarantees for that Senior Debt) but not before all the Senior Debt is paid in full.

16. PROTECTION OF SUBORDINATION

(a) *Continuing subordination* The subordination provisions in this Agreement constitute a continuing subordination and benefit the ultimate balance of the Senior Debt regardless of any intermediate payment or discharge of the Senior Debt in whole or in part.

(b) *Waiver of defences* The subordination in this Agreement and the obligations of the Junior Creditor under this Agreement will not be affected by any act, omission, matter or thing which, but for this provision, would reduce, release or prejudice the subordination or any of those obligations in whole or in part, including without limitation:

(i) any time or waiver granted to, or composition with, the Borrower or other person;

(ii) the taking, variation, compromise, exchange, renewal or release of, or refusal or neglect to perfect, take up or enforce, any rights against, or security over assets of, the Borrower or other person in respect of the Senior Debt or otherwise or any non-presentment or non-observance of any formality or other requirement in respect of any instrument or any failure to realise the full value of any security;

(iii) any unenforceability, illegality or invalidity of any obligation of the Borrower or security in respect of the Senior Debt or any other document or security;

(c) *Immediate recourse* The Junior Creditor waives any right it may have of first requiring the Senior Creditor (or any trustee or agent on its behalf) to proceed against or enforce any other right or security or claim payment from any person before claiming the benefit of this Agreement.

(d) *Appropriations* Until the Senior Debt has been irrevocably paid in full, the Senior Creditor (or any trustee or agent on its behalf) may:

(i) apply any moneys or property received under this Agreement or from the Borrower or from any other person against the Senior Debt in such order as it sees fit;

[(ii) (if it so decides) apply any moneys or property received from the Borrower or from any other person (other than money or property received for the Junior Creditor under this Agreement) against any liability other than the Senior Debt owed to it;]

[*Note*: The above para. (ii) will be relevant only if the Senior Debt does not include all debt owed by the Borrower to the Senior Creditor.]

(iii) hold in suspense any moneys or distributions received from the Junior Creditor under Clauses 5, 6 and 7 or on account of the liability of the Junior Creditor under this Agreement.

(e) *Non-competition* Until the Senior Debt has been irrevocably paid in full, the Junior Creditor will not by virtue of any payment or performance by it under this Agreement or by virtue of the operation of Clause 5, 6 or 7:

(i) be subrogated to any rights, security or moneys held, received or receivable by the Senior Creditor (or any trustee or agent on its behalf) or be entitled to any right of contribution or indemnity;

(ii) claim, rank, prove or vote as a creditor of the Borrower or any other person or their respective estates in competition with the Senior Creditor (or any trustee or agent on its behalf); or

(iii) receive, claim or have the benefit of any payment, distribution or security from or on account of the Borrower or other person.

17. PRESERVATION OF JUNIOR DEBT

Solely as between the Borrower and the Junior Creditor, the Junior Debt shall remain owing or due and payable in accordance with the terms of the Junior Finance Documents, and interest and default interest will accrue on missed payments accordingly.

18. TERMINATION OF SUBORDINATION

By not less than 30 days' prior written notice to the Senior Creditor, the Junior Creditor may terminate this subordination agreement. However the termination will not affect Junior Debt which is incurred prior to the expiry of the notice or which arises as a result of any transaction or under or in connection with any agreement entered into prior to such expiry.

19. RESPONSIBILITY OF SENIOR CREDITOR

The Senior Creditor will not be liable to the Junior Creditor

(a) for the manner of exercise or for any non-exercise of its powers under this Agreement, or
(b) for failure to collect or preserve the Junior Debt.

20. EXPENSES

(a) *Initial costs* The Borrower will forthwith on demand pay the Senior Creditor the amount of all costs and expenses incurred by it in connection with the negotiation, preparation, execution and performance of this Agreement and all waivers in relation to and variations of this Agreement.

(b) *Enforcement costs* Each of the Borrower and the Junior Creditor shall, forthwith on demand, pay to the Senior Creditor the amount of all costs and expenses incurred by it in connection with the enforcement against the Borrower or Junior Creditor (as the case may be) of the Senior Creditor's rights against it under this Agreement.

(c) *Legal expenses and taxes* The costs and expenses referred to above include, without limitation, the fees and expenses of legal advisers and any value added tax or similar tax, and are payable in the currency in which they are incurred.

21. CHANGES TO THE PARTIES

(a) *Successors and assigns* This Agreement is binding on the successors and assigns of the parties hereto.

(b) *Borrower* The Borrower may not assign or transfer any of its rights (if any) or obligations under this Agreement.

(c) *Junior Creditor* So long as any Senior Debt is or may become outstanding, the Junior Creditor will not

(i) assign or dispose of, or create or permit to subsist any security (fixed or floating) over, any of the Junior Debt or its proceeds or any interest in the Junior Debt or its proceeds to or in favour of any person, or

(ii) subordinate any of the Junior Debt or its proceeds to any sums owing by the Borrower to any person other than the Senior Creditor

(iii) transfer by novation or otherwise any of its rights or obligations under any Junior Finance Document or in respect of any Junior Debt to any person

unless in each case that person agrees with the Senior Creditor that he is bound by all the terms of this Agreement as Junior Creditor in a manner satisfactory to the Senior Creditor.

(d) *Senior Creditor* The Senior Creditor may assign or otherwise dispose of all or any of its rights under this Agreement.

(c) *Memorandum on documents* The Junior Creditor will endorse a memorandum of this Agreement on each Junior Finance Document.

22. GENERAL

(a) *Rights of the borrower* The Borrower does not have any rights under or by virtue of this Agreement.

(b) *Perpetuity period* The perpetuity period for the trusts in this Agreement is 80 years.

(c) *Power of attorney* By way of security for the obligations of the Junior Creditor under this Agreement, the Junior Creditor irrevocably appoints the Senior Creditor as its attorney to do anything which the Junior Creditor (i) has authorised the Senior Creditor to do under this Agreement and (ii) is required to do by this Agreement but has failed to do. The Senior Creditor may delegate this power.

(d) *Stamp duties* The Borrower shall pay and forthwith on demand indemnify the Senior Creditor [and the Junior Creditor] against any liability it incurs in respect of any stamp, registration and similar tax which is or becomes payable in connection with the entry into, performance or enforcement of this Agreement.

(e) *Currency indemnity* The Junior Creditor will indemnify the Senior Creditor against losses suffered by the Senior Creditor if any claim by the

Senior Creditor (or any agent or trustee on its behalf) against the Junior Creditor under this Agreement is converted into a claim, proof, judgment or order in a currency other than the currency in which the amount is contractually payable under this Agreement.

(f) *Waivers, remedies cumulative* The rights of the Senior Creditor under this Agreement:

(i) are cumulative and not exclusive of its rights under the general law; and
(ii) may be waived only in writing and specifically.

Delay in exercising or non-exercise of any such right is not a waiver of that right.

(g) *Set-off* The Senior Creditor may set off any matured obligation owed by the Junior Creditor under this Agreement (to the extent beneficially owned by the Senior Creditor) against any obligation (whether or not matured) owed by the Senior Creditor to the Junior Creditor, regardless of the place of payment, booking branch or currency of either obligation. If the obligations are in different currencies, the Senior Creditor may convert either obligation at a market rate of exchange in its usual course of business for the purpose of the set-off.

(h) *Default interest* If the Junior Creditor fails to pay any amount payable by it under this Agreement to the Senior Creditor, it shall, on demand by the Senior Creditor from time to time, pay interest on the overdue amount from the due date up to the date of actual payment, as well after as before judgment, at the rate of [   ].

(i) *Severability* If a provision of this Agreement is or becomes illegal, invalid or unenforceable in any jurisdiction, that shall not affect:

(i) the validity or enforceability in that jurisdiction of any other provision of this Agreement; or
(ii) the validity or enforceability in other jurisdictions of that or any other provisions of this Agreement.

(j) *Counterparts* This Agreement may be executed in any number of counterparts, and this has the same effect as if the signatures on the counterparts were on a single copy of this Agreement.

23. NOTICES

(a) *Service of notices* All notices under or in connection with this Agreement shall be given in writing or by telex or fax. If correctly addressed, any such notice is deemed to be given at the following times:

(i) if in writing when delivered;

(ii) if by telex when dispatched; and

(iii) if by fax when received.

However, a notice given in accordance with the above but received on a non-working day or after business hours in the place of receipt is deemed to be given on the next working day in that place.

(b) *Addresses for notices* The address, telex number and fax number of each party hereto for all notices under, or in connection with, this Agreement, are:

[   ].

A party may change the above by prior written notice to the other parties.

24. JURISDICTION

(a) *Submission* For the benefit of the Senior Creditor, each of the Borrower and the Junior Creditor agrees that the courts of England are to have jurisdiction to settle any disputes in connection with this Agreement, submits to the jurisdiction of the English courts in connection with this Agreement, appoints [   ] as its agent for service of process relating to any proceedings before the English courts in connection with this Agreement and agrees to maintain a process agent in England notified to the Senior Creditor.

(b) *Non-exclusivity* Nothing in this Clause limits the right of the Senior Creditor to bring proceedings against another party hereto in connection with this Agreement:

(i) in any other court of competent jurisdiction; or

(ii) concurrently in more than one jurisdiction.

25. GOVERNING LAW

This Agreement is governed by English law.

IN WITNESS whereof this Agreement has been entered into on the date stated at the head of this Agreement.

FORM 2

SPECIFIC CREDIT TURNOVER SUBORDINATION AGREEMENT
FOR UNSECURED CREDITORS: SHORTER FORM

Note on the form

The senior and junior creditors are unsecured.

Specific credits, *i.e.* the junior creditor subordinates debts owed to him under a specific credit agreement to those owed to the senior creditor under a specific credit agreement.

The senior creditor is a party.

THIS SUBORDINATION AGREEMENT is dated [   ] and made BETWEEN:

(1) [BORROWER] (the "Borrower");

(2) [SENIOR CREDITOR] (the "Senior Creditor" which term includes its successors and assigns);

(3) [JUNIOR CREDITOR] (the "Junior Creditor" which term includes its successors and assigns);

1. DEFINITIONS

In this Agreement:

"Junior Debt" means all present and future liabilities of the Borrower to the Junior Creditor under or in connection with or on rescission of the Junior Credit Agreement;

"Junior Credit Agreement" means the Credit Agreement dated [   ] between the Borrower and the Junior Creditor and all variations thereof;

"Permitted Payments" means payments and receipts (directly or by set-off) of scheduled interest, commissions and costs payable under the Junior Credit Agreement but only so long as no Senior Debt is due and unpaid and no event of default (or event which with giving of notice, lapse of time or other condition might be an event of default) has occurred and is continuing under the Senior Credit Agreement;

"Senior Debt" means all present and future liabilities of the Borrower to the Senior

Creditor, under or in connection
with, or on rescission of, the Senior
Credit Agreement;

"Senior Credit Agreement"   means the Credit Agreement dated
[   ] between the Borrower and
the Senior Creditor and all variations thereof.

2. BORROWER'S UNDERTAKINGS

So long as any Senior Debt is or may become outstanding, the Borrower will not (except as the Senior Creditor has previously consented in
writing)

(a) (subject to Clause 5) pay or repay, or make any distribution in
respect of, or purchase or acquire, any of the Junior Debt in cash or in
property or securities except for Permitted Payments;

(b) permit any of its subsidiaries to purchase or acquire any of the
Junior Debt,

(c) discharge any of the Junior Debt by set-off except for Permitted
Payments;

(d) create or permit or subsist security over any of its assets for any of
the Junior Debt;

(e) vary the Junior Credit Agreement;

(f) take or omit any action whereby the subordination achieved by this
Agreement may be impaired.

3. JUNIOR CREDITOR'S UNDERTAKINGS

So long as any Senior Debt is or may become outstanding, except as the
Senior Creditor has previously consented in writing, the Junior Creditor
will:

(a) (subject to Clause 5) not demand or receive payment of, or any
distribution in respect or on account of, any of the Junior Debt from the
Borrower or any other source or apply any money or assets in discharge of
any Junior Debt, except for Permitted Payments;

(b) not discharge the Junior Debt by set-off except for a Permitted
Payments;

(c) not permit to subsist or receive any security for any of the Junior
Debt;

(d) not permit to subsist or receive any guarantee or other assurance
against loss in respect of any of the Junior Debt;

(e) promptly notify the Senior Creditor of any default or event of
default in respect of the Junior Debt;

(f) unless Clause 5 applies, not

  (i) accelerate any of the Junior Debt;

  (ii) enforce the Junior Debt by execution or otherwise

(iii) initiate or support or take any steps with a view to any insolvency, reorganisation or dissolution proceedings in respect of the Borrower;

(g) not

(i) assign or dispose of, or create or permit to subsist any security over, any of the Junior Debt or its proceeds or any interest in the Junior Debt or its proceeds to or in favour of any person, or

(ii) subordinate any of the Junior Debt or its proceeds to any sums owing by the Borrower to any person other than the Senior Creditor, or

(iii) transfer by novation or otherwise any of its rights or obligations under the Junior Credit Agreement or in respect of any Junior Debt to any person unless in each case that person agrees with the Senior Creditor that he is bound by all the terms of this Agreement as Junior Creditor in a manner satisfactory to the Senior Creditor.

4. TURNOVER OF NON-PERMITTED RECOVERIES

(a) *Non-permitted payment* If

(i) the Junior Creditor receives a payment or distribution in respect of any of the Junior Debt (other than a Permitted Payment) from the Borrower or any other source,

(ii) the Junior Creditor receives the proceeds of any enforcement of any security or any guarantee for any Junior Debt, or

(iii) the Borrower or any of its subsidiaries makes any payment or distribution on account of the purchase or other acquisition of any of the Junior Debt,

the Junior Creditor will hold the same in trust for and pay and distribute it to the Senior Creditor for application towards the Senior Debt until the Senior Debt is irrevocably paid in full.

(b) *Non-permitted set-offs* If any of the Junior Debt is discharged by set-off (except a Permitted Payment), the Junior Creditor will immediately pay an amount equal to the discharge to the Senior Creditor for application towards the Senior Debt until the Senior Debt is irrevocably paid in full.

5. SUBORDINATION ON INSOLVENCY

If the Borrower becomes subject to any insolvency, bankruptcy, reorganisation, administration, assignment to arrangement with creditors, liquidation, dissolution or other similar proceeding or distribution of its assets whether or not involving insolvency, or

(a) the Junior Debt will be subordinate in right of payment to the Senior Debt

(b) the Senior Creditor may, and is irrevocably authorised on behalf of the Junior Creditor to, (i) claim, enforce and prove for the Junior Debt, (ii) file claims and proofs, give receipts and take all such proceedings and do all such things as the Senior Creditor sees fit to recover the Junior Debt and (iii) receive all distributions on the Junior Debt for application towards the Senior Debt

(c) if and to the extent that the Senior Creditor is not entitled to do any of the foregoing, the Junior Creditor will do so in good time as directed by the Senior Creditor

(d) the Junior Creditor will hold all distributions in cash or in kind received or receivable by the Junior Creditor in respect of the Junior Debt from the Borrower or its estate or from any other source in trust for the Senior Creditor and will (at the Junior Creditor's expense) pay and transfer the same to the Senior Creditor for application towards the Senior Debt until the Senior Debt is irrevocably paid in full

(e) the trustee in bankruptcy, liquidator, assignee or other person distributing the assets of the Borrower or their proceeds is directed to pay distributions on the Junior Debt direct to the Senior Creditor until the Senior Debt is irrevocably paid in full. The Junior Creditor will give all such notices and do all such things as the Senior Creditor may direct to give effect to this provision.

[*Note*: Consider a fall-back protection on the lines of Clause 7(d) in Form 1.]

6. VOTING

So long as the Senior Debt is or may become outstanding,

(a) the Senior Creditor may (and is hereby irrevocably authorised to) exercise all powers of convening meetings, voting and representation in respect of the Junior Debt and the Junior Creditor will provide all forms of proxy and of representation needful to that end, and

(b) if and to the extent that the Senior Creditor is not entitled to exercise a power conferred by the above the Junior Creditor (i) will exercise the power as the Senior Creditor directs, and (ii) will not exercise it so as to impair this subordination.

7. CONSENTS

(a) *New transactions* The Junior Creditor will have no remedy against the Borrower or the Senior Creditor by reason of any transaction entered into between the Senior Creditor and the Borrower which violates the Junior Credit Agreement and the Junior Creditor may not object to any such transaction by reason of any provisions of the Junior Credit Agreement.

(b) *Waivers* Any waiver or consent granted by the Senior Creditor will also be deemed to have been given by the Junior Creditor if any transaction or circumstances would, in the absence of such waiver or consent by the Junior Creditor, violate the Junior Credit Agreement.

8. SUBROGATION BY JUNIOR CREDITOR

If the Senior Debt is wholly or partially paid out of any proceeds received in respect of or on account of the Junior Debt, the Junior Creditor will to that extent be subrogated to the Senior Debt so paid (and all securities and guarantees for that Senior Debt) but not before all the Senior Debt is paid in full.

9. PROTECTION OF SUBORDINATION

(a) *Continuing subordination* The subordination provisions in this Agreement constitute a continuing subordination and benefit the ultimate balance of the Senior Debt.

(b) *Waiver of defences* The subordination in this Agreement and the obligations of the Junior Creditor under this Agreement will not be affected by any act, omission, matter or thing which, but for this provision, would reduce, release or prejudice the subordination or any of those obligations in whole or in part, including without limitation:

(i) any waiver granted to, or composition with, the Borrower or other person;

(ii) the taking, variation, compromise, exchange, renewal or release of, or refusal or neglect to perfect, take up or enforce, any rights against, or security over assets of, the Borrower or other person in respect of the Senior Debt or otherwise or any failure to realise the full value of any security.

(iii) any enforceability, illegality or invalidity of any obligation of the Borrower or security in respect of the Senior Debt or any other document or security.

(c) *Immediate recourse* The Junior Creditor waives any right it may have of first requiring the Senior Creditor (or any trustee or agent on its behalf) to proceed against or enforce any other rights or security or claim payment from any person before claiming the benefit of this Agreement. The Senior Creditor (or any trustee or agent on its behalf) may refrain from applying or enforcing any money, rights or security.

(d) *Appropriations* Until the Senior Debt has been irrevocably paid in full, the Senior Creditor (or any trustee or agent on its behalf) may:

(i) apply any moneys or property received under this Agreement or from the Borrower or from any other person against the Senior Debt in such order as it sees fit;

(ii) (if it so decides) apply any moneys or property received from the Borrower or from any other person (other than money or property received for the Junior Creditor under this Agreement) against any liability other than the Senior Debt owed to it;

(iii) hold in suspense any moneys or distributions received from the Junior Creditor under Clauses 4 and 5 or on account of the liability of the Junior Creditor under this Agreement.

(e) *Non-competition* Until the Senior Debt has been irrevocably paid in full, the Junior Creditor will not by virtue of any payment or performance by it under this Agreement or by virtue of the operation of Clauses 4 or 5:

(i) be subrogated to any rights, security or moneys held, received or receivable by the Senior Creditor (or any trustee or agent on its behalf) or be entitled to any right of contribution or indemnity;

(ii) claim, rank, prove or vote as a creditor of the Borrower or other person or their respective estates in competition with the Senior Creditor (or any trustee or agent on its behalf); or

(iii) receive, claim or have the benefit of any payment, distribution or security from or on account of the Borrower or other person.

10. PRESERVATION OF JUNIOR DEBT

Solely as between the Borrower and the Junior Creditor, the Junior Debt will remain owing or due and payable in accordance with the terms of the Junior Credit Agreement, and interest and default interest will accrue on missed payments accordingly.

11. MISCELLANEOUS

(a) *Perpetuity* The perpetuity period for the trusts in this Agreement is 80 years.

(b) *Power of attorney* By way of security for the obligations of the Junior Creditor under this Agreement, the Junior Creditor irrevocably appoints the Senior Creditor as its attorney to do anything which the Junior Creditor (a) has authorised the Senior Creditor to do under this Agreement and (b) is required to do by this Agreement but has failed to do. The Senior Creditor may delegate this power.

(c) *Expenses* The Borrower will forthwith on demand pay the Senior Creditor the amount of all costs, expenses and stamp duties incurred by it in connection with this Agreement and its enforcement.

(d) *Notices* All notices under, or in connection with, this Agreement shall be given in writing or by telex or fax to the following addresses (or such other addresses as may be notified from time to time):
[Addresses]

(e) *Jurisdiction* For the benefit of the Senior Creditor, each of the Borrower and the Junior Creditor agrees that the courts of England are to have jurisdiction to settle any disputes in connection with this Agreement and appoints [   ] as its agent for service of process relating to any proceedings before the English courts in connection with this Agreement. Nothing in this Clause limits the right of the Senior Creditor to bring proceedings against another party hereto in connection with this Agreement in any other court of competent jurisdiction.

(f) *Governing law* This Agreement is governed by English law.

IN WITNESS whereof this Agreement has been entered into on the date stated at the head of this Agreement.

ALL MONEYS TURNOVER SUBORDINATION AGREEMENT FOR SECURED CREDITORS: FULL FORM

Note on the form

The senior and junior creditors are secured on the same assets of the borrower but under separate security documents. Alternatively the security could be granted to a trustee for both creditors: see para. 10.1. In the latter case, the borrower should also covenant with the trustee to pay the junior and senior debt, *i.e.* grant to the trustee a covenant parallel to the covenants given by the borrower to the creditors directly in order to support the security granted to the trustee.

The covenant would state:

"The Borrower covenants in favour of the Trustee to pay the Senior Debt and the Junior Debt to the Trustee when due under the terms of the Senior Finance Documents and the Junior Finance Documents to such bank account as the Trustee may direct, except that until an Event of Default occurs under the Senior Finance Documents and the Senior Creditor notifies the Trustee, the Borrower and the Junior Creditor thereof in writing, the Borrower may (subject to the terms of this Intercreditor Agreement) pay the Senior Debt and the Junior Debt directly to the Senior Creditor and the Junior Creditor respectively and each such payment will be a *pro tanto* discharge of the above payment covenant in favour of the Trustee."

The trust deed should contain

— usual clauses protecting the trustee from liability
— usual powers in favour of the trustee
— provisions requiring the trustee to enforce the security as directed by the senior creditor.

The form covers all moneys, *i.e.* the junior creditor subordinates all present and future liabilities owed to him by the borrower to all present and future liabilities owed by the borrower to the senior creditor.

THIS INTERCREDITOR AGREEMENT is dated [   ] and made BETWEEN:
(1) [BORROWER] (the "Borrower");
(2) [SENIOR CREDITOR] (the "Senior Creditor");
(3) [JUNIOR CREDITOR] (the "Junior Creditor");

1. DEFINITIONS

(a) *Terms defined* In this Agreement:

"Event of Default"   means any event of default or other event entitling the creditor concerned to accelerate the due date of any liability.

"Junior Debt" means all present and future liabilities of the Borrower to the Junior Creditor, absolute, contingent or otherwise, whether or not matured, whether or not liquidated, and whether or not owed solely or jointly by the Borrower or to the Junior Creditor solely or jointly, including without limitation (a) liabilities which the Junior Creditor acquires by purchase, security assignment or otherwise, (b) interest, (c) damages, (d) claims for restitution and (e) costs.

"Junior Finance Documents" means the Junior Security Documents and all other present and future documents and agreements relating to the Junior Debt;

"Junior Security Documents" means

(a) the security documents specified in Schedule 1 to this Agreement,

(b) any existing and future guarantees or the like of, and any document conferring or evidencing security for, any of the Junior Debt, and

(c) any variations, replacements and novations of, and supplements to the foregoing but without prejudice to any restrictions on the same.

"Pending Event of Default" means any event which with giving notice, lapse of time, determination of materiality or fulfilment of any other condition (or any combination of the foregoing) would be an Event of Default.

"Permitted Payments" means the payments and receipts permitted by Clause 4 so long as they are so permitted.

"Senior Debt" means all present and future liabilities of the Borrower to the Senior Creditor, absolute, contingent or otherwise, whether or not matured, whether or not liquidated, and whether or not owed solely or jointly by the Borrower or to the Senior Creditor solely or jointly, including without limitation (a) liabilities which the Senior Creditor acquires by purchase, security assignment or otherwise, (b) interest, (c) damages, (d) claims for restitution and (e) costs.

"Senior Finance Documents" means the Senior Security Documents and all present and future documents and agreements relating to the Senior Debt.

"Senior Security Documents" means:

(a) the security documents specified in Schedule 2 to this Agreement

(b) any existing or future guarantees or the like of, and any existing or future document conferring or evidencing security for, any of the Senior Debt, and

(c) any variations, replacements, and novations of and supplements to the foregoing.

"Subsidiary" means an entity from time to time:

(a) of which another entity has direct or indirect control or another entity owns directly or indirectly more than 50 per cent. of the share capital; or

(b) which is a subsidiary of another under the laws of the jurisdiction of its incorporation.

(b) *Assigns* Without prejudice to any restrictions on assignments or other dispositions, references to the Borrower, the Senior Creditor and the Junior Creditor include their respective successors and assigns.

(c) *Headings* Headings are to be ignored in construing this Agreement.

2. BORROWER'S UNDERTAKINGS

So long as any Senior Debt is or may become outstanding, the Borrower will not (except as the Senior Creditor has previously consented in writing)

(a) (subject to Clause 6) pay or repay, or make any distribution in respect of, or purchase or acquire, any of the Junior Debt in cash or in kind except for Permitted Payments;

(b) permit any of its Subsidiaries to purchase or acquire any of the Junior Debt;

(c) set-off against the Junior Debt except for Permitted Payments;

(d) create or permit or subsist security over any of its assets for any of the Junior Debt except for security under the existing Junior Security Documents;

(e) merge or consolidate into or with any other company;

(f) take or omit any action whereby the subordination achieved by this Agreement may be impaired.

3. JUNIOR CREDITOR'S UNDERTAKINGS

So long as any Senior Debt is or may become outstanding, except as the Senior Creditor has previously consented in writing, the Junior Creditor will not:

(a) (subject to Clause 6) demand or receive payment of, or any distribution in respect or on account of, any of the Junior Debt in cash or kind from the Borrower or any other source or apply any money or assets in discharge of any Junior Debt, except in each case for Permitted Payments and except for the proceeds of security received and applied in the order permitted by Clause 10;

(b) set off any of the Junior Debt except for Permitted Payments;

(c) permit to subsist or receive any security for any of the Junior Debt except for security under the existing Junior Security Documents;

(d) permit to subsist or receive any guarantee or other assurance against loss in respect of any of the Junior Debt except for guarantees and security under the existing Junior Security Documents;

[(e) permit the Junior Debt to be evidenced by a negotiable instrument unless the instrument is legended with this subordination or is deposited with the Senior Creditor;]

[(f) convert any of the Junior Debt into shares of the Borrower.]

4. PERMITTED PAYMENTS

(a) So long as no Senior Debt is overdue and unpaid and no Event of Default or Pending Event of Default has occurred under any Senior Finance Document, (subject to Clause 6) the Borrower may pay and the Junior Creditor may receive and retain payment of, the following:

(i) scheduled payments of interest on the Junior Debt under the Junior Credit Agreement not earlier than the date the same are scheduled to be due in accordance with the original terms of the documents evidencing the same and not exceeding interest at a commercial rate of return;

(ii) [SPECIFY OTHER PERMITTED PAYMENTS]

(b) A payment or receipt includes a payment or receipt by set-off.

5. TURNOVER OF NON-PERMITTED RECOVERIES

(a) *Non-permitted payment* If

(i) the Junior Creditor receives a payment or distribution in cash or kind in respect of or on account of any of the Junior Debt from the Borrower or any other source except for a Permitted Payment

(ii) the Junior Creditor receives the proceeds of any enforcement of any security conferred by the Junior Security Documents otherwise than in the order set out in Clause 10 or payment under any guarantee for any Junior Debt, or

(iii) the Borrower or any of its Subsidiaries makes any payment or distribution in cash or kind on account of the purchase or other acquisition of any of the Junior Debt,

the Junior Creditor will hold the same in trust for and pay and distribute it to the Senior Creditor for application towards the Senior Debt until the Senior Debt is irrevocably paid in full.

(b) *Non-permitted set-offs* If any of the Junior Debt is discharged by set-off (except for a Permitted Payment), the Junior Creditor will immediately pay an amount equal to the discharge to the Senior Creditor for application towards the Senior Debt until the Senior Debt is irrevocably paid in full.

6. SUBORDINATION ON INSOLVENCY

If

(i) any resolution is passed or order made for the winding-up, liquidation, dissolution, administration or reorganisation of the Borrower, or

(ii) the Borrower becomes subject to any insolvency, bankruptcy, reorganisation, receivership, liquidation, dissolution or other similar proceeding, voluntary or involuntary and whether or not involving insolvency, or

(iii) the Borrower assigns its assets for the benefit of its creditors or enters into any arrangement with its creditors generally, or

(iv) the Borrower becomes subject to any distribution of its assets, or

(v) any analogous event occurs anywhere

THEN:

(a) the Junior Debt will be subordinate in right of payment to the Senior Debt

(b) the Senior Creditor may, and is irrevocably authorised on behalf of the Junior Creditor to, (i) claim, enforce and prove for the Junior Debt, (ii) file claims and proofs, give receipts and take all such proceedings and do all such things as the Senior Creditor sees fit to recover the Junior Debt and (iii) receive all distributions on the Junior Debt for application towards the Senior Debt

(c) if and to the extent that the Senior Creditor is not entitled to do any of things mentioned in (b) the Junior Creditor will do so in good time as directed by the Senior Creditor

(d) the Junior Creditor will hold all distributions in cash or in kind received or receivable by the Junior Creditor in respect of the Junior Debt from the Borrower or its estate or any other source in trust for the Senior Creditor and will pay and transfer the same to the Senior Creditor for application towards the Senior Debt until the Senior Debt is irrevocably paid in full

(e) the trustee in bankruptcy, liquidator, assignee or other person distributing the assets of the Borrower or their proceeds is directed to pay distributions on the Junior Debt direct to the Senior Creditor until the Senior Debt is irrevocably paid in full. The Junior Creditor will give all such notices and do all such things as the Senior Creditor may direct to give effect to this provision.

7. TREATMENT OF DISTRIBUTIONS

(a) *Realisation* If the Senior Creditor receives any distribution otherwise than in cash in respect of the Junior Debt from the Borrower or any other source, the Senior Creditor may realise the distribution as it sees fit and the Senior Debt shall not be deemed reduced by the distribution until and except to the extent that the realisation proceeds are applied towards the Senior Debt.

(b) *Transfer of distributions* The Junior Creditor will at its own expense do all such things as the Senior Creditor may require as being necessary or desirable to transfer to the Senior Creditor all payments and distributions which must be turned over or held in trust for the Senior Creditor, including endorsements and execution of formal transfers, and will pay all costs and stamp duties in connection therewith.

(c) *Currencies* If the Senior Creditor receives any payment required to be paid by the Junior Creditor under this Agreement or paid in respect of the Junior Debt in a currency other than the currency of the Senior Debt, the Senior Creditor may convert the currency received into the currency of the Senior Debt at a prevailing market rate of exchange and the Senior Debt shall not be deemed reduced by the payment until and except to the extent that the proceeds of conversion are applied towards the Senior Debt.

(d) *Failure of trust* If for any reason, a trust in favour of, or a holding of property for, the Senior Creditor under this Agreement is invalid or unenforceable, the Junior Creditor will pay and deliver to the Senior

Creditor an amount equal to the payment, receipt or recovery in cash or in kind (or its value, if in kind) which it would otherwise have been bound to hold on trust for or as property of the Senior Creditor.

8. PRIORITY OF SECURITY

(a) *Ranking* Existing and future security conferred by the Senior Security Documents will

(i) rank in all respects prior to existing and future security conferred by the Junior Security Documents, regardless of order of registration, notice, execution or otherwise;

(ii) secure all the Senior Debt in priority to the Junior Debt, regardless of the date upon which the Senior Debt arises, regardless of whether or not the Senior Creditor is obliged to advance moneys included in Senior Debt, and regardless of any intermediate discharge of the Senior Debt in whole or in part.

(b) *Registration and notice* The Junior Creditor will co-operate with the Senior Creditor with a view to reflecting the priority of the security conferred by the Senior Security Documents in any register or with any filing or registration authority and in giving notice to insurers, debtors liable for receivables covered by the security conferred by the Senior Security Documents and other persons.

(c) *Custody of documents* So long as the Senior Security Documents are in force, the Senior Creditor will be entitled to the deposit of any title deeds, share certificates or other title documents, certificates or paper in respect of any assets subject to the security conferred by the Senior Security Documents in priority to the entitlement of the Junior Creditor. The Senior Creditor has no responsibility to the Junior Creditor to require or maintain such deposit.

(d) *Consolidation* The Senior Creditor may consolidate security against the Junior Creditor.

9. ENFORCEMENT OF SECURITY

(a) *Restrictions on enforcement by Junior Creditor* So long as any of the Senior Debt is or may become outstanding, unless Clause 6 applies or unless the Senior Creditor has previously consented in writing, the Junior Creditor will not

(i) accelerate any of the Junior Debt or otherwise declare any of the Junior Debt prematurely payable on an Event of Default or otherwise.

(ii) enforce the Junior Debt by execution or otherwise,

(iii) enforce any security conferred by the Junior Security Documents

or any other security for the Junior Debt by sale, possession, appointment of a receiver or otherwise, or

(iv) initiate or support or take any steps with a view to any insolvency,
liquidation, reorganisation, administration or dissolution proceedings or
any voluntary arrangement or assignment for the benefit of creditors or
any similar proceedings involving the Borrower, whether by petition,
convening a meeting, voting for a resolution or otherwise.

(b) *Enforcement by Senior Creditor* If the Senior Creditor enforces any
security conferred by the Senior Security Documents:

(i) the Junior Creditor will not be entitled to take or have possession of
any such assets or maintain a receiver in possession in respect of such
assets;

(ii) the Senior Creditor will have the entire conduct of any sale of assets
covered by any security created by a Senior Security Document;

(iii) if pursuant to an enforcement the Senior Creditor sells any asset
over which any Junior Creditor (or any trustee or agent on its behalf) has
security for the Junior Debt, or if the Borrower sells such asset at the
request of the Senior Creditor after an Event of Default under the Senior
Credit Agreement, the Junior Creditor will on such sale release its
security over that asset if [the sale is at a fair value and if] the proceeds are
to be applied towards the Senior Debt.

(c) *No foreclosure* The Junior Creditor will not be entitled to the
remedy of foreclosure in respect of any assets subject to the Junior
Security Documents.

(d) *Waiver of marshalling* The Junior Creditor waives any existing or
future right it may have to marshalling in respect of any security held by   .
the Senior Creditor or by a trustee or agent on its behalf.

(e) *No right to require reinstatement* The Junior Creditor waives any
right it may have of requiring that insurance proceeds be applied in
reinstatement of any asset subject to security under the Senior Security
Documents.

(f) *No enforcement* The Senior Creditor may refrain from enforcing the
security conferred by the Senior Security Documents as long as it sees fit.

(g) *Manner of enforcement* If the Senior Creditor does enforce the
security conferred by the Senior Security Documents, it may do so in such
manner as it sees fit, shall not be responsible to the Junior Creditor for
any failure to enforce or to maximise the proceeds of any enforcement,
and may cease any such enforcement.

10. PROCEEDS OF ENFORCEMENT OF SECURITY

Subject to the rights of any prior or preferential encumbrancers or
creditors, the net proceeds of enforcement of the security conferred by

the Senior Security Documents and the Junior Security Document will be paid to the Senior Creditor and applied in the following order:

First   in payment of all costs and expenses incurred by or on behalf of the Senior Creditor in connection with such enforcement;

Second in payment to the Second Creditor for application towards the balance of the Senior Debt in such order as the Senior Creditor may decide;

Third   in payment to the Junior Creditor for application towards the Junior Debt in such order as the Junior Creditor may decide;

Fourth in payment of the surplus (if any) to the Borrower or other person entitled thereto.

11. VOTING

So long as the Senior Debt is or may become outstanding,

(a) the Senior Creditor may (and is hereby irrevocably authorised to) exercise all powers of convening meetings, voting and representation in respect of the Junior Debt and the Junior Creditor will provide all forms of proxy and of representation needful to that end,

(b) if and to the extent that the Senior Creditor is not entitled to exercise a power conferred by the above the Junior Creditor (i) will exercise the power as the Senior Creditor directs, and (ii) will not exercise it so as to impair this subordination.

12. CONSENTS

(a) *New transactions* The Junior Creditor will have no remedy against the Borrower or the Senior Creditor by reason of any transaction entered into between the Senior Creditor and the Borrower which violates or is an Event of Default or Pending Event of Default under any Junior Finance Document and the Junior Creditor may not object to any such transaction by reason of any provisions of the Junior Finance Documents.

(b) *Waivers* Any waiver or consent granted by the Senior Creditor will also be deemed to have been given by the Junior Creditor if any transaction or circumstances would, in the absence of such waiver or consent by the Junior Creditor, violate any Junior Finance Document or constitute an Event of Default or Pending Event of Default under any Junior Finance Document.

13. REPRESENTATIONS AND WARRANTIES OF THE BORROWER

The Borrower represents and warrants to the Senior Creditor

(a) *Status* The Borrower is a limited liability company, duly incorporated and validly existing under the laws of [   ].

(b) *Powers and authority* The Borrower has the power to enter into and perform, and has taken all necessary action to authorise the entry into, performance and delivery of, the existing Junior Finance Documents and this Agreement and the transactions contemplated by those Junior Finance Documents and this Agreement.

(c) *Legal validity* The existing Junior Finance Documents and this Agreement constitute its legal, valid and binding obligations enforceable in accordance with their terms.

(d) *Non-conflict* The entry into and performance by the Borrower of, and the transactions contemplated by, the Junior Finance Documents and this Agreement do not and will not:

(i) conflict with any law or regulation; or
(ii) conflict with the constitutional documents of the Borrower or of any of its Subsidiaries; or
(iii) conflict with any document which is binding on the Borrower or on any of its Subsidiaries or any asset of the Borrower or of any of its Subsidiaries.

(e) *Authorisation* All authorisations, consents, registrations, filings, notarisations and the like required or desirable in connection with the entry into and performance by it, the validity and enforceability of, and of the transactions contemplated by, the Junior Finance Documents and this Agreement have been obtained or effected (as appropriate) and are in full force and effect.

(f) *Security* The Junior Security Documents confer the security expressed to be conferred thereby which is valid and enforceable on the insolvency of the Borrower and which is not subject to any prior or *pari passu* security other than that conferred by the Senior Security Documents.

14. REPRESENTATIONS AND WARRANTIES OF JUNIOR CREDITOR

The Junior Creditor represents and warrants to the Senior Creditor

(a) *Legal validity* This Agreement is within its powers, has been duly authorised by it, constitutes its legal, valid and binding obligations enforceable in accordance with their terms and does not conflict with any law or regulation or its constitution documents or any document binding on it and that it has obtained all necessary consents for the performance by it of this Agreement.

(b) *Disclosure* There has been provided to the Senior Creditor true and complete copies of the existing Junior Finance Documents containing all terms relating to the Junior Debt.

(c) *Ownership* The Junior Creditor is the sole beneficial owner of the Junior Debt and of the benefit of the Junior Finance Documents free of encumbrances, options and subordinations in favour of any person other than the Senior Creditor.

[(d) *Set-off* The Junior Debt is not subject to any set-off, counterclaim or other defence.]

15. REPETITION OF REPRESENTATIONS AND WARRANTIES

The representations and warranties in Clauses 14 and 15 are deemed to be repeated by each of the Borrower and the Junior Creditor respectively on each date so long as any Senior Debt is outstanding with reference to the facts and circumstances then existing.

16. INFORMATION BY JUNIOR CREDITOR

(a) *Defaults* The Junior Creditor will promptly notify the Senior Creditor of the occurrence of any Event of Default or Pending Event of Default under any Junior Finance Document.

(b) *Amount of Junior Debt* The Junior Creditor will on written request by the Senior Creditor from time to time notify the Senior Creditor in writing of details of the amount of the Junior Debt and give the Senior Creditor copies of all Junior Finance Documents as soon as entered into.

17. SUBROGATION BY JUNIOR CREDITOR

If any of the Senior Debt is wholly or partially paid out of any proceeds received in respect of or on account of the Junior Debt, the Junior Creditor will to that extent be subrogated to the Senior Debt so paid (and all securities and guarantees of that Senior Debt) but not before all the Senior Debt is paid in full.

18. PROTECTION OF SUBORDINATION

(a) *Continuing subordination* The subordination provisions in this Agreement constitute a continuing subordination and benefit the ultimate balance of the Senior Debt regardless of any intermediate payment or discharge of the Senior Debt in whole or in part.

(b) *Waiver of defences* The subordination in this Agreement and the obligations of the Junior Creditor under this Agreement will not be affected by any act, omission, matter or thing which, but for this provision, would reduce, release or prejudice the subordination or any of those obligations in whole or in part, including without limitation:

(i) any time or waiver granted to, or composition with, the Borrower or other person;

(ii) the taking, variation, compromise, exchange, renewal or release of, or refusal or neglect to perfect, take up or enforce, any rights against, or security over assets of, the Borrower or other person under the Senior Finance Documents, in respect of the Senior Debt or otherwise or any non-presentment or non-observance of any formality or other requirement in respect of any instruments or any failure to realise the full value of any security;

(iii) any unenforceability, illegality or invalidity of any obligation of the Borrower or security under the Senior Finance Documents, in respect of the Senior Debt or any other document or security;

(c) *Immediate recourse* The Junior Creditor waives any right it may have of first requiring the Senior Creditor (or any trustee or agent on its behalf) to proceed against or enforce any other rights or security or claim payment from any person before claiming the benefit of this Agreement. The Senior Creditor (or any trustee or agent on its behalf) may refrain from applying or enforcing any money, rights or security.

(d) *Appropriations* Until the Senior Debt has been irrevocably paid in full, the Senior Creditor (or any trustee or agent on its behalf) may:

(i) apply any moneys or property received under this Agreement or from the Borrower or from any other person against the Senior Debt in such order as it sees fit;

(ii) (if it so decides) apply any moneys or property received from the Borrower or from any other person (other than money or property received for the Junior Creditor under this Agreement) against any liability other than the Senior Debt owed to it;
[*Note*: The above para. (ii) will be relevant only if the Senior Debt does not include all debt owed by the Borrower to the Senior Creditor.]

(iii) hold in suspense any moneys or distributions received from the Junior Creditor under Clauses 5, 6, 7 and 10 or on account of the liability of the Junior Creditor under this Agreement.

(e) *Non-competition* Until the Senior Debt has been irrevocably paid in full, the Junior Creditor will not by virtue of any payment or performance by it under this Agreement or by virtue of the operation of Clauses 5, 6, 7 or 10:

(i) be subrogated to any rights, security or moneys held, received or receivable by the Senior Creditor (or any trustee or agent on its behalf) or be entitled to any right of contribution or indemnity;

(ii) claim, rank, prove or vote as a creditor of the Borrower or any other person or their respective estates in competition with the Senior Creditor (or any trustee or agent on its behalf); or

(iii) receive, claim or have the benefit of any payment, distribution or security from or on account of the Borrower or other person.

19. PRESERVATION OF JUNIOR DEBT

Solely as between the Borrower and the Junior Creditor, the Junior Debt will remain owing or due and payable in accordance with the terms of the Junior Finance Documents, and interest and default interest will accrue on missed payments accordingly.

20. TERMINATION OF SUBORDINATION

By not less than 30 days' prior written notice to the Senior Creditor, the Junior Creditor may terminate this subordination agreement. However, the termination will not apply to Junior Debt which is incurred prior to the expiry of the notice or which arises as a result of any transaction or under or in connection with any agreement entered into prior to such expiry.

21. RESPONSIBILITY OF SENIOR CREDITOR

The Senior Creditor will not be liable to the Junior Creditor

(a) for the manner of exercise or for any non-exercise of its powers under this Agreement, or

(b) for failure to collect or preserve the Junior Debt, any security or guarantees for the Junior Debt, or any assets subject to any security for the Junior Debt.

22. EXPENSES

(a) *Initial costs* The Borrower will forthwith on demand pay the Senior Creditor the amount of all costs and expenses incurred by it in connection with the negotiation, preparation, execution and performance of this Agreement and all waivers in relation to and variations of this Agreement.

(b) *Enforcement costs* Each of the Borrower and the Junior Creditor shall, forthwith on demand, pay to the Senior Creditor the amount of all costs and expenses incurred by it in connection with the enforcement against the Borrower or Junior Creditor (as the case may be) of the Senior Creditor's rights against it under this Agreement.

(c) *Legal expenses and taxes* The costs and expenses referred to above include, without limitation, the fees and expenses of legal advisers and any value added tax or similar tax, and are payable in the currency in which they are incurred.

23. CHANGES TO THE PARTIES

(a) *Successors and assigns* This Agreement is binding on the successors and assigns of the parties hereto.

(b) *Borrower* The Borrower may not assign or transfer any of its rights or obligations under this Agreement.

(c) *Junior Creditor* So long as any Senior Debt is or may become outstanding, the Junior Creditor will not

(i) assign or dispose of, or create or permit to subsist any security (fixed or floating) over, any of the Junior Debt or its proceeds or any interest in the Junior Debt or its proceeds, or any security therefor, to or in favour of any person, or

(ii) subordinate any of the Junior Debt or its proceeds to any sums owing by the Borrower to any person other than the Senior Creditor

(iii) transfer by novation or otherwise any of its rights or obligations under any Junior Finance Document or in respect of any Junior Debt to any person unless in each case that person agrees with the Senior Creditor that he is bound by all the terms of this Agreement as a Junior Creditor in a manner satisfactory to the Senior Creditor.

(d) *Senior Creditor* The Senior Creditor may assign or otherwise dispose of all or any of its rights under this Agreement.

(e) *Memorandum on documents* The Junior Creditor will indorse a memorandum of this Agreement on the Junior Finance Documents.

24. GENERAL

(a) *Perpetuity period* The perpetuity period for the trusts in this Agreement is 80 years.

(b) *Power of attorney* By way of security for the obligations of the Junior Creditor under this Agreement, the Junior Creditor irrevocably appoints the Senior Creditor as its attorney to do anything which the Junior Creditor (a) has authorised the Senior Creditor to do under this Agreement and (b) is required to do by this Agreement but has failed to do. The Senior Creditor may delegate this power.

(c) *Stamp duties* The Borrower shall pay and forthwith on demand indemnify the Senior Creditor [and the Junior Creditor] against any liability it incurs in respect of any stamp, registration and similar tax which is or becomes payable in connection with the entry into, performance or enforcement of this Agreement.

(d) *Currency indemnity* The Junior Creditor will indemnify the Senior Creditor against losses suffered by the Senior Creditor if any claim by the Senior Creditor (or any agent or trustee on its behalf) against the Junior Creditor under this Agreement is converted into a claim, proof, judgment or order in a currency other than the currency in which the amount is contractually payable under this Agreement.

(e) *Waivers, remedies, cumulative* The rights of the Senior Creditor under this Agreement:

(i) are cumulative and not exclusive of its rights under the general law; and
(ii) may be waived only in writing and specifically.

Delay in exercising or non-exercise of any such right is not a waiver of that right.

(f) *Set-off* The Senior Creditor may set off any matured obligation owed by the Junior Creditor under this Agreement (to the extent beneficially owned by the Senior Creditor) against any obligation (whether or not matured) owed by the Senior Creditor to the Junior Creditor, regardless of the place of payment, booking branch or currency of either obligation. If the obligations are in different currencies, the Senior Creditor may convert either obligation at a market rate of exchange in its usual course of business for the purpose of the set-off.

(g) *Default interest* If the Junior Creditor fails to pay any amount payable by it under this Agreement to the Senior Creditor, it will, on demand by the Senior Creditor from time to time, pay interest on the overdue amount from the due date up to the date of actual payment, as well as before judgment, at the rate of [ ].

(h) *Severability* If a provision of this Agreement is or becomes illegal, invalid or unenforceable in any jurisdiction, that shall not affect:

(i) the validity or enforceability in that jurisdiction of any other provision of this Agreement; or
(ii) the validity or enforceability in other jurisdictions of that or any other provision of this Agreement.

(1) *Counterparts* This Agreement may be executed in any number of counterparts, and this has the same effect as if the signatures on the counterparts were on a single copy of this Agreement.

25. NOTICES

(a) *Service of notices* All notices under, or in connection with, this Agreement shall be given in writing or by telex or fax. If correctly addressed, any such notice is deemed to be given at the following times:

(i) if in writing when delivered;
(ii) if by telex when correctly dispatched; and
(iii) if by fax when received.

However, a notice given in accordance with the above but received on a non-working day or after business hours in the place of receipt is deemed to be given on the next working day in that place.

(b) *Addresses for notices* The address, telex number and fax number of each party hereto for all notices under, or in connection with, this Agreement, are:
    [   ].
A party may change the above by prior written notice to the other parties.

26. JURISDICTION

(a) *Submission* For the benefit of the Senior Creditor, each of the Borrower and the Junior Creditor agrees that the courts of England are to have jurisdiction to settle any disputes in connection with this Agreement, submits to the jurisdiction of the English courts in connection with this Agreement, appoints [   ] as its agent for service of process relating to any proceedings before the English courts in connection with this Agreement and agrees to maintain a process agent in England notified to the Senior Creditor;

(b) *Non-exclusivity* Nothing in this Clause limits the right of the Senior Creditor to bring proceedings against another party hereto in connection with this Agreement.

(i) in any other court of competent jurisdiction; or
(ii) concurrently in more than one jurisdiction.

27. GOVERNING LAW

This Agreement is governed by English law.

IN WITNESS whereof this Agreement has been entered into on the date stated at the head of this Agreement.

MEZZANINE FINANCE

Note on the form

This form is a suggested intercreditor agreement between two syndicates of lenders financing a takeover by the borrower or a management buy-out. One of the syndicates is subordinated to the other. Both syndicates are secured on the same assets, but by separate security documents. Alternatively the security could be granted to a trustee for both sets of lenders: see para. 10.1. In the latter case, the borrower should also covenant with the trustee to pay the senior and the junior debt, *i.e.* a covenant parallel to the covenant given to the creditors directly: see the introductory note to Form 3.

The form envisages that subsidiaries of the borrower, namely, the target company and its subsidiaries, will secure the debts when they are permitted to do so under applicable law: see para. 7.23.

In addition the form contemplates a second tier of subordinated debt in the form of a junior note given to an insider, such as a vendor or a shareholder or director of the borrower. The junior note is unsecured.

The syndicate agreements would normally contain provisions appointing the respective agents for the syndicates, defining their functions and exculpating them from certain liabilities which would otherwise arise under agency law. Otherwise, an agency clause should be included in this Agreement.

THIS INTERCREDITOR AGREEMENT is dated [   ] and made BETWEEN:

(1) [NEWCO] as Borrower;

(2) THE COMPANIES named in Schedule 1 as Charging Subsidiaries;

(3) THE BANKS AND FINANCIAL INSTITUTIONS named in Part I of Schedule 2 as Senior Creditors;

(4) [——————] as Senior Agent;

(5) THE BANKS AND FINANCIAL INSTITUTIONS named in Part II of Schedule 2 as Mezzanine Creditors;

(6) [——————] as Mezzanine Agent; and

(7) [——————] as Junior Creditor.

IT IS AGREED AS FOLLOWS:

1. DEFINITIONS AND INTERPRETATION

1.1 *Definitions*

In this Agreement:

"Borrower" means [Newco] (registered number [   ]) whose registered office is at [   ].

"**Business Day**" has the meaning given to it in the Senior Credit Agreement.

"**Charging Subsidiary**" means [each of] [   ] and also any New Obligor.

"**Encumbrance**" means any type of mortgage, charge, incumbrance or other security interest and any preferential arrangement having the effect of security.

"**Event of Default**" means any event of default or other event entitling the creditor concerned to accelerate the due date of any liability of any Obligor.

"**Group**" means the Borrower and its Subsidiaries from time to time.

"**Junior Creditor**" means [   ].

"**Junior Debt**" means all present and future liabilities (actual or contingent) payable or owing by the Obligors to the Junior Creditor under or in connection with the Junior Note, whether or not matured and whether or not liquidated.

"**Junior Note**" means the [description of Vendor Note to be inserted].

"**Majority Mezzanine Creditors**" means the Majority Banks as defined in the Mezzanine Credit Agreement.

"**Majority Senior Creditors**" means the Majority Banks as defined in the Senior Credit Agreement.

"**Mezzanine Credit Agreement**" means the Mezzanine Credit Agreement dated [   ] between the Borrower, the Charging Subsidiaries, the Mezzanine Creditors and the Mezzanine Agent providing for a credit facility of up to £[   ].

"**Mezzanine Creditor**" means each of the banks and financial institutions named in Part II of Schedule 2 in all capacities in which any Obligor is under any liability to them.

"**Mezzanine Debt**" means all present and future liabilities (actual or contingent) payable or owing by the Obligors to the Mezzanine Creditors under or in connection with the Mezzanine Finance Documents whether or not matured and whether or not liquidated and includes all claims arising on rescission of any Mezzanine Finance Document.

"**Mezzanine Discharge Date**" means the date, as determined by the Mezzanine Agent, on which all Mezzanine Debt has been fully and irrevocably paid or discharged to the satisfaction of the Mezzanine Agent whether or not as the result of an enforcement.

"**Mezzanine Finance Documents**" means the Mezzanine Credit Agreement and the Mezzanine Security Documents.

"**Mezzanine Security Documents**" means:

(i) the security documents specified in Schedule 3;

(ii) any present or future document conferring or evidencing any Encumbrance, guarantee or other assurance against financial loss for, or in respect of, any of the Mezzanine Debt.

"New Obligor" has the meaning given to it in Clause 23.3 (New Obligors).

"Obligor" means the Borrower and each Charging Subsidiary.

"Potential Event of Default" means any event which with giving of notice, lapse of time, determination of materiality or fulfilment of any other condition (or any combination thereof) would be an Event of Default.

"Senior Agent" means [   ] in its capacity as agent for the Senior Creditors under the Senior Credit Agreement.

"Senior Credit Agreement" means the Senior Credit Agreement dated [   ] between the Borrower, the Charging Subsidiaries, the Senior Creditors and the Senior Agent providing for a credit facility of up to £[   ].

"Senior Creditors" means the banks and financial institutions named in Part I of Schedule 2 in all capacities in which any Obligor is under any liability to them.

"Senior Debt" means all present and future liabilities (actual or contingent) payable or owing by the Obligors to the Senior Creditors under or in connection with the Senior Finance Documents together with (subject to Clause 15.4 (Limits on Senior Debt)):

(i) any refinancing, novation, refunding, deferral or extension of any of those liabilities;

(ii) any further advances which may be made by a Senior Creditor to any Obligor under any agreement expressed to be supplemental to the Senior Credit Agreement plus all interest, fees and costs in connection therewith;

(iii) any claim for damages or restitution in the event of rescission of any of those liabilities or otherwise in connection with the Senior Finance Documents;

(iv) any claim against any Obligor flowing from any recovery by an Obligor of a payment or discharge in respect of those liabilities on grounds of preference or otherwise; and

(v) any amounts (such as post-insolvency interest) which would be included in any of the above but for any discharge, non-provability, unenforceability or non-allowability of the same in any insolvency or other proceedings.

"Senior Discharge Date" means the date, as determined by the Senior Agent, on which all Senior Debt has been fully and irrevocably paid or discharged to the satisfaction of the Senior Agent whether or not as the result of an enforcement.

"Senior Finance Documents" means the Senior Credit Agreement and the Senior Security Documents.

"Senior Security Documents" means:

(i) the security documents specified in Schedule 4; and

(ii) any present or future document conferring or evidencing any Encumbrance, guarantee or other assurance against financial loss for, or in respect of, any of the Senior Debt.

1.2 *Amendments*

References in this Agreement to this Agreement or to any provisions of this Agreement or to any other document shall be construed as references to this Agreement, that provision or document as in force for the time being and as amended, varied or supplemented from time to time but without prejudice to any restrictions in this Agreement on amendments, variations or supplements.

1.3 *Interpretation*

(a) References to the Obligors, the Senior Creditors, the Mezzanine Creditors and the Junior Creditor include their respective successors and assigns.

(b) Headings shall be ignored in the interpretation of this Agreement.

(c) In this Agreement, unless the context otherwise requires:

 (i) references to Clauses and Schedules are to be construed as references to the Clauses of, and Schedules to, this Agreement;

 (ii) words importing the singular shall include the plural and vice versa.

2. UNDERTAKINGS OF OBLIGORS

Until the Senior Discharge Date, except as the Majority Senior Creditors have previously consented in writing, no Obligor will:

(a) pay, prepay or repay, or make any distribution in respect of, or purchase or acquire, any of the Mezzanine Debt or Junior Debt in cash or in kind except, in the case of Mezzanine Debt only, as permitted by Clause 5 (Permitted Mezzanine Payments)

(b) permit any member of the Group to purchase or acquire any of the Mezzanine Debt or the Junior Debt;

(c) discharge any of the Mezzanine Debt or Junior Debt by set-off except, in the case of Mezzanine Debt only, if and to the extent that it is permitted to be paid by Clause 5 (Permitted Mezzanine Payments);

(d) create or permit or subsist any Encumbrance over any of its assets for any of the Mezzanine Debt or Junior Debt except for, in the case of the Mezzanine Debt only, Encumbrances under the Mezzanine Security Documents;

(e) amend, vary, waive or release any term of the Mezzanine Finance Documents or the Junior Note; or

(f) take or omit any action whereby the subordinations contemplated by this Agreement may be impaired.

3. UNDERTAKINGS OF MEZZANINE CREDITORS

Until the Senior Discharge Date, except as the Majority Senior Creditors have previously consented in writing, no Mezzanine Creditor will:

(a) demand or receive payment, prepayment or repayment of, or any distribution in respect of (or on account of) any of the Mezzanine Debt in cash or in kind from an Obligor or any other source or apply any money or property in discharge of any Mezzanine Debt, except in each case:

(i) to the extent permitted by Clause 5 (Permitted Mezzanine Payments); and

(ii) for the proceeds of enforcement of the Mezzanine Security Documents received and applied in the order permitted by Clause 12 (Proceeds of Enforcement of Security);

(b) discharge the Mezzanine Debt by set-off except if and to the extent that the Mezzanine Debt is permitted to be paid by Clause 5 (Permitted Mezzanine Payments);

(c) permit to subsist or receive any Encumbrance or any guarantee or other assurance against financial loss for, or in respect of, any of the Mezzanine Debt other than under the Mezzanine Security Documents specified in Schedule 3; or

(d) amend, vary, waive or release any term of the Mezzanine Finance Documents or the Mezzanine Debt.

4. UNDERTAKINGS OF JUNIOR CREDITOR

So long as any Senior Debt or Mezzanine Debt is or may become outstanding, except as the Majority Senior Creditors have previously consented in writing, the Junior Creditor will not:

(a) demand or receive payment, prepayment or repayment of, or any distribution in respect of (or on account of) any of the Junior Debt in cash or in kind from an Obligor or any other source or apply any money or property in discharge of any Junior Debt;

(b) discharge the Junior Debt by set-off;

(c) permit to subsist or receive any Encumbrance or any guarantee or assurance against financial loss for, or in respect of, any of the Junior Debt; or

(d) amend, vary, waive or release any term of the Junior Note or the Junior Debt.

5. PERMITTED MEZZANINE PAYMENTS

Subject to Clauses 6 (Suspension of Permitted Payments) and 7 (Turnover), the Borrower may pay and the Mezzanine Creditors may receive and retain payment of, the following:

(a) scheduled payments of interest on the Mezzanine Debt under the

Mezzanine Credit Agreement not earlier than the date the same are scheduled to be due in accordance with the original terms of the Mezzanine Finance Documents;

(b) [payments of increased costs under Clause [   ] of the Mezzanine Credit Agreement [and of additional amounts in respect of taxes under Clause [   ] of the Mezzanine Credit Agreement];

(c) commissions and fees payable under Clause [   ] of the Mezzanine Credit Agreement; and

(d) costs and expenses payable under Clause [   ] of the Mezzanine Credit Agreement.

6. SUSPENSION OF PERMITTED PAYMENTS

6.1 *Payment default and acceleration*

Subject to Clause 8 (Subordination on Insolvency), no Obligor may make any payments permitted by Clause 5 (Permitted Mezzanine Payments):

(a) if and so long as any of the Senior Debt is overdue and unpaid; or

(b) if any of the Mezzanine Debt has been declared due and payable under Clause [   ] (Events of Default) of the Mezzanine Credit Agreement (or otherwise become prematurely due and payable) until such time as such declaration or other premature acceleration has been rescinded.

6.2 *Non-payment defaults*

Subject to Clause 8 (Subordination on Insolvency), no Obligor may make any payments permitted by Clause 5 (Permitted Mezzanine Payments) after an Event of Default or Potential Event of Default has occurred under the Senior Credit Agreement (other than non-payment of the Senior Debt when due) and the Senior Agent has on the instructions of the Majority Senior Creditors served a written notice (a "Stop Notice") on the Mezzanine Agent and the Borrower specifying such Event of Default or Potential Event of Default (each a "Non-payment Default") suspending permitted payments until the earlier of:

(a) more than [180] days has elapsed from receipt by the Mezzanine Agent or the Borrower of the Stop Notice;

(b) the Non-payment Default has been cured or waived by the Majority Senior Creditors in writing or has ceased to exist; or

(c) the Senior Agent acting on the instructions of the Majority Senior Creditors has by notice in writing to the Borrower and the Mezzanine Agent cancelled the Stop Notice.

7. TURNOVER

7.1 *Non-permitted payments*

If before the Senior Discharge Date:

(a) any Mezzanine Creditor receives a payment or distribution in cash or in kind of, in respect of or on account of, any of the Mezzanine Debt not permitted by Clause 5 (Permitted Mezzanine Payments) from an Obligor or any other source;

(b) the Junior Creditor receives a payment or distribution in cash or in kind of, or on account of the Junior Debt from an Obligor or any other source;

(c) any Mezzanine Creditor receives the proceeds of any enforcement of any security conferred by the Mezzanine Security Documents otherwise than in the order set out in Clause 12 (Proceeds of Enforcement of Security); or

(d) any Obligor or any member of the Group makes any payment or distribution in cash or in kind on account of the purchase or other acquisition of any of the Mezzanine Debt or the Junior Debt,

the receiving Mezzanine Creditor or Junior Creditor (as appropriate) will hold the same in trust for and pay and distribute it upon demand to the Senior Agent for application towards the Senior Debt.

7.2 *Non-permitted set-offs*

If any of the Mezzanine Debt or Junior Debt is discharged by set-off (otherwise than if and to the extent a payment of the Mezzanine Debt is permitted by Clause 5 (Permitted Mezzanine Payments)), the Mezzanine Creditor concerned or, as the case may be, Junior Creditor will immediately pay an amount equal to the discharge to the Senior Agent for application towards the Senior Debt until the Senior Debt is irrevocably paid in full.

8. SUBORDINATION ON INSOLVENCY

8.1 *Subordination events*

If:

(a) any resolution is passed or order made for the winding-up, liquidation, dissolution, administration or reorganisation of any Obligor;

(b) any Obligor becomes subject to any insolvency, bankruptcy, reorganisation, receivership, liquidation, dissolution or other similar proceeding voluntary or involuntary (and whether or not involving insolvency);

(c) any Obligor assigns its assets for the benefit of its creditors or enters into any arrangement with its creditors generally; or

(d) any Obligor becomes subject to any distribution of its assets, or if any analogous event occurs anywhere,

the provisions of Clause 8.2 (Subordination) shall apply.

8.2 *Subordination*

In any of the circumstances mentioned in Clause 8.1 (Subordination Events):

(a) the Mezzanine Debt and Junior Debt will be subordinate in right of payment to the Senior Debt;

(b) the Junior Debt will be subordinate in right of payment to the Mezzanine Debt;

(c) the Senior Agent (or, if not, each Senior Creditor) may, and is irrevocably authorised on behalf of the Mezzanine Creditors and Junior Creditor to, (i) claim, enforce and prove for the Mezzanine Debt and the Junior Debt, (ii) file claims and proofs, give receipts and take all such proceedings and do all such things as the Senior Agent or the Senior Creditor sees fit to recover the Mezzanine Debt and the Junior Debt and (iii) receive all distributions on the Mezzanine Debt and the Junior Debt for application towards the Senior Debt;

(d) if and to the extent that the Senior Agent or a Senior Creditor is not entitled to claim, enforce, prove, file claims or proofs, or take proceedings for the Mezzanine Debt and the Junior Debt (otherwise than by reason of the Mezzanine Creditors being secured creditors), the Mezzanine Creditors and Junior Creditor will do so in good time as reasonably requested by the Senior Agent acting in accordance with the instructions of the Majority Senior Creditors;

(e) each Mezzanine Creditor and Junior Creditor will hold all distributions in cash or in kind received or receivable by the Mezzanine Creditor and Junior Creditor in respect of the Mezzanine Debt and the Junior Debt from the Obligor concerned or its estate or from any other source in trust for the Senior Creditors and upon demand will pay and transfer the same to the Senior Agent for application towards the Senior Debt until the Senior Debt is irrevocably paid in full; and

(f) the trustee in bankruptcy, liquidator, assignee or other person distributing the assets of that Obligor or their proceeds is directed to pay distributions on the Mezzanine Debt and the Junior Debt direct to the Senior Agent on behalf of the Senior Creditors until the Senior Debt is irrevocably paid in full. The Mezzanine Creditors and Junior Creditor will give all such notices and do all such things as the Senior Agent may reasonably request to give effect to this provision.

[*Note*: Consider the addition of a Clause on the lines of Clause 7 of Form 3 (Treatment of distributions).]

9. PRIORITY OF SECURITY

9.1 *Ranking*

All existing and future security conferred by the Senior Security Documents will:

(a) rank in all respects prior to existing and future security conferred by the Mezzanine Security Documents, regardless of order of registration, notice, execution or otherwise; and

(b) secure all the Senior Debt in priority to the Mezzanine Debt, regardless of the date upon which the Senior Debt arises, regardless of whether a Senior Creditor is obliged to advance moneys included in Senior Debt, and regardless of any fluctuations in the amount of Senior Debt outstanding or any intermediate discharge of the Senior Debt in whole or in part.

9.2 *Registration and notice*

The Mezzanine Agent will co-operate with the Senior Agent with a view to reflecting the priority of the security conferred by the Senior Security Documents in any register or with any filing or registration authority and in giving notice to insurers, debtors liable for receivables covered by the security conferred by the Senior Security Documents and other persons.

9.3 *Custody of documents*

Until the Senior Discharge Date, the Senior Agent will be entitled to (but not obliged to take) the deposit of any title deeds, share certificates or other title documents, certificates or paper in respect of any assets subject to the security conferred by the Senior Security Documents in priority to the entitlement of the Mezzanine Agent.

9.4 *Consolidation*

The Senior Agent and the Senior Creditors may consolidate security against the Mezzanine Creditors and the Junior Creditor.

10. ENFORCEMENT BY MEZZANINE AND JUNIOR CREDITORS

10.1 *Restrictions on enforcement*

Until the Senior Discharge Date, subject to Clause 11 (Permitted Enforcement) and unless the Majority Senior Creditors have previously consented in writing, no Mezzanine Creditor or Junior Creditor will:

(a) accelerate any of the Mezzanine Debt or Junior Debt or otherwise declare any of the Mezzanine Debt or Junior Debt prematurely payable on an Event of Default or otherwise unless the Senior Agent has declared the Senior Debt prematurely due and payable under Clause [ ] (Events of Default) of the Senior Credit Agreement:

(b) enforce the Mezzanine Debt or Junior Debt by execution or otherwise;

(c) crystallise any floating charge in the Mezzanine Security Documents;

(d) enforce any security conferred by the Mezzanine Security Documents by sale, possession, appointment of a receiver or otherwise except as permitted by Clause 10.2 (Joint Enforcement);

(e) initiate or support or take any steps with a view to any insolvency, liquidation, reorganisation, administration or dissolution proceedings or any voluntary arrangement or assignment for the benefit of creditors or any similar proceedings involving an Obligor, whether by petition, convening a meeting, voting for a resolution or otherwise.

10.2 *Joint enforcement*

Notwithstanding Clause 10.1, the Mezzanine Creditors may enforce any security conferred by the Mezzanine Security Documents over assets of an Obligor if the Senior Agent has enforced security conferred by the Senior Security Documents over the same assets, but any enforcement by the Mezzanine Creditors shall be subject to any enforcement remedies of the Senior Agent or the Senior Creditors. Without limiting the above:

(a) the Mezzanine Agent will not (and no Mezzanine Creditor will be entitled to) take or have possession of any such assets or maintain a receiver in possession in respect of such assets so long as the Senior Agent requires possession or wishes to maintain a receiver in possession of those assets;

(b) the Senior Agent will have the entire conduct of any sale of those assets; and

(c) if pursuant to an enforcement the Senior Agent or any Senior Creditor sells any asset over which any Mezzanine Creditor (or any trustee or agent on its behalf) has security for the Mezzanine Debt, or if the Obligor concerned sells such asset at the request of the Senior Agent after an Event of Default under the Senior Credit Agreement, the Mezzanine Agent and the Mezzanine Creditors will on such sale release their security over that asset if the sale is, in the opinion of the Senior Agent, at a fair value and if the proceeds are to be applied towards the Senior Debt.

10.3 *No foreclosure*

The Mezzanine Agent and the Mezzanine Creditors shall not be entitled to the remedy of foreclosure in respect of any assets subject to the Mezzanine Security Documents.

10.4 *Waiver of marshalling*

The Mezzanine Creditors waive any existing or future right they may have to marshalling in respect of any security held by a Senior Creditor or by a trustee or agent on its behalf.

10.5 *No right to require reinstatement*

Each Mezzanine Creditor waives any right it may have of requiring that insurance proceeds be applied in reinstatement of any asset subject to security under the Senior Security Documents.

11. PERMITTED ENFORCEMENT

The Mezzanine Creditors may take any action in relation to the Mezzanine Debt which would otherwise be prohibited by Clause 10.1 (Restrictions on enforcement) if (but only if):

(a) an Event of Default has occurred under the Mezzanine Credit Agreement as result of:

(i) non-payment when due of any amount under the Mezzanine Finance Documents;

(ii) breach by the Borrower [by a margin of not less than [20] per cent.] of any of the financial covenants in Clauses [ ] and [ ] of the Mezzanine Credit Agreement;

(iii) an acceleration of the Senior Debt;

(iv) a petition for an administration order in relation to the Borrower having been presented to the court; or

(v) any resolution having been passed or order made for the winding-up of the Borrower;

(b) the Mezzanine Agent has given notice in writing ("Enforcement Notice") to the Senior Agent (who shall promptly notify the Senior Creditors) of the occurrence of such Event of Default; and

(c) not less than [180] days has elapsed from the date the Senior Agent received the Enforcement Notice and such Event of Default is still continuing and has not been waived by the Majority Mezzanine Creditors.

12. PROCEEDS OF ENFORCEMENT OF SECURITY

Subject to the rights of any prior or preferential encumbrancers or creditors the net proceeds of enforcement of the security conferred by the Senior Security Documents and the Mezzanine Security shall be paid to the Senior Agent and applied in the following order:

First in payment of all costs and expenses incurred by or on behalf of the Senior Agent or any Senior Creditor in connection with such enforcement;

Second in payment to the Senior Agent for application towards the balance of the Senior Debt in such order as the Majority Senior Creditors may direct;

Third in payment to the Mezzanine Agent for application towards the Mezzanine Debt in such order as the Majority Mezzanine Creditors may direct;

Fourth in payment of all other liabilities owing to the Senior Creditors;

Fifth in payment of the surplus (if any) to the Obligor concerned or other person entitled thereto.

13. ENFORCEMENT OF SECURITY BY SENIOR CREDITORS

13.1 *No enforcement*

The Senior Agent and the Senior Creditors may refrain from enforcing the security conferred by the Senior Security Documents as long as they see fit.

13.2 *Manner of enforcement*

If the Senior Agent or any Senior Creditor does enforce the security conferred by the Senior Security Documents, it may do so (without prior consultation with the Mezzanine Creditors) in such manner as it sees fit and solely having regard to the interests of the Senior Agent and the Senior Creditors. Neither the Senior Agent nor any Senior Creditor shall be responsible to the Mezzanine Creditors or Junior Creditor for any failure to enforce or to maximise the proceeds of any enforcement, and may cease any such enforcement at any time.

14. VOTING

Until the Senior Discharge Date:

(a) the Senior Agent acting on the instructions of the Majority Senior Creditors may (and is hereby irrevocably authorised to) exercise all powers of convening meetings, voting and representation in respect of the Mezzanine Debt and Junior Debt and each Mezzanine Creditor and the Junior Creditor will provide all forms of proxy and of representation needful to that end;

(b) if and to the extent that the Senior Agent is not entitled to exercise a power conferred by the above each Mezzanine Creditor and the Junior Creditor (a) will exercise the power as the Senior Agent acting in accordance with the instructions of the Majority Senior Creditors reasonably directs, and (b) will not exercise them so as to impair this subordination.

15. CONSENTS

15.1 *New transactions*

Neither the Mezzanine Creditors nor the Junior Creditor will have any remedy against any Obligor or the Senior Creditors by reason of any transaction entered into between the Senior Creditors (or any of them) and any Obligor which violates or is an Event of Default under the Mezzanine Finance Documents or the Junior Note. Neither the Mezzanine Creditors nor the Junior Creditor may object to any such transaction by reason of any provisions of the Mezzanine Finance Documents or the Junior Note.

15.2 *Waivers*

Any waiver or consent granted by the Majority Senior Creditors under the Senior Finance Documents will also be deemed to have been given by the Mezzanine Creditors and the Junior Creditor if any transaction or circumstances would, in the absence of such waiver or consent by the Mezzanine Creditors or the Junior Creditor, violate any Mezzanine Finance Document or constitute an Event of Default or Potential Event of Default under the Mezzanine Credit Agreement or the Junior Note.

15.3 *Entrenched Clauses*

However Clauses 15.1 and 15.2 shall not apply so as to deem the Mezzanine Creditors to:

(a) consent to any action or transaction to be done or entered into by any member of the Group which would be in breach, or to waive an Event of Default committed as a result of any action, event or transaction in breach, of any of the following Clauses of the Mezzanine Credit Agreement:

  (i) [   ] (repayment);
  (ii) [   ] (interest);
  (iii) [   ] (information);
  (iv) [   ] (compliance certificates);
  (v) [   ] (maintenance of consents and authorisations);
  (vi) [   ] (restrictions on dividends);
  (vii) [   ] (financial covenants) provided that any such breach is by a margin of not less than [20] per cent. of any relevant amount or ratio; or
  (viii) [   ] (negative pledge) unless the security is granted to or for the benefit of the Senior Creditors or the Mezzanine Creditors receive second-ranking security over the relevant assets (which must be subordinated on the same terms *mutatis mutandis* as are contained in this Agreement).

(b) waive any Event of Default constituted by an event, fact or circumstance falling within any of the following sub-clauses of Clause [   ] (Events of Default) in the Mezzanine Credit Agreement:

  (i) [   ] (non-payment);
  (ii) [   ] (non-compliance) if the relevant Event of Default has been committed in consequence of a breach of or failure to observe obligations contained in any of the Clauses of the Mezzanine Credit Agreement which are entrenched by virtue of, but only to the extent specified in, Clause 15.3(a) above;
  (iii) [   ] (cross-acceleration) if the relevant Event of Default arises as a consequence of an acceleration of the Senior Debt which has not been rescinded;
  (iv) [   ] (insolvency, etc.) if the relevant Event of Default arises as a consequence of a presentation of a petition for an administration order in respect of the Borrower or a resolution having been passed or an order made for the winding up of the Borrower.

15.4 *Limits on Senior Debt*

The principal amount of the Senior Debt which qualifies as Senior Debt shall not exceed the amount of loans contemplated by the original terms of the Senior Credit Agreement *less* any repayments of the principal of those loans actually made by the Borrower from time to time in circumstances where the sum repaid may not be readvanced *plus*:

  (i) £[   ];

(ii)[any capitalised interest in respect of the Senior Debt],

but taking, for this purpose, any Senior Debt advanced in a currency other than Sterling at its Sterling equivalent determined by the Senior Agent by reference to a market rate at the time of the advance.

16. REPRESENTATIONS AND WARRANTIES OF MEZZANINE CREDITORS

Each Mezzanine Creditor represents and warrants to each Senior Creditor that this Agreement (i) is within its powers and has been duly authorised by it, (ii) constitutes its legal, valid and binding obligations and (iii) does not conflict in any material respect with any law or regulation or its constitutional documents or any document binding on it and that it has obtained all necessary consents for the performance by it of this Agreement.

17. INFORMATION BETWEEN SENIOR AND MEZZANINE CREDITORS

17.1 *Defaults*

Each of the Senior Agent and the Mezzanine Agent will notify the other of the occurrence of any Event of Default or Potential Event of Default under the Senior Creditor Agreement and the Mezzanine Credit Agreement respectively but only if the Senior Agent or the Mezzanine Agent (as the case may be) has received written notice specifying the event concerned or if the event is non-payment of principal or interest which is more than five Business Days overdue.

17.2 *Amounts of debt*

Each of the Senior Agent and the Mezzanine Agent will on written request by the other from time to time notify the other in writing of details of the amount of the Senior Debt and the Mezzanine Debt so far as known to it.

17.3 *Other information*

Each Obligor authorises the Senior Agent and the Mezzanine Agent to disclose to each other and to the Mezzanine Creditors and the Senior Creditors all information relating to that Obligor, its subsidiaries or related entities coming into the possession of any of them in connection with the Senior Finance Documents or the Mezzanine Finance Documents.

18. SUBROGATION BY MEZZANINE AND JUNIOR CREDITORS

(a) If the Senior Debt is wholly or partially paid out of any proceeds received of or on account of the Mezzanine Debt or the Junior Debt, the

Mezzanine Creditors and the Junior Creditor (as the case may be) will to that extent be subrogated to the Senior Debt so paid (and all securities and guarantees for that Senior Debt) but not before all the Senior Debt is irrevocably paid in full.

(b) The Junior Creditor will not be entitled to be subrogated under this Clause until all the Mezzanine Debt is irrevocably paid in full.

(c) Forthwith on the Senior Discharge Date, references in this Agreement:

(i) to the Senior Agent or the Senior Creditors shall be deemed to be references to the Mezzanine Agent and the Mezzanine Creditors;

(ii) to the Senior Discharge Date shall be deemed to be references to the Mezzanine Discharge Date; and

(iii) to the Majority Senior Creditors will be deemed to be references to the Majority Mezzanine Creditors.

19. PROTECTION OF SUBORDINATION

19.1 *Continuing subordination*

The subordination provisions in this Agreement constitute a continuing subordination and benefit the ultimate balance of the Senior Debt regardless of any intermediate payment or discharge of the Senior Debt in whole or in part.

19.2 *Waiver of defences*

The subordination in this Agreement and the obligations of each Mezzanine Creditor and the Junior Creditor under this Agreement will not be affected by any act, omission, matter or thing which but for this provision, would reduce, release or prejudice the subordination or any of those obligations in whole or in part, including without limitation:

(a) any time or waiver granted to, or composition with, an Obligor or other person;

(b) the taking, variation, compromise, exchange, renewal or release of, or refusal or neglect to perfect, take up or enforce, any rights against, or security over assets of, any Obligor or other person under the Senior Finance Documents or otherwise or any non-presentment or non-observance of any formality or other requirement in respect of any instruments or any failure to realise the full value of any security;

(c) any unenforceability, illegality or invalidity of any obligation of an Obligor or security under the Senior Finance Documents or any other document or security.

19.3 *Immediate recourse*

Each Mezzanine Creditor and the Junior Creditor waives any right it may have of first requiring any Senior Creditor (or any trustee or agent on its behalf) to proceed against or enforce any other rights or security or claim payment from any person before claiming the benefit of this subordination, of the security conferred by the Senior Security Documents or of the obligations of the Mezzanine Creditors and the Junior Creditor under this Agreement. Each Senior Creditor (or any trustee or agent on its behalf) may refrain from applying or enforcing any money, rights or security.

19.4 *Appropriations*

Until the Senior Debt has been irrevocably paid in full, each Senior Creditor (or any trustee or agent on its behalf) may:

(a) apply any moneys or property received under this Agreement or from an Obligor or from any other person against the Senior Debt in such order as it sees fit;

(b) (if it so decides) apply any moneys or property received from an Obligor or from any other person (other than money or property received for the Mezzanine Creditors or the Junior Creditor under this Agreement) against any liability other than the Senior Debt owed to it;

(c) hold in suspense any moneys or distributions received from the Mezzanine Creditors or the Junior Creditor or on account of the liability of any Mezzanine Creditor or the Junior Creditor (as appropriate) under this Agreement.

20. PRESERVATION OF JUNIOR DEBT

The Mezzanine Debt or Junior Debt concerned shall, solely as between the Obligors and the Mezzanine Creditors, or as the case may be, the Junior Creditor, remain owing or due and payable in accordance with the terms of the Mezzanine Finance Documents or, as the case may be, the Junior Note, and interest and default interest will accrue on missed payments accordingly.

21. POWER OF ATTORNEY

By way of security for the obligations of each Mezzanine Creditor and the Junior Creditor under this Agreement, each Mezzanine Creditor and the Junior Creditor irrevocably appoints the Senior Agent and each Senior Creditor as its attorney to do anything which the Mezzanine Creditor or the Junior Creditor (a) has authorised the Senior Agent or the Senior Creditor to do under this Agreement and (b) is required to do by this Agreement but has failed to do. The Senior Agent and each Senior Creditor may delegate this power.

22. EXPENSES

22.1 *Initial costs*

The Borrower will forthwith on demand pay the Senior Agent and the Mezzanine Agent the amount of all costs and expenses incurred by either of them in connection with the negotiation, preparation, execution and performance of this Agreement and any other documents referred to in this Agreement.

22.2 *Enforcement costs*

Each Obligor, each Mezzanine Creditor and the Junior Creditor shall, forthwith on demand, pay to each Senior Creditor the amount of all costs and expenses incurred by it in connection with the enforcement against the Obligor, Mezzanine Creditor or the Junior Creditor (as the case may be) of such Senior Creditor's rights against it under this Agreement.

22.3 *Legal expenses and taxes*

The costs and expenses referred to above include, without limitation, the fees and expenses of legal advisers and any value added tax or similar tax, and are payable in the currency in which they are incurred.

23. CHANGES TO THE PARTIES

23.1 *Successors and assigns*

This Agreement is binding on the successors and assigns of the parties hereto.

23.2 *Obligors*

No Obligor may assign or transfer any of its rights (if any) or obligations under this Agreement.

23.3 *New Obligors*

If any member of the Group (a "New Obligor") guarantees or otherwise becomes liable for any Senior Debt or Mezzanine Debt or grants security for any Senior Debt or Mezzanine Debt, the Borrower will procure that such Obligor will become a party hereto as a New Obligor by the execution of an Obligor Deed of Accession in the form set out in Schedule 5.

23.4 *Mezzanine Creditors*

Until the Senior Discharge Date, no Mezzanine Creditor will:

(a) assign or dispose of, or create or permit to subsist any security over, any of the Mezzanine Debt owing to it or its proceeds or any interest in that Mezzanine Debt or its proceeds, or any security therefor, to or in favour of any person; or

(b) subordinate any of the Mezzanine Debt owing to it or its proceeds to any sums owing by an Obligor to any person other than the Senior Creditors;

(c) transfer by novation or otherwise any of its rights or obligations under any Mezzanine Finance Document to any person, unless in each case that person agrees with the parties hereto that he is bound by all the terms of this Agreement as a Mezzanine Creditor in a manner satisfactory to the Senior Agent or by the execution of a Mezzanine Creditor Deed of Accession in the form set out in Schedule 6.

23.5 *Junior Creditor*

The Junior Creditor shall not:

(a) assign or dispose of, or create or permit to subsist any security over, any of the Junior Debt owing to it or its proceeds or any interest in that Junior Debt or its proceeds, or any security therefor, to or in favour of any person; or

(b) subordinate any of the Junior Debt owing to it or its proceeds to any sums owing by an Obligor to any person other than the Senior Creditors and the Mezzanine Creditors; or

(c) transfer by novation or otherwise any of its rights or obligations under the Junior Note to any person.

23.6 *Senior Creditors*

Each Senior Creditor may assign or otherwise dispose of all or any of its rights under this Agreement.

23.7 *Novated Senior Creditors*

If a Senior Creditor wishes to novate or transfer any of its rights or obligations under the Senior Finance Documents to another person, that other person may become a party hereto by executing a Senior Creditor Deed of Accession in the form set out in Schedule 7.

23.8 *Agents*

Neither the Senior Agent nor the Mezzanine Agent may resign or be removed except as specified in the Senior Credit Agreement or the Mezzanine Credit Agreement (as the case may be) and only if a replacement Senior Agent or Mezzanine Agent agrees with all other parties hereto to become a replacement agent under this Agreement by execution of an Agent's Deed of Accession in the form set out in Schedule 8.

23.9 *Authorisations*

Each Obligor authorises the Senior Agent and the Mezzanine Agent to execute each Deed of Accession referred to in this Clause 23 on its behalf. Each Senior Creditor and Mezzanine Creditor authorises the Senior Agent and the Mezzanine Agent respectively to execute each Deed of Accession on its behalf. The Junior Creditor authorises the Senior Agent and the Mezzanine Agent to execute each Deed of Accession on its behalf. Each Mezzanine Creditor authorises the Senior Agent to execute a Senior Creditor Deed of Accession on its behalf.

23.10 *Variation of form of accession*

The Senior Agent may agree changes to the forms of Deeds of Accession referred to above.

23.11 *Memorandum on documents*

Each of the Senior Agent and the Mezzanine Agent will endorse a memorandum of this Agreement on the Senior Finance Documents and the Mezzanine Finance Documents respectively and the Junior Creditor will endorse a memorandum of this Agreement on the Junior Note.

24. STATUS OF OBLIGORS

24.1 *Priorities*

Each of the Obligors joins in this Agreement for the purpose of acknowledging the priorities, rights and obligations recorded in this Agreement and undertakes with each of the other parties hereto to observe provisions of this Agreement at all times and not in any way to prejudice or affect the enforcement of such provisions or do or suffer anything which would be inconsistent with the terms of this Agreement.

24.3 *No rights*

None of the Obligors shall have any rights hereunder and none of the undertakings herein contained on the part of the Senior Creditors, the Mezzanine Creditors or the Junior Creditor are given (or shall be deemed to have been given) to, or for the benefit of, the Obligors.

25. NOTICES

Every notice, request, demand or other communication under this Agreement shall be in writing delivered personally, by first-class prepaid post, facsimile or telex and shall be sent to the address, telex or facsimile number of the person concerned set out under its name on the signing pages hereto or such other address, telex or facsimile number as is notified by it to the parties to this Agreement.

26. WAIVERS, REMEDIES CUMULATIVE

The rights of each party under this Agreement:

(a) are cumulative and not exclusive of its rights under the general law; and
(b) may be waived only in writing and specifically.

Delay in exercising or non-exercise of any such right is not a waiver of that right.

27. JURISDICTION

[Adapt Clause 24 of Form 1.]

28. GOVERNING LAW

This Agreement is governed by English law.

IN WITNESS whereof this Agreement has been entered into on the date stated at the beginning of this Agreement.

SCHEDULE 1

CHARGING SUBSIDIARIES

SCHEDULE 2

PART I

SENIOR CREDITORS

PART II

MEZZANINE CREDITORS

SCHEDULE 3

MEZZANINE SECURITY DOCUMENTS

SCHEDULE 4

SENIOR SECURITY DOCUMENTS

SCHEDULE 5

NEW OBLIGOR

DEED OF ACCESSION

SCHEDULE 6

MEZZANINE CREDITOR

DEED OF ACCESSION

SCHEDULE 7

SENIOR CREDITOR

DEED OF ACCESSION

SCHEDULE 8

AGENT'S DEED OF ACCESSION

SIGNATORIES

THE BORROWER

[NEWCO]

By:
Address:

THE CHARGING SUBSIDIARIES

[   ]

By:
Address:

THE SENIOR AGENT

[SENIOR AGENT]

By:
Address:

THE SENIOR CREDITORS

[SENIOR AGENT]

By:
Address:
By:
Address:

THE MEZZANINE AGENT

[MEZZANINE AGENT]

By:
Address:

THE MEZZANINE CREDITORS

[MEZZANINE AGENT]

By:

Address:

By:

Address:

THE JUNIOR CREDITOR

[JUNIOR CREDITOR]

By:

Address:

FORM 5

CONTRACTUAL SUBORDINATION

Note on the form

The subordination agreement is solely between the debtor and the junior creditor. The senior creditor is not a party.

The junior creditor subordinates claims arising under a specific credit agreement to all other liabilities of the debtor.

The subordination on the insolvency of the common debtor is achieved by rendering the junior debt conditional on the payment of the senior debt.

THIS SUBORDINATION AGREEMENT is dated [   ] and made BETWEEN:
(1) [BORROWER] (the "Borrower");
(2) [JUNIOR CREDITOR] (the "Junior Creditor");

1. INTERPRETATION

(a) *Definitions* In this Agreement:

"Junior Credit Agreement"	means the credit agreement dated [ ] between the Borrower and the Junior Creditor for a credit of £[ ] and includes all variations, replacements, novations of and supplements to the credit agreement but without prejudice to any restrictions on the same.
"Junior Debt"	means all present and future liabilities of the Borrower under or in connection with (or on rescission of) the Junior Credit Agreement.
"Permitted Payments"	means the payments permitted by Clause 4 so long as the same are so permitted.
"Senior Creditor"	means each holder of any Senior Debt;
"Senior Debt"	means all present and future liabilities payable or owing by the Borrower (whether actual or contingent, jointly or severally or otherwise howsoever), other than subordinated liabilities.

(b) *Headings* Headings are to be ignored in construing this Agreement.

2. BORROWER'S UNDERTAKINGS

So long as any Senior Debt is outstanding, the Borrower will not

(a) pay or repay, or make any distribution in respect of, or purchase or acquire, any of the Junior Debt in cash or kind except for Permitted Payments;

(b) permit any of its Subsidiaries to purchase or acquire any of the Junior Debt;

(c) set off against the Junior Debt except for Permitted Payments;

(d) create or permit or subsist security over any of its assets for any of the Junior Debt;

(e) vary the Junior Credit Agreement.

3. JUNIOR CREDITOR'S UNDERTAKINGS

So long as any Senior Debt is outstanding, the Junior Creditor will not:

(a) demand or receive payment of, or any distribution in respect or on account of, any of the Junior Debt in cash or kind, or apply any money or assets in discharge of any Junior Debt, except for Permitted Payments;

(b) set off any of the Junior Debt except for Permitted Payments.

4. PERMITTED PAYMENTS

Subject to Clause 6, whether by actual payment or by set-off, the Borrower may pay and the Junior Creditor may receive and retain payment of (i) scheduled payments of principal and interest on the Junior Debt not earlier than the scheduled due dates in accordance with the original terms of the Junior Credit Agreement (for which purpose a mandatory or voluntary acceleration or prepayment is not a scheduled payment); (ii) [SPECIFY OTHER PERMITTED PAYMENTS] PROVIDED THAT:

(a) The Borrower may not make any payments otherwise permitted by this Clause if and so long as any of the Senior Debt is [more than 30 days] overdue and unpaid;

(b) The Borrower may not make any payments of principal otherwise permitted by this Clause unless the auditors of the Borrower have reported to the Borrower not less than 14 days before the payment that the Borrower would be solvent both at the time of and immediately after the payment. For this purpose the Borrower shall be considered to be solvent if it is able to pay all Senior Debt as it falls due and if the value of its assets is more than the amount of its liabilities, taking into account its contingent and prospective liabilities.

5. SUBORDINATION ON INSOLVENCY

If an order has been made or effective resolution has been passed for the liquidation, winding-up, bankruptcy, administration, rehabilitation, reorganisation or dissolution of the Borrower or any analogous event has occurred, the rights of the Junior Creditor in respect of the Junior Debt will be subordinated to the Senior Debt. Accordingly any payment in respect of the Junior Debt is conditional upon the Borrower being solvent both at the time of and immediately after the payment and shall not be made unless this condition is satisfied. For this purpose, the Borrower shall be considered to be solvent only if the Borrower is able to pay all the Senior Debt in full.

[*Note*: the Agreement may state that the only remedy of the Junior Creditor for the recovery of the Junior Debt is to petition for the winding up of the Borrower.]

6. RETURN OF NON-PERMITTED RECOVERIES

(a) *Non-permitted payment* If

(i) the Junior Creditor receives a payment or distribution in cash, in property, securities or otherwise in respect of or on account of any of the Junior Debt (other than a Permitted Payment);

(ii) the Junior Creditor receives the proceeds of any enforcement of any security for any Junior Debt, or

(iii) the Borrower or any of its subsidiaries makes any payment or distribution, in cash or kind, on account of the purchase or other acquisition of any of the Junior Debt,

the Junior Creditor will hold the same upon trust and immediately return the same to the Borrower or its estate. Thereupon the relevant payment or distribution or receipt will be deemed not to have been made or received.

(b) *Non-permitted set-offs* If any of the Junior Debt is discharged by set-off (except for a Permitted Payment), the Junior Creditor will immediately pay an amount equal to the discharge to the Borrower or its estate. Thereupon the discharge will be deemed not to have taken place.

7. RELIANCE BY SENIOR CREDITORS

The Borrower and the Junior Creditor declare in favour of each Senior Creditor that the terms of this Agreement are in inducement and consideration to each Senior Creditor to give or continue credit to the Borrower or to acquire Senior Debt. Each Senior Creditor may accept the benefit of this Agreement by giving or continuing credit to the Borrower or acquiring Senior Debt. Each of the Borrower and the Junior Creditor waives reliance and notice of acceptance. For the purpose of such inducement, each of the Borrower and the Junior Creditor agrees not to vary the terms of this Agreement nor to take or omit any action whereby the subordination achieved by this Agreement may be impaired.

[*Note*: This clause attempts to create an estoppel in favour of Senior Creditors who rely on the Agreement. Perhaps another method would be for the Borrower and the Junior Creditor each to declare a trust in favour of the Senior Creditor of the benefit of the undertakings given to it by the other.]

9. JUNIOR CREDIT AGREEMENT

This Agreement overrides anything in the Junior Credit Agreement to the contrary.

10. SUCCESSORS AND ASSIGNS

(a) *Successors and assigns* This Agreement is binding on the successors and assigns of the parties hereto.

(b) *Junior Creditor* So long as any Senior Debt is outstanding, the Junior Creditor will not

(i) assign or dispose of, or create or permit to subsist any security over, any of the Junior Debt or its proceeds or any interest in the Junior Debt or its proceeds to or in favour of any person, or

(ii) transfer by novation or otherwise any of its rights or obligations in respect of any Junior Debt to any person

unless in each case that person agrees with the Borrower that he is bound by all the terms of this Agreement as Junior Creditor.

11. PERPETUITY PERIOD

The perpetuity period for the trusts in this Agreement is 80 years.

12. JURISDICTION

[Adapt Clause 24 in Form 1.]

13. GOVERNING LAW

This Agreement is governed by English law.

This Agreement has been entered into on the date stated at the head of this Agreement.

FORM 6

SUBORDINATED CAPITAL NOTE ISSUES BY BANKS: SUBORDINATION CLAUSES

Note on the form

This form sets out the subordination clauses in a trust deed constituting an issue of subordinated capital notes by a bank intended to qualify as capital of the appropriate class for capital adequacy purposes: see para. 11.1.

1. *Subordination on winding-up*

On a winding-up of the Bank, the claims of the Trustee, the Noteholders and Couponholders against the Bank in respect of the Notes and the Coupons shall be postponed to the claims of all depositors and other creditors (other than holders of subordinated indebtedness, if any) of the Bank. Accordingly no amount shall be payable to the Noteholders or the Couponholders out of the amounts in respect of the Notes or Coupons paid to the Trustee in the winding-up until the claims of all depositors and other creditors (other than as aforesaid) of the Bank admitted in the winding-up have been satisfied [and the rights of the Noteholders and the Couponholders shall be conditional upon those claims being satisfied]. Any amounts in respect of the Notes and the Coupons paid to the Trustee *pari passu* with the amounts payable to other creditors in the winding-up shall be held by the Trustee upon trust:

FIRST in payment or satisfaction of the costs, charges, expenses and liabilities incurred by the Trustee in or about the execution of the trusts of these presents and any unpaid remuneration of the Trustee;

SECONDLY in payment of claims of all depositors and other creditors (other than as aforesaid) of the Bank in the winding-up to the extent that such claims are admitted to proof in the winding-up (not having been satisfied out of the other resources of the Bank); and

THIRDLY as to the balance (if any) in payment *pari passu* and rateably of the amounts owing on or in respect of the Notes and the Coupons.

2. *Recoveries payable to liquidator*

(a) The trust secondly mentioned in Clause 1 may be performed by the Trustee paying over to the liquidator for the time being in the winding-up of the Bank the amount to be distributed on terms that such liquidator shall distribute the same accordingly and in that event the Trustee shall not be bound to supervise such distribution. The receipt of such liquidator for the same shall be a good discharge to the Trustee for the performance by it of the trust secondly mentioned in Clause 1.

(b) The Trustee shall be entitled and it is hereby authorised to call for and to accept as conclusive evidence thereof a certificate from the liquidator for the time being of the Bank as to:

(i) the amount of the claims of the depositors and other creditors referred to in Clause 1 (other than as therein mentioned); and

(ii) the persons entitled thereto and their respective entitlements.

3. *Winding-up of Bank*

(a) At any time after the Notes shall have become due and repayable under Condition [ ] of the Notes and have not been repaid, the Trustee may, at its discretion and without further notice, institute proceedings for the winding-up of the Bank, but it shall not be bound to institute any such proceedings unless (i) it shall have been so directed by an Extraordinary Resolution or so requested in writing by the holders of at least one-fifth in principal amount of the Notes then outstanding and (ii) it shall have been indemnified to its satisfaction against all proceedings, claims and demands to which it may be liable and all costs, charges and expenses which may be incurred by it in connection therewith.

(b) No remedy against the Bank, other than the institution of proceedings by the Trustee for the winding-up of the Bank, shall be available to the Trustee or the Noteholders or Couponholders for the recovery of amounts owing on the Notes and the Coupons and no Noteholder or Couponholder shall be entitled to institute proceedings for the winding-up of the Bank, or to prove in such winding-up, except that if the Trustee, having become bound so to proceed, fails to do so or being able to prove in such winding-up, fails to do so, in each case within a reasonable time, then any such holder may, if such failure is continuing and on giving an indemnity satisfactory to the Trustee (against all proceedings, claims and demands to which it may be liable and all costs, charges and expenses which may be incurred by it in connection therewith) in the name of the Trustee (but not otherwise) himself either institute proceedings for the winding-up of the Bank or prove in such winding-up.

CHECK-LIST

Note: This check-list is intended as a quick reminder of some of the main legal and drafting points involved in subordination agreements.

Numbers in brackets are references to numbered paragraphs in the text.

1. Form of subordination (2.3 *et seq.*)

— Turnover subordination trust of proceeds?
— Contractual or "contingent debt" subordination?
— Turnover debtor-creditor subordination?

2. Turnover subordination trust

Junior creditor holds proceeds of junior debt as property of senior creditor. (2.4)

— Is the trust of proceeds a security interest created by junior creditor? (5.1 *et seq.*)

— registration or filing?
— negative pledges binding on junior creditor?
— freeze on security on rehabilitation proceedings involving junior creditor (*e.g.* British administrations and United States Chapter 11)?
— overreached by administrative receiver?

— Is formal notice of transfer of proceeds necessary for its validity? (12.1 *et seq.*).

— Priority of transfer against competing assignees or garnishors of proceeds? (7.21, 7.24).
— Do future proceeds belong to junior creditor's estate if he becomes insolvent? (4.1).
— Can the senior creditor vote the junior debt? (3.5 *et seq.*).
— Perpetuity rule?—this prevents use of subordination trust for perpetual subordinated debt issues (11.4).
— Is the subordination capable of being defeated by set-off between junior creditor and common debtor? (6.1 *et seq.*).

3. Contractual (or "contingent debt") subordination

Payment of junior debt on insolvency of the common debtor is contingent on senior debt being paid in full (2.5).

— Necessarily a subordination to all creditors (2.5).
— Senior creditor does not have benefit of double-dip resulting from turnover of proceeds (2.8).

— Is the contingency valid on common debtor's insolvency? (3.1 *et seq.*).

— Is the subordination capable of being defeated by set-off between junior creditor and common debtor? (6.1 *et seq.*).

4. Debtor-creditor subordination

Junior creditor pays senior creditor amounts *equal to* recoveries on junior debt if the common debtor is insolvent (2.4(b)).

Senior creditor is unsecured creditor of junior creditor.

5. Taxation

— Any withholding tax on junior interest? (11.2).

— Can the debtor deduct interest on junior debt in computing taxable profits?

— Any issue taxes on issue of junior debt? (1.4).

— Any stamp duties on subordination agreement as transfer of proceeds? (11.3).

6. General

— Is the subordination a preference or transaction at an undervalue by junior creditor? (4.2 *et seq.*).

— Corporate powers (especially junior creditor)? (11.6).

— Corporate authorisations?

— Is subordinated debt excluded from debtor's borrowing limits? Is it equity for the purposes of the debtor's financial ratios?

— Does the subordination comply with official requirements to enable subordinated debt to qualify as capital, *e.g.* bank capital adequacy, official solvency ratios, etc.? (11.1 *et seq.*).

— Does the turnover subordination infringe any anti-disposal covenant binding on junior creditor? (5.7).

— Is the subordination revocable by junior creditor if the senior creditor is not a party? (7.20).

— Should there be a trustee for the junior debt:

— regulatory or stock exchange requirement for a (qualified) trustee? (10.2)

— foreign recognition of trusts? (10.5)

— conflicts of interest? (10.7 *et seq.*)

— trustee is private lender (disgorgement risk)? (10.11)

— bondholder community statutes? (10.16 *et seq.*).

— Is the junior debt convertible into shares? (11.5)

7. Terms of subordination agreements

(1) *Senior debt*

— all present and future debt, or specific debt, or class of debt? (1.5)

— are the following included in senior debt?

— senior debt acquired by purchase?

— refinancings or variations of specific senior debt? (7.13 *et seq.*)

— increases in specific senior debt? (up to a limit?) (7.12; 8.5)

— debt springing up on return of preferential payment of senior debt?

— non-provable senior debt, *e.g.* post-insolvency interest, claims subject to rule against double-proof? (9.8)

— damages on rescission of senior debt? (11.7)

— exclusion of other subordinated debt? (2.15)

(2) *Junior debt*

— all present and future debt owed to junior creditor or specific debt or class of debt (1.6)

— are damages on rescission of junior debt subordinated? (11.7)

— is debt acquired by purchase included?

— turnover to apply to recoveries from all sources, *e.g.* third-party guarantees or security? (2.11)

(3) *Permitted payments on junior debt* (2.1; 7.5 *et seq.*)

— scheduled interest and principal?—exclude voluntary and compulsory prepayments and accelerations (default acceleration, illegality clause, substitute basis clause, poison pills, change of control, etc.)

— fees, costs, commissions?

— tax grossing-up, increased costs, breakage costs, indemnities, stamp duties?

— salaries and fringe benefits?

— supplier debt?

— rent?

Suspension of permitted payments if—

— senior debt unpaid?

— senior pending event of default, actual event of default or acceleration (limited freeze period in mezzanine finance?)

— junior pending event of default, actual event of default or acceleration? (Cross-default this in senior loan)

— solvency ratio not met?

(4) *Debtor's undertakings*

— non-payment of junior debt except permitted payments. Cover purchase of debt by debtor and its subsidiaries; cover compensation deals and distributions in kind (7.4 *et seq.*)

— no set-off against junior debt (6.1 *et seq.*)

— no security for junior debt? (7.21)

— no corporate mergers?

— no impairment of subordination? (7.2)

— (in junior board issues) all other subordinated debt to be equally subordinated? (7.3)

— representations and warranties? (7.19)

(5) *Junior creditor's undertakings*

— no receipt of junior debt except permitted payments (2.1; 7.5 *et seq.*)
— no set-off discharging junior debt (6.1 *et seq.*)
— pay senior creditor amounts equal to set-offs received (6.9)
— no security for junior debt? (8.16)
— no guarantees for junior debt? (1.7)
— note subordination on junior negotiable instruments? (7.21)
— no conversion of junior debt into equity? (11.5)
— no transfer of or security over junior debt unless transferee agrees to be bound? (7.2 *et seq.*)
— no subordination of junior debt to another creditor? (7.4)
— turnover to senior creditor of non-permitted recoveries on junior debt and all recoveries on insolvency of common debtor
— conversion of turnovers in kind or in foreign currency (2.12)
— pay senior creditor amounts equal to recoveries if turnover or trust obligation is invalid? (2.4)
— no acceleration of junior debt?—unless senior debt also accelerated or debtor's insolvency instituted (7.5 *et seq.*)
— no enforcement of junior debt by execution? (7.5 *et seq.*)
— no initiation of insolvency proceedings? (7.5 *et seq.*)
— (in mezzanine finance) can junior creditor exercise any remedy after junior event of default and [180] days have elapsed? (7.5 *et seq.*)
— prove for junior debt in timely manner? (3.5 *et seq.*)
— vote junior debt as directed by senior creditor? (3.5 *et seq.*)
— notify senior creditor of details of junior debt and of junior events of default?
— no variation of junior debt?—especially definition of junior debt, subordination, amount, time and currency of payments, covenants, events of default and acceleration rights (7.20)
— ability of senior creditor to override covenants and events of default in junior credit agreement? (7.14 *et seq.*)
— (in mezzanine bank finance) any entrenched junior covenants (information, dividends, financial ratios, negative pledge, disposals)? Tolerances and thresholds? Should junior creditor be allowed covenants? (7.14 *et seq.*)
— representations and warranties? (7.19)

(6) *Protective clauses*

— subrogation by junior creditor? (9.2)
— suspense account for turnover proceeds? (9.3)
— waiver of defences? (9.4)
— exclusion of contribution between junior creditors? (9.5)
— termination of subordination as regards future debt owing to junior creditor? (9.6)
— no exhaustion of recourse by senior creditor? (9.7)

— turnover to cover non-provable senior debt? *e.g.* post-insolvency interest? (9.8)

— free appropriation of payments by senior creditor? (9.10)

(7) *General*

— breakage costs if turnover received by senior creditor during a funding period? (2.14)

— limited cross-acceleration clause in junior credit agreement? (7.17)

— events of default in senior credit agreement—non-compliance or breach of warranty under subordination agreement; inefficacy of subordination; default under junior debt instrument; acceleration of junior debt? (7.26)

— preservation of junior debt? (7.27)

— expenses?

— assignments by senior creditor?

— novations by senior creditor? Trustee necessary if the senior debt is secured? (10.1)

— deeds of accession for new debtors, junior creditors and senior creditors? (7.22)

— powers of attorney (for voting, recovery of proceeds, etc.)?

— stamp duty indemnity?

— currency indemnity?

— default interest?

— waivers, remedies cumulative, severability, counterparts?

— notices?

— governing law and jurisdiction?

8. Secured debt

— Subordinate the junior debt as well as the junior security? (8.1)

— Is variation of mandatory statutory priorities possible? Consider order of registration, notification to debtors, notification to insurers (8.2 *et seq.*)

— Trustee to hold security for senior and junior creditors? (10.1 *et seq.*)

— Can senior creditor add new money to prior security? (8.5)

— Restrictions on enforcement rights of junior creditor? *e.g.* sale, foreclosure, possession, receiver—unless senior creditor has enforced? (8.6 *et seq.*)

— Order of application of realisation proceeds

— Junior creditor to co-operate in private sale? (6.8)

— Senior creditor's responsibilities to junior creditor? *e.g.* protection of senior security, no releases, deposit of title deeds, maximisation of enforcement proceeds? (8.11)

— Senior creditor's right to consolidate securities? (8.12)

— Application of insurance proceeds? (8.13)

— Waiver of marshalling by junior creditor? (8.15)